A Girl's Own
ADVENTURE
ACROSS AFRICA ANY WAY ANY HOW

A Girl's Own

ADVENTURE

ACROSS AFRICA ANY WAY ANY HOW

Jacqueline Tomlins

NEW
HOLLAND

First published in Australia in 2003 by
New Holland Publishers (Australia) Pty Ltd
Sydney • Auckland • London • Cape Town

14 Aquatic Drive Frenchs Forest NSW 2086 Australia
218 Lake Road Northcote Auckland New Zealand
86 Edgware Road London W2 2EA United Kingdom
80 McKenzie Street Cape Town 8001 South Africa

10 9 8 7 6 5 4 3 2 1

National Library of Australia Cataloguing-in-Publication Data:

Tomlins, Jacqueline Ruth, 1962–
   A girl's own adventure: across Africa any way any how

   ISBN 1 86436 779 2

   1. Tomlins, Jacqueline Ruth, 1962–. —Journeys—Africa
   2. Africa—Description and travel. I. Title

916

Publishing Manager: Anouska Good
Senior Editor: Monica Ban
Designer: Karl Roper
Cartographer: Ian Faulkner
Production Manager: Wendy Hunt
Printed in Australia by Griffin Press, Adelaide

This book was typeset in Aldine 11pt

Cover: Sarah cartwheeling over the dunes at Sossusvlei, Namibia

CONTENTS

For Sarah
For doing a hundred things they have not dreamed of...

ACKNOWLEDGEMENTS

It is a long road from the idea of a book to its publication—especially the first time. I offer my thanks to the following people who helped along the way.

The Eleanor Dark Foundation who provided me with an Editorial Mentorship enabling me to spend a week at Varuna, The Writer's House in Katoomba, New South Wales. Peter Bishop, executive director, who kept faith with my manuscript and Louise Thurtell, whose help in preparing it for publication was invaluable. I cannot imagine a more inspiring experience for a writer than spending time at Varuna.

My parents—Tony Tomlins and Grace Roberts—who, long before it was fashionable, left the safe shores of England and set out on their own adventure—this travelling business starts with them. Eva and Michael Nichols—Sarah's parents—who invited me to stay at their beautiful cottage on Lake Catchacoma in southern Ontario where I wrote the first drafts of this book.

Elizabeth Flann who read the manuscript in its early stages and suggested I keep going. Andrea Goldsmith who taught me much about writing in the course I undertook at Deakin University. Later, over lunch, she indulged my new-writer's angst, offered quiet encouragement and suggested Varuna. Clare Allan-Kamil who has always given time, advice and guidance in a spirit of enormous generosity. I see her hovering at the sidelines of my writing life waving a small bright flag with 'Jacqui' written on it. Lee FitzRoy who is enthusiastic about all my writing ventures and who provided feedback in the thoughtful, positive way writers always hope for. Rachel Tham and Lynda Poke who read sections of the manuscript at a weekend by the beach and laughed out loud. My sister, Susan Tomlins, my sister-in-law, Françoise Godet, Sarah's colleague, Kristina Anderson and my Varuna buddy, Nicole Hayes, who all read it and said the right things.

Maria Berry and Jacki Ford who have long been the best of friends and great travelling companions. Thanks girls for the time together in Africa and for accepting my portrayal of you, and your relationship, with such good grace. Fancy South America...?

And of course, Sarah, who made this African adventure what it was, who went to work everyday so I could stay home and write about it, who happily told everyone she was 'the butt of all the jokes', who ticked and crossed my drafts and handed them back for rewrites, and who never doubted—not for a minute—the manuscript would eventually grace our bookshelf. Thanks Babe, for all that and more. Was there ever a better person to share a girl's own adventure?

*If adventures do not befall a young lady in her own village,
she must seek them abroad.*

Jane Austen

*To have an adventure is not just to hug the right side of a notional
dividing line, it's to cross an entire physical and emotional landscape, rainforest
to icecap, euphoric thrill to misery and back again. It makes
the memory of everyday life seem both enticingly safe and boringly
routine. But once you've had a glimpse of that seductive scenery, you
can't just draw the blinds and go back to your armchair.*

Rosie Thomas, 'The Ascent of Woman'
Good Weekend, 6 March 1999

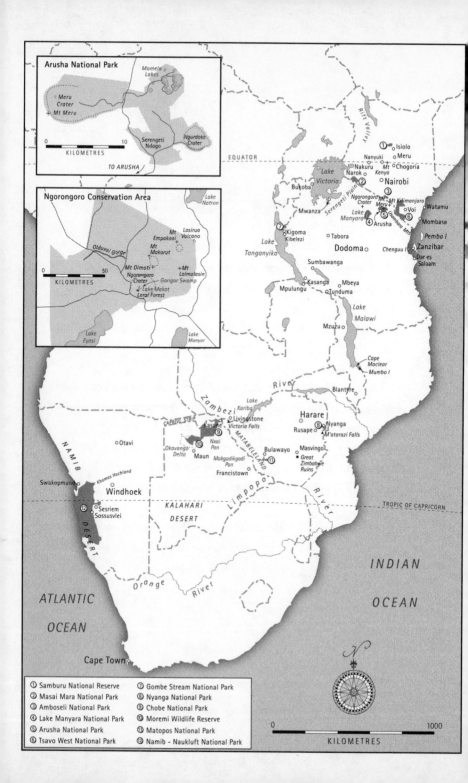

Arusha National Park

Momela Lakes
Meru Crater
+ Mt Meru
Serengeti Ndogo
Ngurdoto Crater

0 ———— 10
KILOMETRES

TO ARUSHA

Ngorongoro Conservation Area

Lake Natron
Mt Empakaai
Losirua Volcano
Olduvai Gorge
Mt Makarut
Mt Olmoti +
+ Mt Lalmalasin
Ngorongoro Crater
Gorigor Swamp
Lake Makat
Lerai Forest
Lake Eyasi
Lake Manyar

0 ———— 50
KILOMETRES

EQUATOR

Rift Valley
① Isiolo
Nanyuki ○ Meru
Nakuru Mt ○ Chogoria
Lake Narok Kenya
Victoria ② ○ Nairobi
Bukoba ③
Mwanza Serengeti Plain Ngorongoro ○ Mt Kilimanjaro
Crater Meru + ⑤ Voi ○ ○ Watamu
Lake ④ ⑥
Manyara Arusha Usambara Mts Mombasa
⑦ Kigoma Pemba I
Kibelezi ○ Tabora Dodoma ○ Chenguu I Zanzibar
Lake Dar es
Tanganyika Sumbawanga Salaam

Kasanga ○ Mbeya
Mpulungu ○ Tunduma
Lake
Malawi
Mzuzu ○

Cape Maclear
Mumbo I
Zambezi River
○ Blantyre
Lake Kariba
○ Livingstone Harare ⑧ Nyanga
CAPRIVI STRIP Kasane Victoria Falls Rusape ○ M'atarazi Falls
⑨
Otavi ○ ⑩ Nxai Pan
Okavango Maun Bulawayo Masvingo ○
Delta Makgadikgadi ⑪ ■ Great
Pan Zimbabwe
NAMIB Khomas Hochland Francistown Ruins
MATABELELAND

Swakopmund ○ Windhoek
Sesriem KALAHARI Limpopo River TROPIC OF CAPRICORN
⑫ Sossusvlei DESERT

DESERT
Orange River

ATLANTIC INDIAN

OCEAN OCEAN

Cape Town ○

N

① Samburu National Reserve	⑦ Gombe Stream National Park
② Masai Mara National Park	⑧ Nyanga National Park
③ Amboseli National Park	⑨ Chobe National Park
④ Lake Manyara National Park	⑩ Moremi Wildlife Reserve
⑤ Arusha National Park	⑪ Matopos National Park
⑥ Tsavo West National Park	⑫ Namib – Naukluft National Park

0 ———————— 1000
KILOMETRES

PROLOGUE

IT'S DIFFICULT TO ignore the exciting, cosmopolitan atmosphere, the go! go! go! of Perth International Airport, but we do our best. With half an hour of family farewells to get through, we need to focus.

I can see Mum fumbling with something under the table and can hear the crinkling of a paper bag. She looks at Dad to check if this is the right moment. He winks and nods energetically, smiles at me, and at Mum.

I am all anticipation.

From beneath the table she pulls a brightly coloured bundle and dangles it in front of me at arm's length. I tilt my head, squint, sit back trying to work out what it is. 'We wanted you...sniff...to take some Australian sunshine with you...sniff,' she says.

I focus on the obscure fluffy offering suspended in front of my nose. What is she on about? She jiggles it ever so slightly—as if that might explain something—and I take another look. Aah...*it's the sun*...cunningly disguised as a large cuddly toy—a bright round, yellow face, smiley eyes and short green arms that wobble as she holds it.

'Perth sunshine,' she says, eyebrows raised, head nodding in perfect unison with Dad.

Of course... because Africa doesn't have much sunshine of its own.

'That's...lovely Mum. Thanks,' I say, carefully avoiding Sarah's eyes.

'It has a sucker you see. You can stick it to the inside of your car.' Dear sweet Mother somehow failed to notice in the extensive preparations for our backpacking adventure that we didn't actually pack a car.

As she blows her nose and pats her eyes I take the oversize smiley from her and sit it awkwardly in my lap. I try to decide which frivolous item in my pack—the first-aid kit, the camp-stove, or my waterproof jacket—I'll have to leave behind in order to squeeze it in. Alternatively, I could pop it in an envelope to my sister with instructions to lose it in a cupboard until I return in six months—which is what I did.

It was a year and a half ago now that Sarah and I made the decision to travel around Africa, though I'm still not quite sure I understand *how* we made it. 'It's about time we had a serious talk about money,' I'd said.

Sarah had flopped onto the kitchen table with a huge sigh, 'You know it's not my best thing, Jac.'

'I know Hon, but seriously.'

'Yeah, yeah. Mid-thirties, crappy car, no house, no savings.'

I'd dried the last plate, slipped it into the cupboard and hung up the tea towel. 'The Datsun's seen better days, we couldn't retire for a week on our current superannuation, and we are the only people we know who haven't bought a house.'

Sarah had smiled indulgently and wandered into the bathroom to examine her split ends.

'We need to save some money Hon,' I'd shouted after her.

'Oh...I suppose so.'

I'd grabbed a piece of paper and started scribbling figures. With both of us working, debts mostly paid off, we should be able to put away a decent amount each month. I estimated the mortgage on a three bedroom place in a yuppyish part of town and calculated the down payment. It would take eighteen months to save enough for ten per cent, maybe even fifteen.

'If we both keep working full-time and you make Senior Associate soon, and I do some more freelance stuff in my spare time, and we're careful, we could pay it off in twenty years.'

I'd heard a faint 'Uh huh' from down the hallway and sat staring at the huge figure circled in red biro at the end of my calculations. If we saved that, it would be more money than I'd ever had in my life.

'Let's go to Africa,' I'd said.

Sarah had poked her head out of the bathroom. *'What?'*

'Instead of buying a house, let's go to Africa.'

She'd fixed her eyes on mine. Nodded. Smiled. 'OK.'

We'd both travelled before, of course. I'd done the Europe thing as a student, toured North and Central America on my way to Australia from the UK, and seen a little of Asia. Growing up in Canada, Sarah had spent summers in Europe and the States. Later, she'd been to Egypt and Morocco, and lived for a year in the Middle East. But we'd never travelled together. My family had left England a few years before and settled in Perth and I'd followed them out after a few years working in London and ended up in Melbourne. We'd had a couple of short trips to Western Australia to see them—like this one—and rushed visits to Toronto to catch up with Sarah's family. But none of that is what you'd call *travelling*.

In the five years we'd been together we'd had other things to think about: study, careers and—when Sarah's scholarship ran out and she had to go back to Canada—maintaining a long-distance relationship. Finally, after trips back and forth, and four-figure phone bills she'd applied for immigration and moved, temporarily at least, to Australia.

For a while, life in Melbourne had been quite settled, and we'd taken advantage of long weekends and the occasional week off to explore our newly adopted home. But to be honest, life as a responsible adult was not generally as exciting as we might have hoped. It was as if, even though we were both in our thirties, we still felt like students, and Australia was just a stopover on the big overseas trip. Melbourne was a great city to live in, but I missed my friends in England, and Sarah longed for her beloved Canada. If nothing else, the Africa trip would see the endless comparisons between Australia, Canada and the UK put on hold. Travelling was a reprieve from the eternal debates about where we wanted to live.

It wasn't as if Sarah needed much persuading to give up being a lawyer for a while, and I was fed up with my job and burnt out. After ten years of professional caring I'd had enough. I wanted people to take responsibility for their own lives or, at least, find someone else to help sort them out. Lately, I'd started to lock my office while I was still in it, and once even turned out the light so no one would knock. All of a sudden, long-service leave and a vague promise of promotion didn't have quite the same appeal and, besides, there were huge parts of the world I still hadn't seen.

Secretly, I think we both fancied ourselves a bit rugged and Africa seemed so terribly adventurous—lions and tigers and all that. The only real connection I had to the place was that I'd once been arrested outside the South African Embassy in Trafalgar Square at an anti-apartheid demonstration, but that's another story. People always said there was something about Africa—that once you travelled there it got into your blood. I wanted to see if it would get into mine.

I look across at Mum trying to find her brave face. 'We'll be back before you know it, Mum,' I say.

'I know Jacqui…I'm OK…Really. You girls have a *lovely* time.'

Dad places a protective arm around her shoulder and we wander towards the exit. We make the hugs brief, and with a long backward glance, wave goodbye as the doors slide shut.

On board, we grab headsets and *Who Weekly* magazines and squeeze into our seats. A map of Australia appears on the screen, and I am acutely aware that instead of turning left and heading back to Melbourne, we will turn right and head out across the Indian Ocean.

CHAPTER 1

THE DESCENT INTO HELL

ARRIVING IN NAIROBI in the dead of night is like stumbling into a medieval vision of hell. The darkened streets teem with people in sweat-stained T-shirts, laceless shoes and torn and ragged trousers. Our cab jolts in and out of potholes and skirts around rocks and jagged chunks of wood that litter the road. There are no street lights, just the glaring yellow headlights of battered cars and *matatus*—the beaten up old combies used as taxis. They are painted with garish images—horned devils, thunderbolts of lightning—and slogans: 'Descend not into hell: Jesus saves'.

Not in Nairobi, clearly.

Groups of young men sit on the pavement or slouch against rough wooden stalls selling rubber stamps and cigarettes, and cheap plastic watches laid out on up-turned crates. A row of glassless shop fronts display grease-soaked chicken and chips, barely visible under thick layers of flies, and hot dogs that glow with fluorescent pink sauce. Even with the cab window wound up tightly, there is a foul smell, like week-old dustbins left out in summer. The air is thick with dirt and dust and smoke, and the people shuffle through a dark, yellow haze.

I click the lock on the door, wrap the strap of my day-pack around my feet and edge towards Sarah. The road in the centre of town is flooded and the city's detritus floats by: plastic bags spilling with moulding food, half-chewed, blackened corn husks, disintegrating cardboard boxes and bundles of matted rags. Flames envelop great piles of rotting rubbish three metres high and fill the air with acrid smoke. Municipal workers in dark blue overalls stand in a circle, periodically shovelling garbage onto the pyre. I squeeze Sarah's hand tightly. Christ. This is not quite what I expected.

As we turn towards our hotel, an old man leans into the road and vomits violently. Behind him, groups of women, and children with snot-encrusted noses, crouch in makeshift cardboard shelters. Above the noise of the street, half a dozen different horns blast continually and, somewhere in the distance, I can hear a child screaming. 'We're here,' Sarah says and I realise we have stopped outside the hotel. I grab my pack and make a dash for the entry while Sarah pays. She follows me in and throws a reassuring glance. 'I think I just remembered what culture shock is,' I say.

Our room is reasonably clean, if you don't look too closely at the floor, up the walls, in the shower, or behind the wardrobe. A multi-holed mosquito net falls limply around two wooden beds covered with threadbare sheets, and on the side table—where there should be a Gideon's *Bible*—there is a packet of condoms. From the window, I can see into the next lot where another huge pile of rubbish is ablaze. The window doesn't actually shut and I am only mildly reassured by the fact that we are on the second floor.

We dump our gear, undo our boots and take a few long deep breaths. Sarah unpacks some toiletries, drags the two single beds together and, after a quick change, we duck in under the mosquito net. She carefully lines up the corners of the net and tucks the edges under the mattress in the way described by the nice man in the army surplus shop back home. We lie back, listening to the *matatus* tooting for business, and watching the mosquitoes buzzing outside the net, searching for the easiest way in.

I realise we have left the light on, and we untuck the net so we can switch it off. It's a little more difficult to fix it up in the dark because you can't quite see the corners to line them up. We tuck it back under the mattress, pulling it vaguely straight and settle back—the *matatus* now accompanied by ghetto blasters churning out dull, thudding rap.

Everything is rather more clearly focussed than it should be which, given that I'm still wearing my glasses, makes some sense. I untuck the net again, grope around for my case and pop it on the bedside table. The re-tuck, in darkness, with no specs is really quite awkward. Sarah clambers over me and attempts to tuck in the bottom corner, but in so doing pulls the top corner out. We perform an awkward dance, shuffling from one end of the bed to the other until we are finally tucked in.

We lie, deadly still, anxious that any movement might upset the delicate balance of the net. For a few minutes we listen to the sounds of the night, trying to take in the fact that after all the saving, the preparation and packing, we've finally made it. 'We're in Africa, Babe.'

'I know.'

'And guess what?'

'What?'

'I need to pee.'

I awake feeling refreshed and excited—somehow I must have slept through the noise—and the view from the window is far less scary in the quiet light of early morning. As I shower, I notice I'm covered in small red bites and wonder whether the performance with the mosquito net was really worth it.

We head down to the main office and meet the manager who is friendly and helpful. He shows us some key places to visit on the map and locks our valuables in the office safe. We must carry nothing with us when we go out, he explains, no backpacks, cameras, watches or jewellery, not even earrings or sunglasses. 'Tourists are robbed frequently, in daylight, in quiet and busy places,' he says. 'Take a small amount of cash in your pocket and leave your purse or money belt here. Always look as if you know where you are going, take a taxi if you are not sure, and never go out at night.' He asks how long we have been in Kenya and winces visibly when we tell him. I suspect he thinks, in the nicest possible way, that we are young and white and stupid and, quite frankly, just now I have to agree with him.

We choose a place for breakfast and Sarah checks it out on the map. 'It's not far,' she says, 'an easy five minute walk'. Directions are not Sarah's best thing, and my look has just the tiniest hint of scepticism. 'No really, I've worked out a route,' she says. As we step out of the hotel we are immediately surrounded by eight or ten touts waving safari brochures and barking names and places and prices in our faces. We wade through them, shaking off all but one, a young guy, at least six foot tall, who follows closely behind. In my head I start to recite the 'Dangers and annoyances' section of the guidebook and wonder how we can lose him.

We take a couple of sharp turns, duck down an alley, and hover in a doorway looking to see if we've given him the slip. We have, but we've also given breakfast the slip—our café could be anywhere. We loiter amidst a crowd of shoppers, absolutely no idea where we are, where our hotel is, where breakfast is. I recall the manager's advice and reflect that whipping out the map, and asking for directions might not be the best course of action just now.

From nowhere the tout appears, strolling up the road towards us. He smiles, introduces himself as 'Kepher' and asks if he may escort to us to the 'Growers Café', a good place for breakfast often frequented by tourists. I'm hungry, we have no idea where we are, and Kepher doesn't look as if he's going to mug us. 'OK,' we mumble reluctantly.

We order coffee—which comes weak and milky in a pint glass—some cake and a banana, which are the only things we recognise. Kepher waits outside, watching. We pull out the map, establish our location and pinpoint half-a-dozen safari companies. 'It shouldn't be that difficult to work out a route,' I say, 'and stick to it.'

'What about our guy?' asks Sarah, nodding towards Kepher.

'I'll tell him we're not interested. We just need to be assertive.'

'Yep. You're right. We'll be really firm.'

We put one foot outside the café door and he is upon us, remonstrating and cajoling, brochure in hand. 'No thank you,' I say, politely. 'We do not require your help.'

'Listen,' he says. 'I presume you want to book a safari, yes? Let's make a deal.'

He will escort us around town, take us to every safari company we want, as long as we agree to visit 'Savuka', the company he works for. We don't have to buy from them and we don't have to pay him a shilling.

I think about our combined lack of a sense of direction, of Sarah's little problem with left and right, of the hundreds of touts out there who will see us coming. Maybe it's not such a bad idea. 'What do you think, Doll?'

'Sounds like a good deal.'

'OK,' we say, 'we'll take it. Thanks.'

We have a great day, entirely hassle-free, escorted by Kepher who keeps the other touts, shoe-shine boys and beggars at bay. We discuss the forthcoming elections, learn some political history, and a few words of Swahili. He is charming, funny and true to his word. After three hours and eight safari companies—half of which are hidden away in office buildings we would never have found—we arrive at Savuka. Because, for some reason, God decides to smile on us today, they offer the best safari at the cheapest price. Kepher makes his commission and we make a friend. We say goodbye and agree to meet for a drink the following day.

We have a day before we head off and, buoyed by our tour with Kepher, set out for town by ourselves. It is Christmas and election time in Nairobi and there is much evidence of both. Posters on every available wall declare support for Mwai Kibaki, the popular opponent of the long-standing, slightly less than squeaky clean president, Daniel Arop Moi. Plastic Santas and snowmen deck the shop fronts, and Boney M's 'Mary's Boychild' blares out from the *matatu* radios. It is also Independence Day and the city is covered with Kenyan flags, a shield with crossed spears on three bold stripes: black for the people, green for the land and red for the blood spilled fighting for liberation.

People in overalls, in smart business suits, in brightly coloured *kangas*—the African sarongs—head off to work or to do their shopping. Newspaper sellers display copies of the *Daily Nation* and the *Kenya Times*, and a soapbox preacher warns of Armageddon. A line of children in smart blue and white uniforms is escorted across the road by their teacher, carefully avoiding any proximity to the street kids, and a battered pick-up screeches to a halt disgorging a group of Boy Scouts in khaki shorts and loosely knotted scarves.

Young women, barely sixteen, with babies on their backs, sit with small piles of tomatoes or onions at their feet, and hawkers usher us towards stalls lined with carved giraffes and hippos: 'Free look Madam. Madam, please, free look.' The street corners are guarded by old men and women with grotesque physical deformities and groups of children high on glue and lighter fuel. Requests for cash are constant and hands frequently brush our pockets, eyes focused on our waists, searching for money belts. A desperate looking teenage boy thrusts his face into mine so close I can smell the sour stench of his breath. He is holding a filthy plastic bottle containing a dark liquid which he threatens to throw unless we give him money. We brush him off and weave quickly in and out of the crowd, dodging the other kids, until he is diverted by someone else.

Nairobi is affectionately known as 'Nairobbery' among independent travellers, though I'm really not sure that's our biggest danger. The *matatus* speed though the tiniest gap in traffic, regularly skidding around corners and mounting the kerbs. An old Mazda shoots out of a side alley into the main road and, literally, runs over a young man, the wheel bouncing over his kneecap.

We attempt to cross the nightmarish Moi Avenue and, as I step off the pavement, a beaten up Datsun appears out of nowhere, heading straight for me. He slams on the brakes and skids to a halt, his front bumper brushing against my trouser leg. I stand perfectly still, looking down at the rusted chrome nudging my knee. Sarah grabs my arm and hauls me back onto the pavement. 'You OK Jac?!'

'Er…Yeah…Fine.' I take a few deep breaths and try not to recall the stories about Third World hospitals told to us before we left. 'Let's go to the Growers eh?'

Over lunch we discover there is a cholera outbreak in the city slums and, though we have no intention of visiting the slums, the news is mildly disconcerting. Back home we were assured that cholera was not a danger and that the vaccine for it didn't work anyway. Like many other travellers, we have an official stamp in Latin in our vaccination book, *Cholera non-datum* (Cholera not given) which usually manages to fool health officials, but isn't particularly helpful if we want to drink water any time in the next few days.

We share our table with an English couple who are trying to climb one mountain in every country in southern Africa to raise money for Oxfam. They are accompanied by their guide, Paul, with whom we discuss the possibility of climbing Mount Kenya after our safari. The elections are on 29 December and we would rather be out of town. By the end of lunch we have agreed with Paul on a date and price and arrange to withdraw a hundred dollars as a deposit for the trip. We say goodbye to the Oxfam couple who ask where we are staying. 'Ah…we met a young New Zealand couple who were staying there, but they

THE DESCENT INTO HELL

woke up covered in red spots from the bed bugs.'

'Hmm…How interesting,' I say, rolling up my sleeve. 'Do you think they looked anything like this?'

Withdrawing money in Nairobi is a dangerous activity. There are two automatic teller machines on the street, but they are surrounded by a large cluster of stoned children and dishevelled men. We enter the bank and stand in the twenty-two person queue. At the business counter, a middle-aged man rolls up his trouser leg and pulls out two fat wads of American dollars from his socks. The teller meticulously checks every bill, holding it up to the light and, by the time we reach the front of our queue, he is up to ten thousand dollars and still counting. Some people in Kenya clearly have money.

We hand over our one hundred dollars to Paul in return for a scrappy receipt which provides little comfort. He is 'freelance' and has no real address or telephone number. He assures us he will make the necessary arrangements and call at our hotel when we return from safari. Sarah puts our remaining cash in her boots and we say goodbye, laying bets on the chances of ever seeing him again.

We join Kepher in the early evening for a beer at a local bar, a dark scruffy room with red painted walls and plastic tables and chairs. It is not, I suspect, a place frequented by tourists, or by women. Kepher is from Lake Victoria, the home of the Luo. He speaks to his family in his tribal language, to other Africans in Swahili, 'the uniting tongue', and he addresses us in perfect English. He has eleven brothers and sisters, the children of his father and his father's three wives. 'Do the wives get jealous?' I ask. 'It depends on how my father treats them,' he explains. 'As long as he pays them equal attention there is no problem.'

Kepher came to Nairobi to look for work and thought he could make a living from tourists. He gets a commission from Savuka based on the type of safari the person he brings books. He is very happy with our eleven days—most people book no more than five. Savuka is one of the few African-run companies, which is why he likes to work for them. Most, it seems, are owned by Indians, and for Kepher 'African' doesn't include Indian.

Nairobi is a dangerous place, he says, especially for travellers, and he tries to look out for the tourists he meets and stop the street kids hassling them. He and the other touts often pick the kids up, give them flyers, show them the safari offices, and tell them how to approach westerners. This way the kids can earn some money, the tourists are hassled less and the safari companies get more business. It's a small thing he can do to make Nairobi a bit safer and life a little better for the kids.

After our drink, Kepher walks us to the cinema where we pay a dollar to see *Broken Arrow*, a second-rate American action movie. We obey the polite notice at the beginning of the screening: 'Please stand for the national anthem. This is mandatory,' and note that a solitary Englishwoman in front of us fails to do so. It strikes me that this is fairly unwise and falls into the same category as taking photographs of military installations or saying rude things about religious leaders. You can't be too careful if you want to avoid having to explain yourself to some overenthusiastic, gun-carrying minor official.

As the opening credits flutter onto the screen and the soundtrack splutters into action, an enthusiastic, gun-carrying minor official appears from nowhere and approaches the Englishwoman. He whispers something in her ear, places an assertive hand on her arm and escorts her out of the cinema. I raise my eyebrows at Sarah. I hope she returns soon.

The random slaughter of the movie fails to capture my attention and my eyes drift towards the exit. After fifteen minutes my compatriot is still not back. I have visions of spending the night at the British Embassy trying to explain the disappearance of a woman whose name I don't know, and whom I have never met, and persuading the ambassador that she has been abducted by the manager of Twentieth Century Cinemas. Fortunately, after another ten minutes, she returns, unhurt, but looking as if she won't be sitting through the National Anthem again anytime soon.

After two hours immersed in Western culture it is a shock to step back onto the streets of Nairobi. Our hotel is only five minutes away, but this is the first time we have been out at night by ourselves. We assess the risk: we're carrying nothing of value, there is a large number of respectable people leaving the cinema with us, and there is no taxi immediately in sight. We walk, briskly, down Mama Ngina Street to Moi Avenue where our respectable group disperses and leaves us in the late-night crowds that congregate at the top of Tom Mboya Avenue. 'Hmm…' I say to Sarah, 'do the words "sticking out" and "sore thumb" mean anything to you?'

She grabs my hand and we dash across the road, zig-zagging between the *matatus* with their lights flashing and horns screeching. We tiptoe over two filthy, ragged old men sleeping on the pavement and shove through a dozen kids gathered around a ghetto blaster. The giant puddle we passed on the first night has turned into a small pond and plastic food containers float across it like ducks on a lake. We elbow our way past the bag sellers, the beggars, and dodge the pick-pockets who, with no attempt at disguise, brush up against us and slide their hands around our waists.

I grip Sarah's hand tightly and we sprint the last fifty metres, jumping over Coke crates and splashing though the gutters. My heart is racing as we turn into our hotel and I lean against the wall and catch my breath. 'Good evening,' says the nice man behind the desk, 'and how are you liking Nairobi?'

CHAPTER 2

RACING RHINOS IN NAKURU

IT IS A GREAT relief to leave Nairobi the next morning and head towards the Rift Valley where the hills are green and fertile and the air smells fresh. We park high on the steep scarp of the eastern ridge, look down the valley and across to the shallower, more gentle incline of the west. It is mid-morning and the sun is high, filling the valley with a faint blue haze. Down below, circles of rondavels form giant Olympic rings, and a herd of cattle moves across the floor like a faint brown smudge. Dark green splotches of acacia surround a cluster of white satellite dishes, a violent intrusion that drags this ancient valley into the twentieth century. I beckon Sarah towards me, drape my arms around her shoulders and linger over the exquisite view. This is where we all began—the site of our earliest ancestors—and it's somehow reassuring to know we originated in such a beautiful place.

We are heading for Narok, on our way to the Masai Mara, Kenya's most famous game park. Our van is surprisingly good—for a budget safari. It's new, clean and comfortable with well-sprung seats and a pop-up lid for game viewing. On our way out of Nairobi we pick up

Allan and Scott, two sailors on leave from the Australian Navy. In the course of introductory chit-chat we somehow find ourselves discussing Australian politics. It soon becomes apparent we hold rather different views and, in the interests of safari harmony, I divert the conversation to something more benign. It isn't a good start, and I am not terribly excited by the thought of being cooped up in a van with them for five days.

The other member of our group is a tall, skinny red-haired Irishman who is wearing black suit trousers, a white dress shirt with a ruffle front, and leather winklepicker shoes. His suitcase, which is wedged behind our chair, is about three feet square. He introduces himself as 'Darren' and explains, in one breath, that he has been moochin' around Mombasa and moochin' around Lamu and he thought he'd come and mooch around Masai Mara, and that he hasn't really packed for safari, but he'd met a guy who said it was fun so he decided to mooch on up. The Navy boys and I exchange a glance and there are raised eyebrows throughout the van.

We stop for lunch at a concrete table and chair arrangement at the back of a petrol station. White sliced bread, tiny slithers of tomato, and something in lurid pink that I used to call 'pork luncheon meat' as a child—though I suspect this stuff has never been anywhere near a pig. We meet the Prints, an English family—Mark and Cath and their two children Luke, nine and Angel, seven—who are also on a Savuka safari and on their way to the Mara. The kids have spotted a large bowl of chips provided to the members of a different, and we suspect, some-what more up-market safari company, on an adjacent concrete table. Clearly our US$45 a day does not stretch to chips.

There is some confusion after lunch as Francis, our guide, begins unloading our van and piling suitcases, packs, boxes of food, cooking utensils, kerosene lamps and two dozen eggs into a beaten up vehicle parked in the corner. We stand, perplexed, as a group of strangers is loaded into our comfortable, shiny van and packed off to Nairobi.

Francis ushers us into a dusty, dented Toyota Hi-Lux, scraping the mud off the windows so we can see out.

The vinyl on the chairs is torn around the edges and the padding is wafer thin. The springs have gone in a couple of places and the backs are at a forty-five degree angle to the floor, making sitting somewhat taxing on the stomach muscles. Our gear seems to have taken up rather more space than before, providing even greater opportunities for intimacy with our fellow travellers. I shove the giant frying pan at my feet under the chair, and attempt to create some back support with a rolled up mattress. This is it—home for the next eleven days. The shiny new bus—that wouldn't know a safari if it drove over one—is heading back to town.

We drive at sixty kilometres an hour on the flat, forty up the hills and a hundred and twenty going down so we can get a good run up the approaching inclines. The road is rough and, as we near Masai Mara, increasingly waterlogged. As we enter the park we have our first animal sighting: giraffe, wildebeest and zebra. It is dusk and the animals are far off, but we are all terribly excited and get through two rolls of film anyway. Except for Darren who didn't bring a camera.

Our accommodation for the next two nights is a canvas ridge-pole tent erected under a corrugated 'A' frame roof. Inside, on the concrete floor, are two single beds separated from the 'ensuite' by a canvas flap that doesn't quite close. I poke my head around to find a cracked toilet, no seat, but a working flush and a mouldy shower dripping cold water. Fortunately, the light doesn't work so I am spared further details.

There is a communal tent adjacent to ours, and after unpacking our gear we head over for dinner. We sit at a long trestle table: us, the Navy boys, Darren, Cath, Mark and the kids. Scott and Allan buy beers all round and we hoe into our spaghetti bolognaise and carrot and cabbage accompaniment. Darren chats with Allan across the table and I attempt to carry on a conversation with Cath down the other end. Sarah is bobbing up and down, not wanting to miss out on anything, and Mark is showing the kids how to dangle their spaghetti in the air and aim it into their mouths from a great height. Everyone is ever so slightly manic, like the first night at school camp. For the first time in ages, I feel a certain, rather delightful, *frisson*.

After dinner, we settle a little. I sneak a rollie when Sarah isn't looking and Cath tells us about a gay pub crawl she once did in Dublin with her best friend. I love the way some people let us know that they know, and that it's OK. Our Navy boys, of course, have not yet twigged.

Before we left for Africa, we heard dozens of stories about the crowds on Masai Mara, solitary lions surrounded by twenty vehicles and photographers with huge, peering telephoto lenses. Today, there are only a handful of vans, the unseasonal rain and the elections having kept people away. The official advice of the various embassies back home was to avoid Kenya throughout December and January, because of the likelihood of violence.

Just past the entrance to the park, we see hundreds of Thompson's gazelle, their tiny black tails wagging like cranked-up metronomes. A cheetah mother and cub stretch out in the grass ten metres from the van and Francis turns off the engine as they roll in mud, amble across the road and flop down in front of us. A little further on there is a brand-new baby wildebeest, only hours old, the afterbirth still wrapped around the mother's legs. The wildebeest, it seems, congregate *en masse*, and like to hang out with the zebra who stand in their classic pose, heads resting on each other's rump. Sarah tells me they were the inspiration for Dr Dolittle's 'Push me, Pull you'. In the distance, the flat green plains are interrupted by splashes of red, the bright blankets worn by the Masai men. Periodically they jump high in the air, the sudden movement and colour frightening away lions and cheetahs.

Inside the park our van grinds to a halt as the engine knocks violently and we pile out with orders from Francis to stay close. Within seconds, we are surrounded by the Masai who appear out of nowhere—young men, blankets knotted across their shoulders, carrying sticks and small carved clubs. The women follow, draped in brightly coloured beads, one with a bottle of Estee Lauder nail varnish hung around her neck. A group of children rush towards us with their hands stretched out, 'Give me sweet. Give me pen.' Cath rummages through her pack and produces some apples and a couple of packets of two-minute noodles which she gives to the older women. 'Boiling water,' she says. 'Put them in a pot and pour on boiling water.'

Cath kneels down and holds the hands of one of the raggedy kids. He has two open sores on his mouth and snot and sleep encrusted around his nose and eyes. She gives him some dried fruit and plays clapping games, though she really wants to grab her first-aid kit and clean him up. Mark is exchanging a very expensive pocket knife for a club for Luke, and stripping off his shirt for some beads for Angel. I negotiate a deal for photographs with one of the young men: two pens and an empty white plastic film canister, which immediately becomes an earring, fitting perfectly into the enlarged hole in his lobe.

Allan and Scott help Francis fix the van while Sarah supervises. Darren loiters by the edge of the road not quite sure of his role. As the engine turns over and everyone starts to push, he digs his winklepickers into the mud and dirties his shirt against the van. He is clearly very excited about the opportunity to prove his manliness in front of the Navy boys, and delighted when the wheel spins and sends a perfect arc of mud up one trouser leg.

Back on board, Allan and Scott stare out across the plain with binoculars and, not surprisingly in light of their profession, are very good at spotting small things on the horizon. They see a pair of ears in the distance which Francis confirms belong to a lion, but doesn't count it as a sighting—too far away. Darren spots a number of dead tree trunks, and a small clump of grass waving in the breeze, but we don't count those either. A group of giraffe run elegantly, as if in slow motion, across our path. 'They're the supermodels of the animal kingdom,' says Darren. 'You get the feeling they think they're rather superior to everyone else.'

We spot a pair of crested cranes with yellow and red mohicans, an Egyptian vulture with dark circles of kohl around its eyes, and a rather formal, strutting Secretary bird. With Francis' assistance we attempt to differentiate the 'DLAs', (Deer Like Animals): topi, oryx, bush, water and reed bucks, gerenuck, hartebeest, Thompson's and Grant's gazelles, Roan and Sable antelope, eland and impala. The males and females are quite different of course, which doubles the number we have to learn.

Back at camp, we meet Dana, a nineteen-year-old Israeli woman, who is travelling by herself after finishing her military service. Next to her is an American, Eliza, who is tall, skinny and immaculately dressed in a pair of clean, sharp chinos and a pristine white singlet. She has that healthy, glossy magazine-type skin and, even in the dull light, her hair shines. She and Sarah spend ten minutes rubbing each other the wrong way in the manner of first contact between Canadians and Americans. Her friend, Ana, is from Brazil, and is rather more laid-back. They are with another Savuka group and will tag along with us to Nakuru and Samburu. After that, we'll all return to Nairobi, drop off Allan, Scott, Darren and Dana, and Sarah and I will continue on with Eliza and Ana to the southern parks for five days. I remind Sarah that since she has been living in Australia she has, despite herself, often defended Americans and this might be a good time to extend some Christmas goodwill to all. She grunts and returns to her fish curry, with the carrot and cabbage combo.

After dinner, I do UK bonding with the Prints—the 'New' Labour government, the state of the English football team, and the demise of the Royals. After a few beers, I start saying 'Nah wot a min?' at the end of sentences, and by the end of the evening I have lost all my aitches and recovered my glottal stops. We find our way into a discussion about class which has our Navy boys completely confounded. That we can slot ourselves very specifically into a complex hierarchy based on an assessment of our parents' occupation, our income, education and accent, is not something with which Australians easily identify.

They are both from the country and joined the Navy to see the world which they have done. Allan rejected the opportunity of university in favour of hands-on training in sonar radar. He's done well, been promoted a couple of times and was decorated for service in the Gulf War, but he struggles with taking orders. He has a pilot's licence and fantasises about moving to Africa to fly tourists across the savannah. Scott sits quietly in the corner, taking it all in.

Cath is teaching the Masai barman basic maths so he can calculate the cost of multiple beers. She pulls some coloured pencils and a notebook from Angel's bag and draws up a table with pictures of Coke and beer bottles down one side, and amounts in neat, primary school teacher writing, on the other. Mark is in a trading frenzy with the other Masai; he's already swapped two T-shirts, a box of camping knick-knacks and a Maglite torch with batteries for a variety of carved weapons and motley blankets. Cath is starting to worry about his walking boots and hauls him back to our table before he gives up the entire content of their packs. Darren is flitting maniacally between conversations, not wanting to miss out. He has finally twigged Sarah and I are a couple, and is feeling terribly astute.

We are up, breakfasted on fried eggs and in the van by 7.00 a.m., everyone a little worse for wear from the beer and late night. It has rained and the roads are a foot deep in mud. It's a struggle even to get out of the camp, but Francis has clearly done this before, and in twenty minutes, we are bumping back onto the Mara.

The Prints' van breaks down and, as we travel in convoy, we all pile out and chat with the Masai while the guides tinker with the engine. The Masai have been in contact with Western tourists for decades and have adapted to our presence. You must barter with them for photographs, and if you want to visit a village or watch traditional dancing, you pay a fixed price in American dollars. Over the years, they have lost much of their tribal land to the game parks, and younger Masai have drifted away to the towns. Undoubtedly, tourism is perverting, if not destroying, their traditional culture. Now, they hanker after anything Western, and will barter for a string of paper clips, a pack of cards, a T-shirt, or an empty plastic film canister.

The Prints' van has had it, which means that Cath, Mark, the two kids and their day-packs must squeeze in with Allan, Scott, Darren, Sarah and me. Everybody is damp and sweaty and the windows fog with warm breath. Luke and Angel sit on Allan and Scott's laps, and two dozen eggs, a stove and a rolled up mattress sit on mine. I can't see much from this position, but when I arch my neck and twist around a bit, I spot a pair of hyenas, a pack of black-backed jackal and a family of warthogs. We also have our first elephant sighting—a mother and baby—who are somewhat easier to see.

On the way back to camp we stop at one of the many luxury lodges where the non-budget safari people enjoy superb views of the savannah from the comfort of a shady terrace. In the evenings, they sip gin and tonic and watch the animals congregate around an artificial waterhole lit by spotlights. A handful of smart guests hover around the bar as Cath, Mark and the kids, the Navy boys, Darren, Sarah and I deposit Masai Mara mud over their newly swept flagstone floor.

We head for the toilet and enjoy the novelty of clean stalls with seats, paper on a roll, hot water and soap. On the terrace we order cold Cokes and rearrange the wicker settees. Sarah spots a pristine swimming pool with stepping stones stretching from one side to the other and hovers at its edge. 'No, Doll,' I say. '*Please.*' She plants her size ten muddy boot right in the middle of the first stone and dances across the water. Angel and Cath follow, and the three of them splash merrily, their barely suppressed giggles floating over to the bar.

On the way out we traipse past the reception like a long line of refugees and, just in case our tone lowering hasn't been fully effective, Luke, in the inimitable style of a nine-year-old boy, lets out a long deep burp that floats around the high ceiling and lands amongst the G and T drinkers at the bar. 'Guys,' I say, 'let's get out of here. I think we've out-stayed our welcome.'

It is supposed to be a half-day drive but it's 3.00 p.m. before we return to camp. We have a choice of activities for the afternoon: a guided walk through traditional Masai hunting grounds, or a visit to a traditional Masai village. Cath and Mark take the kids to the village, and the rest of us opt for a traditional lie-down.

By seven o'clock it is dark, the Prints are not back and Francis is worried. He leaves instructions for us to stay put, and heads off to look for them. Moments after he leaves, they arrive, the kids high on the shoulders of two local Masai. The van had broken down again and they had to walk for an hour in the dark escorted by some local villagers who guided them through the bush to camp. They are all exhausted and Cath has the air of a woman mildly deranged.

The traditional village was a nightmare—mud everywhere, up to the kids' knees and a foul smell of goats, dung, stale urine and body odour. They had been besieged by people trying to sell them jewellery; five or six Masai women swooping down on Angel, grabbing her hands and slipping bracelets on her arms. Cath had smiled patiently until another woman had leant over and tied strings of beads around Angel's neck. When Cath said she didn't want to buy, they refused to take them off and became aggressive, until in the middle of it all, poor Angel had burst into tears. They didn't really see much of the village because the kids were so distressed and the mud so thick. The van packing up, and the walk back in the dark was the final straw. Cath had reassured the kids there was no danger from wild animals and that the strange, grunting and roaring noises they could hear were just distant giraffe and zebra.

She bundles up the kids and packs them off to the tent just as Francis returns with the empty van, visibly relieved to see them back at camp. 'There was a leopard,' he says, 'in the fork of the tree where they broke down. He looked like he'd been in there quite a while.' There is silence at the table. 'Maybe we just won't mention that to Cath,' I say.

We are invited to watch a performance of traditional dancing, but after hearing about the traditional village fiasco I am sceptical. There is a degree of coercion however, and though none of us are enamoured of the idea, we trot off to the campfire and sit in a circle. The various Masai men who hang around the camp change out of their jeans and T-shirts into their red blankets and exchange their beers for small wooden clubs. They begin to chant and shuffle round the fire, bouncing from one foot to another, and jumping up and down in their traditional Nike hightops. We watch politely, the old guy from Salt Lake City who joined us this evening nodding off and snoring loudly.

The performance continues in the same vein for a further twenty minutes. I have no way of knowing, of course, but I suspect that what we are witnessing here is not a strictly authentic, traditional Masai ritual. They bob round the fire once more and shuffle off into the bush while we cough up our five bucks. Moments later they return to the bar in their civvies, grab their beers and count their money.

In the morning—over the ever-popular fried egg breakfast—we say goodbye to Francis who is taking the Prints back to Nairobi, and are introduced to Winjau, our guide for the next nine days. It has rained all night and the drivers are clearly worried about getting off the Mara. It takes half an hour to drive the vans out of the camp parking area, and we agree to travel in close convoy back to Narok and up to Lake

Nakuru, about three hundred kilometres to the north. After fifteen minutes we are stuck again and bail out, trudging though ankle deep mud while the drivers try to fix the engine. We lean up against the van—Scott and Allan at the back, Mark and I at the front—and heave, shove, slide and slip. Sarah hovers, providing important advice.

It takes four hours to do the one hundred kilometres back to Narok and most of that time we spend shouting orders at each other to dig and push, pausing only to scrape splatters of wet mud from every part of our body. We are sweaty and exhausted and brown from head to toe but, not so secretly, we are all enjoying ourselves. As I watch Scott and Allan teasing Sarah about her supervisory role, and listen to the endless laughter I realise, somehow, we have broken down the barriers with our Navy boys.

The drive from Narok to Nakuru is terrifying. The road is sealed, or at least it was about twenty-five years ago. We overtake on corners, curves, while going uphill and into oncoming traffic. There is much horn blowing, light flashing, swearing and gesticulating, and frequent dashes onto the pot-holed gravel shoulder to avoid collision. Fortunately, the tarmac is short-lived and we are soon back onto mud and puddles where we must drive somewhat more slowly.

Our camp at Nakuru is protected by a concrete-walled complex which we enter via locked metal security doors topped with barbed wire. Inside, it is only slightly less like a prison—so much for the romantic image of African safari. Winjau explains that, unlike on the Mara, we are close to villages here, and tourists have occasionally been robbed. As we pile off the bus, Dana the young Israeli, sidles up to me and whispers in my ear. She's been so scared on her own the last two nights on Masai Mara she's barely slept at all. Can she share with us? We are allocated tents: Darren with Scott and Allan, Ana with Eliza, and Sarah and I with Dana.

We dump our gear and give a moment's thought to a shower. The ablutions block is a rather nasty concrete structure housing a variety of small wildlife: a great croaking mass of frogs, a couple of lizards and a few long-legged spiders. The water is icy and dribbles from a rusty shower head. We give it the flick, and meet the boys at the concrete table and chairs in the concrete bar. Eliza and Ana join us shortly after, entering the room in a pink cloud of fresh deodorant and shampoo. Eliza is wearing pressed, cream trousers and a long-sleeved cotton top, and might have stepped out of an Abercrombie & Kent catalogue. 'Did you *see* an ironing board in her pack?' I ask Sarah. 'Perhaps she stretches them out by hand and breathes on the places that are wrinkly.'

Eliza sits at the top of the table and pontificates about the 'Eco-challenge', an annual endurance competition held in different parts of the world over seven days. Teams are required to complete a strenuous and demanding course involving hiking, climbing, cycling and paddling, carrying all their gear for a week and camping in the bush between stages. 'We trained for eighteen months,' she says. 'I ran ten kilometres before breakfast, worked-out in the gym during lunch and cycled over a hundred kilometres most weekends. My team managed to reach day six which was a great achievement.'

'Oh dear,' I mumble to Sarah. 'I think it's going to be a difficult eight days.'

Dinner is a vegetable mush made with tomatoes, onions and cucumber, and accompanied by the clearly rather popular carrot and cabbage combo. This is only day three and the food has deteriorated markedly—and it wasn't terribly good to start with.

It is our last night with the Navy boys and Darren, and I confess to Sarah that I have grown quite fond of them. Over a beer, Allan talks about his girlfriend—he split with her recently after she slept with someone else on his ship. He was shaken by her betrayal and thinks it will take some time before he will trust again. He talks about his hometown, how proud he felt returning in his uniform, having travelled all over the world when his old friends were still on the dole or stuck in dead-end jobs. He has decided though, over the last few days, to leave the Navy—maybe he'll try university, maybe he'll travel more.

In the morning, we brave the ablutions block. It is some days since I showered and I am sticky with sweat and sunscreen and have sprinkles of mud all the way up the backs of my legs. Sarah undresses on the concrete slab and steps into the gathering of tiny frogs. As she turns the tap I flush the toilet and water spurts and gurgles into the bowl. '*Jac!*' Sarah shouts, 'you've just used all the water.'

'Sorry, Doll. But it's not like there was much to start with.' We pull on our stale, dusty trousers and two-day-old T-shirts and wipe the sleep from our eyes with a damp tissue.

We breakfast on fried eggs again, and something approximating toast. I have already eaten more eggs in the past week than I did in the six months before we left Australia. Eliza suggests they would be much better off providing Granola and yoghurt; it's far healthier and, she is sure, no more expensive. 'Yes,' I agree. 'An excellent idea—fresh muesli would be lovely. Perhaps we could pick some up from that Safeway we passed in the shopping mall on the way into the park.'

We head out to Lake Nakuru, one of a series of shallow soda lakes that litter the floor of the Rift Valley. It is home to over two million flamingos and, from a distance, looks as if it has been edged with streams of pink ribbon. As we drive closer, the individual shapes of the flamingos emerge, and the sound of their honking drowns our conversation. We step out of the van on to the white crusty mud, and look across the water where puffs of pink hover like so many sticks of candy floss at the fairground. As we approach, they beat their wings in perfect unison, and lift off into the sky forming a huge red moving cloud that momentarily casts us all in shadow.

Winjau has spotted a white rhino and her cub a few hundred metres from the van who are heading our way. He shouts to us in an I-don't-want-to-seem-worried-but-get-the-fuck-over-here-quickly kind of way and Sarah, I, and the boys, turn and walk briskly towards him. He waves at Eliza and Ana and the old guy who slept through the traditional dancing, who have wandered off down the lake to take photographs. The rhino is ambling towards us nudging her baby in front of her—about the same distance from the van, as we are from the other side. She breaks into a trot, kicking up chalky dust, her huge horn bobbing up and down as she runs. We, likewise, break into a trot, trying to remain calm despite speculating on the damage resulting from an encounter with that horn. I calculate that a trotting rhino is probably faster than a trotting tourist. Sarah and the boys obviously reach the same conclusion, at the same time, and we all start to sprint in unison.

I try to remember the 'What to do if charged by a wild animal' section of my guidebook. It was different for each one. Stay completely still and make no eye contact? Climb the nearest tree? Run in zig-zags as fast as you can? This would not be the time to mix them up.

We reach the van, red-faced, adrenaline pumping, with the rhino thirty metres off. She decides she's had enough fun for one day and screeches to a halt like Bugs Bunny. She spins around and heads back to the other side of the park. In the distance, Eliza and Ana snap a few more pictures, re-apply their sunscreen and mosey back to the van. 'Hi guys, don't you love this place? It's just *so* relaxing.'

I check with Winjau for future reference. 'Rhinos are very short sighted,' he says. 'You must run short distances and keep changing direction. That way you will lose them. If you stay still, you will die. For lions it's the opposite. Never run from a lion. They don't generally attack people, but if you behave like prey, they will treat you like prey, and bring you down. If a lion comes close, take a deep breath and stay still. He might sniff around, but after a while he'll wander off.'

We drive up to Baboon Cliffs where we can see the lakes, and their pink ribbons stretching for miles. From here Dana, Scott, Allan and Darren head back to Nairobi and we proceed to Samburu with Eliza and Ana. Dana has decided to join us for the Mount Kenya climb, and we arrange to meet her back at our hotel at the end of our safari. We sit with the others on a rock and pose for group photographs, arms hung loosely around each other's shoulders. Winjau fiddles with our gear making sure everything is in the correct vehicle while we hover, snapping a few final shots. We give the boys a hug, exchange addresses and promise letters and Christmas cards, though we all know it's highly unlikely we'll ever see each other again.

In the afternoon, we drive north through the Central Highlands region which is richly fertile and heavily cultivated. It is very different from the grasslands in the south and the steep scarps of the Rift Valley. Rich, deep soil covers the rolling hills, and tea and coffee plantations extend from the road far into the distance. The original Kikuyu inhabitants lost much of their land here to the British and other white settlers during colonisation. Some was redistributed to the farmers after Independence, but many of the large holdings are still owned by whites.

The climate is perfect for intensive cultivation and there is always a robust, overseas market for tea and coffee. The richness of the region brings home the desperateness of Kenya's plight. There is wealth here, and so much potential, but the majority of the people remain poor. President Moi, we are told, is one of the ten richest people in Africa. Most of the country's wealth is in his overseas bank accounts. 'A couple of years ago,' Winjau explains, 'the government levied a tax to pay for road improvements. When the British left, the roads were in a reasonable state, but nothing has been done since. The money was stolen by politicians and bureaucrats and the roads are still terrible. We pay taxes, but nothing is ever fixed, nothing ever gets better.'

We have to be through the Central Province and at our camp site near Samburu National Game Reserve before dark. At night, the road is lined with Somali bandits, and attacks on safari vehicles are common. The bus is playing up again and we pull into Nanyuki for a pit stop. While Winjau looks for a mechanic, we sit down to lunch at 'Mother's Choice Café', the cabbage and carrot thing again, and something that looks like mashed potato, but is bright green.

Nanyuki is the base for climbing Mount Kenya, but apart from a great view of the mountain it has little to recommend it. We are hassled at every step to buy carvings and batiks, or to employ guides and porters for a climb. It is a shock to be in a town—even after only a few days in the bush—and I am watching my back again. Ana and Eliza are spending up. Whatever the price quoted, five hundred shillings or five thousand, Eliza's opening bid is one hundred. It's an unconventional method, but very effective. They buy masks, some decorated gourds, three batiks, a large carved hippo and giraffe, a set of bongo drums and sundry small wooden animals. Sarah and I loiter, poke at the necklaces and carvings, but don't actually manage to buy anything.

The van is fixed, temporarily at least, but Winjau is tense; we have lost time and only have a few hours of light left. 'What if we don't get through in time?' I ask.

'We will have to stay in a hotel and continue in the morning.'

Hallelujah, I think, clean sheets and hot showers.

We are stopped by police on the border of the Northern Province and told we are too late to proceed. They direct us to Isiolo, where we check into the best hotel in town, a kind of run-down backpackers, but it has both beds and showers, and it's a long time since I was clean.

I sleep like the dead from 9.00 p.m. until the wake-up call at 5.30 a.m. Sarah fumbles with my mosquito net and slides in bed beside me to whisper early morning sweet nothings. Delightful though she is, I resist her attempts to rouse me, and explain that she has made a mistake. I am on holiday and, on holiday, people have lie-ins and get up *later* than when they work, not earlier. I, in fact, will sleep until at least 10.00 a.m., then rise, in a leisurely fashion, and read today's newspaper over a fresh pot of tea.

Four hours earlier than I intend, I am up, sitting in the dining room where a large plastic reindeer wishes me Merry Christmas. I reject the weary fried eggs, pile weak coffee powder into a mug of tepid milk and try to wake up.

We proceed through the Northern Province without incident—the road is littered with army personnel and it seems all the banditos have been scared off. Winjau stops periodically to fiddle with the engine and we are immediately surrounded by men selling Somali daggers who are abusive when we don't buy.

Samburu Reserve is very different from the broad, flat expanse of Masai Mara. The big brown Ewaso Nyiro River lined with flat-topped acacias runs through it, and low, gentle hillocks edge the park. It is the end of the short rains and the vegetation is a rich deep green. A large group of reticulated giraffe amble in front of us, munching at the acacia thorns. The giraffe's main defence against predators is his built-in early warning system, Winjau explains. He can see much further than most animals and can run fast enough to get out of danger. Lions are lazy, they want their prey very close; cheetahs are more dangerous because they are willing to put in a little more effort and will attack from further away. We see pairs of elephants, too, enormous great bulls that look completely different from those on the Mara. They take on the colour of the soil from rolling in the mud, and here they are a bright orange, like the enormous termite mounds that erupt intermittently along the roadside.

We drop into the Samburu Lodge where a group of Americans in khaki shorts and four-pocket shirts throw disdainful looks our way. Sarah washes out a T-shirt in the cloakroom, steals some toilet paper, and we sit for an hour in the posh lounge on the strength of one Coke a piece. A group of Samburu, in traditional dress, appears in the dining room, chanting and dancing around the tables as the guests slice into their salmon steaks. They weave out of the dining room and end up in the bar where, like the Masai, they grab their beers and revert to their slightly less traditional selves.

Over margarine sandwiches—the wafer thin tomato slices seem to have disappeared altogether—we talk to Winjau about something other than wildlife. He has been a guide for eleven years now, working mostly for Savuka. When he was young, his brother took him to the Masai Mara and Samburu where he fell in love with the country. At college, he took courses in botany and zoology and continued to explore the other parks. He now has a number of private clients who return each year for photographic safaris.

I imagine, by African standards, he is comfortably middle-class. His wife used to be a steward on Kenyan Airlines, but on the birth of their first son, she changed to a ground staff position so she could look after him. Now though, says Winjau, he is looking for another wife. Eliza commiserates; she was in a long-term relationship herself that ended twelve months ago. She asks him what went wrong and Winjau is perplexed. There is nothing wrong with his first wife, or their marriage, he is looking for another wife, *in addition to*, the first. 'Aah...simultaneously,' says Eliza, as the penny drops.

His second wife must meet with the approval of his first; in fact, it is at her insistence that he finds another. She will help with the household duties and with raising the children. If either wife dies in childbirth—which is not uncommon in Africa, though less likely in this case—the remaining wife will become mother to all. Sometimes, if a woman already has children and doesn't want any more, she will look for a husband who has all the children he wants. Divorce, he says, is practically unheard of. If there are problems, the extended family will provide support and encouragement to the couple to sort things out. Family is very important. It feels good to talk; on this sort of trip you can spend a lot of time surrounded by people, but never get past the formalities.

By early evening, I am exhausted again. It is day six of our eleven-day safari and I am beginning to feel the effects of our daily pre-dawn starts, the fried egg and coleslaw diet, grotty toilets and inadequate ablution facilities. My stomach is churning and I haven't been to the toilet properly for days.

The quality of our camps has also taken a dive. The ground is hard and dusty with little shade, the water supply is erratic, and the toilets mostly unusable. We sit with Eliza and Ana at a rickety picnic table under a sagging canvas awning, a thick cloud of bugs buzzing around a solitary kerosene lantern. Eliza's Eco-challenge enthusiasm is beginning to wane, and none of us is very cheery.

Dinner is rice with a meat and vegetable stew which isn't bad if you avoid the rice, which is a little crunchy, and don't eat the meat, which I suspect is left over from lunch earlier in the day. More interested in my meal than I is the variety of small wildlife with whom I share the table. A few moths flutter around my plate and drop down to try some carrot. A praying mantis checks out my onions, and dozens of tiny beetles make kamikaze raids into my gravy. My head torch provides them with perfect landing lights, but I am reluctant to tackle this meal in the dark.

I make a desperate attempt to extricate the beetles and the moths, to find a mouthful of food with nothing alive or very recently dead. I push a flailing mosquito over the edge and pick out three drowning flies, labouring in their final death throes. Just as soon as I remove them, others take their place.

As I stab frenetically with my fork, I realise I am fighting a losing battle. I am tired and haven't the will to go on. I admit defeat and offer up my meal in surrender. The beetles announce 'party time' to the rest of the gang, and the moths, praying mantis and various unidentified bugs, follow them into my dinner while I tuck into my fifth banana of the day. Later, our cook ambles to the table and lifts the lid of the rice and stew. He stares at my plate and is clearly not happy. I want to explain, but don't have the energy so I smile meekly instead. He wanders back to the cooking tent muttering something about 'tourists' and 'picky'.

Unfortunately, I have to try the toilets again. Generally, if they are really bad we can find a spot just outside in some bushes, and dig a shallow hole with the heel of our boot. Not so here. A narrow wooden shack houses a concrete hole in the ground which is spread with faecal matter and shimmering with feeding flies. The stench is unbearable. I cover my nose and mouth with a bandanna and squat, desperately hoping that whatever happens here, happens quickly. As I struggle out, I dry retch and my eyes begin to water. I have goose bumps all over my body and fight the urge to vomit. I meet Sarah on the track coming my way. She takes one look at me, slips her arm through mine, and accompanies me back to the tent. 'I think I'll wait 'til tomorrow's lodge,' she says.

I stretch out on my sleeping bag and stare up at the roof of the tent. I can feel Sarah lying stiffly by my side. 'Are you…having a good time, Doll?' There is a long pause while I watch a stray mosquito working out his approach to my ankles. 'Yes,' she says, in a somewhat uncertain tone. 'I am. Really. It's just…you know…the food, and the toilets, and the not great washing facilities.'

'Do you think…we might have overdone it with the eleven days?'

'Maybe. We were a bit excited, eh?'

'We were, but you know, I'm tired and all, but I do feel terribly rugged.'

In darkness the following morning, I prepare what passes on safari for a shower. I take a large green, plastic bucket and pour an inch of cold water into the bottom from a jerry can. I carry it over to our tent and place it on the ground, remove the cheap soap from my kit bag and lather my hands. I realise I have a torch strapped to my head still and am wearing my glasses which makes washing my face a little tricky. I rinse and dry my hands, grab my boot and place my light and specs carefully on top. I start again with the soap, which slips out of my hand and into the dirt. I retrieve it and rinse it in my precious inch of water, but it retains the feel of a scouring pad. I close my eyes and imagine I am using a gently exfoliating, apricot facial scrub. I can't quite bring it off, especially as the water I used to rinse my face also gently exfoliates. I feel a minuscule amount better, and proudly announce to Sarah that I have washed, *with* soap. She kisses me on the neck, her smile turning to a grimace, 'Yes I can tell,' she says wiping her lips on the back of her hand. 'I said I *used* soap, I didn't say any thing about rinsing it off.'

Eliza emerges from her tent, her once crisp khakis now baggy and stained, her shining hair now lank and greasy. 'I'm not sure I can do much more of this,' she says, disappearing into the bush.

We pack up our gear and pile into the van for the six hundred kilometre ride back to Nairobi.

Nairobi is still grim, and arriving in the daylight doesn't make it any more pleasant. Winjau drops us at a Wimpy Bar for lunch while he goes to the office. The place is packed with businessmen, but we are spotted by the eager beaver young manager who, seeing there are no tables available, ushers us quickly into his office. Papers and stationery are hastily removed from his desk and replaced by menus and cutlery. He grabs a couple of chairs, squeezes them into place and invites us to sit. Burger and chips is about the last thing I want at the moment, but unfortunately the pan fried chicken with spinach and snow peas tossed in garlic and olive oil and served on a bed of basmati rice with a green salad is off, so burger and chips it is.

Back at the Savuka office, Eliza and Ana are trying to bail out of the final five days. They love the parks…really…and are having a great time…mostly, but they need showers, proper toilets and somewhere to wash their clothes. They're not sure they can go on. The Savuka lady insists they cannot have their money back and a compromise is reached: they'll continue to Amboseli and Tsavo with us, but instead of camping, we will drop them at the nearest lodge where they'll book a room for a sum equal to our weekly budget. Sarah and I feel completely smug having outdone the Eco-challenger and silently congratulate ourselves on being so rugged. Quite frankly, though, if we could afford it, I'd swap rugged for luxury in an instant.

CHAPTER 3

CHRISTMAS AND KILIMANJARO

THE JOURNEY TO Amboseli National Park is exhausting. Winjau has been driving since daybreak, and the two hours spent in Nairobi rearranging Eliza and Ana's accommodation has put us way behind schedule. It is supposed to be the end of the dry season, but Africa's weather patterns, like everyone else's, have been affected by 'El Niño'. For reasons that have never been adequately explained to me, it has caused drought in Australia and prolonged the wet in East Africa. Consequently, where there were roads, there are now swamps and we hit water at every turn. In order to get to Eliza and Ana's lodge we have to take a long and tortuous wet detour.

We step down from the van just as the sun sets. A wide, wooden walkway leads through a canopy of tropical ferns lit by hanging lanterns. At the entrance, we are welcomed by a young man in crisp white livery who takes Eliza's bags and ushers us across the flagstones to the desk. A waiter appears from nowhere with a tray of fresh pineapple juice in tall champagne flutes and offers them around.

The reception is built in rough-hewn wood, like a log cabin, and decorated with huge carvings of giraffe and subtle watercolours of the savannah. Wicker settees and armchairs with deep cushions are sprinkled about the bar and terrace, and well-dressed, middle-aged guests sip cocktails with miniature umbrellas. High above, a thatched ceiling spirals up into a cone and fills with the strains of 'Oh come all ye faithful'. It is quite beautiful, redolent of class and money, of quiet comfort and luxury.

I am suddenly aware that Sarah is calling and I drag myself back to the desk. 'How much?' I ask.

'Two-hundred a night.'

'Shame…are you sure there's nothing cheaper?'

'Sorry Jac.'

'Maybe they'd let us camp in the grounds?'

'I don't think so, somehow.'

'Pity…Back to the tent then I suppose.'

We pile into the van and stop a few hundred metres from the lodge at a huge puddle covering the road. Winjau climbs out and pokes the water with a long stick to check its depth. He climbs back in, and we drive through, the water almost covering the wheels. Half a kilometre further on we stop again, test the puddle and proceed, repeating the exercise a dozen times until we reach our camp site. It is pitch black when we arrive and we are exhausted and road weary. We muster some energy to erect the tent and after another hastily prepared meal, involving the usual carrot and cabbage and a banana, crawl into bed.

It is hot and humid and the air is completely still. I haven't showered in days and I lie writhing in accumulated layers of sun block, insect repellent, dirt and sweat. My hair bears a striking resemblance, in sight and touch, to a toilet brush. I stick to myself, and to Sarah on the unfortunate occasions when we happen to touch. The ground is hard and uneven and we have placed an old blanket from the van under our thermarests. It is coarse and prickly and smells faintly of wet dog. I shove a rolled-up jacket on top of the rocky outcrop at my hip in an attempt to relieve the sharp pressure on my side. There is too much gear in the tent and my feet are vying for space with the camera bag and my dirty underwear and trousers. My head is pushed up into one corner where it is positioned at a ninety-degree angle to my body. I lie on my back and pretend to be comfortable, reminding myself that I am on holiday and having a good time.

The tent is stifling and I can barely breathe, but my fresh air options are limited: my boots and four-day-old socks nestled in the vestibule, the wet dog blanket, or the spot just near my head which my camping predecessor obviously used as his own personal toilet.

I doze fitfully for an hour, becoming increasingly agitated with my inability to sleep. My Restless Leg Syndrome kicks in and I start to wriggle, alternately tensing and relaxing the muscles in my calves. I wake Sarah, not for the first time. 'I can't sleep,' I say.

'I can,' she replies.

It finally cools down enough that I can slip into my sleeping bag liner, tucking the silk between my legs so they don't touch each other. It is a bit caught up in everything and I have to pop a few things on top of Sarah before I can extricate it. A faint voice rises from beneath a mass of down sleeping bag, 'If you don't stop I will have to kill you and bury you under an acacia tree.'

I lie back down, the sheer frustration of not being able to sleep having now far surpassed any physical discomfort. I am incapable of relaxing and feel completely awake. Then, out of the misery of this whole gruesome night, I start to cry, and in minutes, fall asleep.

I wake at 6.00 a.m., unsurprisingly feeling like shit. It is still dark, but Sarah is up and chirpy. I announce that I will require a bowl of water—though I know there is barely any left in the jerry can—a towel and my toilet bag, and until they are forth-coming I will not be leaving the tent. Sarah smiles and wanders off into the bush. I settle on top of my sleeping bag and feel quietly sorry for myself; all I want is a shower and a decent cup of tea. Not much to ask for Christmas.

Sarah returns eventually, placing a plastic bowl filled with fresh, clean water in front of the tent and hands me my toiletries. I stand in my boxers and vest and perform an all-over body wash in front of a group of Masai men who stare, utterly bemused. I dunk my head completely in the water, tipping the bowl as I stand, and soaking my clothes. I grab my toothbrush. 'Where's the water?' I demand.

'Borehole, bit of a way down there.'

I trek off into the bush, feeling somewhat refreshed. The path meanders though the scrub, past the edge of a village and through three or four dense groves of trees, but there is no sign of a pump. The sun is just beginning to rise and the Masai gather, leaning on their sticks and picking their teeth with twigs. I walk further down the track, around a huge flooded bend and into a clearing where I spot the pump and clean my teeth. I nod and smile at the kids who draw in close to watch. As I negotiate my way back, it dawns on me that Sarah has just done this fifteen-minute walk lumbering my precious water in a huge great bowl. I think, perhaps, I owe her.

We force down another fried egg breakfast and strike camp, shoving the tents in the back of the van and piling our packs roughly on top. It is a beautiful morning and we perk up as we drive through the park to the lodge. Eliza and Ana are restored to their former shining hair and gleaming teeth in fresh white cotton. We ask about their night, but they are reticent, and I wonder if it wasn't quite up to their usual standard.

Amboseli is different again from Samburu and Masai Mara. There is generally more water here than in the northern parks, and at the moment, because of the extended rains, it looks more like wetlands than savannah. We watch the hippos bobbing up for air in the shallow lakes that have formed on either side of the road. They are enormous creatures, though we see only their ears and eyes and occasionally the length of their backs. 'Hippos kill more people in Africa than any other animal,' Winjau explains. 'Tourists often pitch their tents by the hippo runs along the river, because it looks like a nice clear spot. At night, they leave the water and wobble on to the bank, stepping on anything in their way, including your tent. Or, sometimes, they just come up for air in the spot where you happen to be canoeing.'

On the plains, there are literally hundreds of elephants, and we climb up to an observation point and sit for an hour watching them drift through the grasses below. They march in long lines, the younger, smaller elephants walking between the older ones, the bulls flanking the edge of the herd. Periodically, the leader pauses for everyone to catch up and the juveniles trot up to their mothers like a scene from *The Jungle Book*.

Away from the elephants there are zebra, wildebeest, baboons, guineafowl, warthogs, and an abundance of DLAs. I have never been a great animal person, but there is something quite special about seeing them here—so close—and in their own environment. The only thing we haven't seen, however, is lions. 'I'm sick of prey,' says Eliza. 'I want predators.' I leave her squinting through binoculars for the big five and crash on the back seat. I give Sarah instructions to wake me if we see anything big, or if Kilimanjaro emerges from the clouds. We don't and it doesn't.

We drop Eliza and Ana off and they confess the lodge is beautiful and they had a superb night: a long hot shower, a cold beer, a great meal and an excellent sleep. They didn't want to tell us in case it made us feel worse, especially with it being Christmas and all. 'No, no,' I say. 'No problem. Not at all. We had a great night. Lovely. Very comfortable. Really. Slept like a baby.'

We have our first down-time the whole trip, three hours to ourselves, and I am inordinately relieved. I grab a mattress and lie in the shade of an acacia tree, dozing happily in the languid air of the afternoon, delighted at the prospect of being still and doing nothing.

By the time we set out for our evening game drive, I am remarkably refreshed—it doesn't take much. The clouds are huge and billowing and the setting sun fills the air with gold dust. There are elephants everywhere—close to the road and scattered far off in the distance—bulls with huge thick tusks and mud-caked matriarchs guarding their offspring. They leave great holes in the grass, their enormous feet sinking into the soft, wet mud. I kneel on my seat and stare out of the pop-up roof, breathing in the beauty of the animals, and the light on the hills.

Slowly, the cloud clears from the top of the mountains and Kilimanjaro emerges—a perfect, flat-topped volcano rising from the plain, dwarfing the elephant herds and the rainforest, and overwhelming the eastern edge of the park. The sun illuminates its unmistakable snow-covered peak, which shines like Donne's 'gold to airy thinness beat'. A cold, damp wind whips across my face as I stare mesmerised by the remarkable splendour that is Kilimanjaro. I wouldn't have missed this moment for the world: the long drives, the poor food, the mud, the dirt and discomfort, have all been worth it.

By the time we head back, dusk has fallen and the sky has filled with dark, towering storm clouds. A perfect cumulonimbus anvil rises on the horizon and great shuddering claps of thunder echo around the mountain. We pull down the lid of the van and wind the windows up tight. With every bolt of lightning the clouds suddenly brighten to pink, then plunge back into deep dark purple, as if God were sitting with his finger on a light switch. We arrive back at camp, fall out of the van and into bed. Tonight, sleep comes quickly and stays.

It is Christmas Eve morning and Sarah and I head over to the borehole. We take it in turns to pump and wash, doing the best we can, half-dressed. The Masai appear again, and this time it seems that word has gone round there is a show on. A cluster of young men appears, and a circle of women with babies gathers at the edge of the clearing.

Thirty or forty people stare amusedly, pointing, smiling, commenting. As I duck my head under the water, the laughter picks up and spreads until we are surrounded by a small tribe of giggling Masai. We cannot help but laugh ourselves. I run my fingers through my hair and towel dry my face and hands. I would love to understand Swahili just now. 'Man those white chicks are weird. Don't they wear some strange shit.'

'Yeah. That one with the long hair, why do you think she has it like that?'

'Beats me. And *what* is she putting under her arms?'

At breakfast I approach our cook and tentatively ask whether we might have the eggs done a different way. He looks at me blankly, clearly non-plussed by my question. 'Maybe scrambled?' I say, 'or…'

'Poached?' he interrupts.

'Yes! Poached would be great. Thanks.'

I wander over to Sarah and plonk myself at the table. '*Poached*,' I whisper proudly.

As we contemplate the possibility of our first grease free breakfast, our cook retrieves the eggs from a box and takes a huge frying pan from the van. He grabs a large can of oil and slugs in into the pan, and we watch as he pours…and pours…until the oil is a good inch deep.

'Oh God!' I groan. 'He's not really…'

'…Poaching them in oil?'

We pick up Eliza and Ana and head for Tsavo West, a much less visited park in the southern corner of the country. Once we are clear of the lodge Eliza holds up three small plastic bags crammed full of freshly baked croissants. 'I stole them from the buffet for you,' she says, handing them around. They are the nicest thing we've eaten in days.

Over our second and much nicer breakfast, we chat. Eliza was posted to Rio de Janeiro by her company and has been there for almost two years. She loves Brazil, its easy, laid-back lifestyle, its romanticism, the colour and passion of its people. Just before she left for Africa she was offered a big-bucks job in New York, but she has fallen in love with a beautiful, bronze Brazilian and now doesn't know what to do. We pass the journey easily—relationships, work, travel—and, after their initial frosty start, it seems Eliza and Sarah have reached *détente*.

We take a wrong turn through a group of villages nestled beneath a range of green conical hills. The houses are very different from the Masai huts up on the Mara. Most are made of wood rather than thatch and look well built and substantial. They are spread out along neat tracks that line fields of abundant healthy maize. The earth is a rich dark brown, the colour of coffee, and the vegetation is a vibrant green and yellow. For the first time, the kids look well-fed, though this doesn't stop them running by the bus with up-turned palms and their persistent demand of 'Give me sweet'.

It is an easy and pleasant drive, though by the time we reach the lodge the sky has darkened. We follow Eliza and Ana into the lobby and are arrested by the spectacular view from the dining room: a small herd of impala, some baboons, a pair of spotted hyena and a large gathering of water birds, edge a natural oval water hole. A huge open grassy plain surrounds them, and a steep slope behind rises up to meet the clouds. 'You picked a nice spot for dinner,' I say to Eliza.

'You could join us,' she replies. It's way beyond our budget and Winjau would either have to wait around or eat with us, and I'm not sure he would be comfortable with either. 'Thanks, but we'll head back.'

Eliza negotiates a price with the manager, grabs her cabin key and turns to us as we leave. 'You know,' she says, 'I admire your resilience. I just can't cope with this much dirt, with not being able to shower, and having to eat such awful food. The Eco-challenge was one thing, but this is something else.' I smile, try to feel vindicated, but Eliza gets to spend Christmas Eve in luxury and we get to spend it in a cramped and stifling tent, so who wins here?

We drive back along the track in the dark and I try not to think about another sticky night with no shower. The jaunts to and from the lodge are adding an extra couple of hours driving every day, on top of the huge distances we are already covering. It's late and we are all pretty zonked. As we round a corner I see some movement in the bushes picked up by the headlights. 'What?' says Sarah.

'I think I saw something.' A lion, a full grown male with a shaggy mane, ambles across the road in front of the van. He is huge—his paws twice the size of my hands—and has a long thin scar down his left haunch. It can't be more than five seconds before he disappears, but we are completely thrilled. Predators! At last! Our reward for not staying at the lodge. Eliza will be gutted.

Two minutes later—and the proximity of the aforementioned predator is not lost on us—we turn into our camp site and watch a herd of zebra and Thompson's gazelle scurry off into the bush. In the darkening twilight I can just make out one skinny thorn tree and a toilet block. There is a shower, but no water. Winjau disappears in search of food and we erect the tent in the dark. A number of white South Africans arrive in four wheel drives, unloading huge tents and mattresses, tables and chairs and spreading themselves out across the site. We sit by our tent listening to Christmas carols drift over from a radio and watch the stars.

Winjau returns, having found something for dinner, and we hover round him eager to discover our Christmas treat. He is carrying a small bundle cupped in his hands, which he presents for our inspection. I lean over and pull back the layers of old newspaper in which it is wrapped. It is reddish, bloody and certainly looks as if it once belonged to an animal, though beyond that, it resembles nothing with which I am familiar. 'What is it?' I ask.

'Steak.'

'Steak?'

'Yes. Steak from the local village.'

'Funny. Doesn't look like steak.'

'Oh yes. Steak. Definitely steak.'

'*Really?*'

'Yes…Steak…of goat. Goat steak.'

Ah! Steak of goat. Great. Yes. Fabulous. Not sure about you, but *just* what I fancied. Yup. Goat. Terrific. There are worse things than goat, I know, but it is Christmas and we have been eating crap now for two weeks.

I try to keep an open mind and pop a succulent, tender, goat morsel onto the end of my fork. Mmm…it's kind of…bouncy. As I clamp my teeth around it, my jaw springs apart in a kind of repeated boing! boing! boing! I slide it into my cupped hand and drop it onto the dirt as discreetly as I can. 'Fantastic, Winjau,' I say. 'Thanks for all your efforts.'

The air is heavy and humid and as we prepare for bed I long for rain. At about 1.00 a.m. it comes, a huge tropical downpour. Somehow the tent pegs on one side have worked loose and the fly sheet starts to flap wildly. My waterproof is locked in the van, so I unzip the fly screen, and re-peg the whole thing in my vest and boxers. It takes no more than a minute, but by the time I get back in, I am soaked through and have an acacia thorn sticking out of my foot. The rain has formed a small stream beneath us and the tent floor is now a waterbed. We float on our thermarests.

I lie back, hoping the extra money we spent on a Macpac will pay off. We stay dry, but as soon as the rain stops, the humidity rises and I wish it were raining again. I arrange my sleeping bag liner to minimise contact between the various parts of my body, and pretend to sleep. I am aggravated by the mosquitoes that must have snuck in when I was re-pegging. After fifteen minutes of swatting I grow suspicious; there shouldn't be this many. In the darkness I extend my arm towards the fly screen, but I reach through the vestibule to the outside of the tent.

There is no fly screen. I failed to re-zip it and the mozzies have been enjoying an unexpected Christmas dinner and spreading malarial good cheer everywhere. I fumble around in the dark, trying to locate the end of the zip and close it up.

I really must stop doing things without my glasses.

We are up and out early, meeting Eliza and Ana and pretending it isn't really Christmas Day. It is another ferociously fast drive down the 'highway', the main north south route linking Nairobi to Mombasa. By the roadside, I count four overturned tankers—burned out and gutted—and a couple of rusting minivans.

In order to accommodate Eliza and Ana in their next lodge we have to find a different camp site, the usual one is over two hours drive away. Winjau knows a place we may be able to stay.

We arrive at what can most accurately be described as a scrap yard—a large patch of dirt littered with disused cars and wrecked safari vans, hunks of contorted metal and bundles of rusting wire. At one end there is a concrete, corrugated iron garage furnished with green formica tables and orange plastic chairs. There is no grass anywhere—there being no water—just a sloping area of dried mud where we may pitch our tent.

A young man wearing torn polyester trousers and a faded Michael Jackson T-shirt clears the phlegm from his throat and spits in the dirt by way of welcome. We plonk ourselves in the chairs and spread Christmas lunch on the formica table, rummaging through sweaty plastic bags full of stale bread and left-over salad. Sarah forks cold baked beans from a tin and I chew through a coleslaw sandwich. 'At least there's bread,' I say. Sarah looks up suddenly from her beans, 'Oh Jac, did you check it?' I stop, mid chew and spit my mouthful onto the ground. 'What?'

'It was green, Babe.' I tuck into a raw carrot and we admit to a low moment.

We head out for a game drive, via Eliza and Ana's lodge. It's hot, we don't expect to see much and I grab the back seats and lie down for a nap. I am awoken by Ana shouting in Portuguese and gesticulating wildly. I jump up to see a lioness disappearing into the bush, and a full-grown male lying just by the side of the road. He sits and stares, making eye contact with each of us in turn. He raises his head, yawns and shakes his mane and we whip out the cameras, paparazzi style. We are so close that a few strides would see him on the bonnet, but he remains still, clearly far less impressed by us, than we are with him.

Back at the car yard, we sit around the formica waiting for dinner. The humidity is unbearable and the mosquitoes are biting through my socks and enjoying the insect repellent underneath. I share out the two bottles of warm beer I've been carrying since Nairobi in an attempt to engender some Christmas spirit. Michael Jackson switches his radio to an English speaking channel for our benefit and we listen to a lively discussion about AIDS and sexually transmitted diseases on the KBC. I am thinking about turkey and roast potatoes, about stuffing and parsnips and gravy, of a room full of wrapping paper and presents, of my nieces and nephews playing Twister and Mah Jong, of Mum before we left, 'Ooh Jacqui, you'll have a *lovely* time in Africa at Christmas.'

Sarah has an amazing capacity to be chirpy, even in the most adverse of circumstances. After another sticky and restless night she is up at 5.45 a.m., pottering around the tent. She wakes me with a smile as if she has just brought in the paper and put the kettle on for a cup of tea. Which she hasn't. Over fried eggs, we listen to the news and discuss the Middle East peace process with Winjau. 'It's tragic about Rabin,' he says, 'Netanyahu is too hard line. They should look at Egypt, at what Anwar Sadat achieved.' I am surprised at how well-informed he is. I know I shouldn't be, but I am. We discuss the parallels with tribal Africa and Kenya's colonial history. Winjau's father still deeply resents the English, but Winjau was brought up in a different political climate where the sense of black inferiority wasn't perpetuated in the same way. He has many friends of all nationalities, including English.

Out of the blue, he asks me whether a lot of women have their hair like me now—my hair is short and straight, cut closely around my ears and neck. I am trying to work out what he means when he clarifies his question, 'You know, since she was killed in the crash.' I glance at Sarah to see if he is really saying what I think. She nods. Ah yes, Princess Diana. Of course. Funny, I have often thought she and I bore more than a passing resemblance. 'Many African women,' he says, 'use a "relaxer" on their hair so they can have a "Lady Di" style.'

We pack up and head for Voi, a nothing little town with a rough dirt road and a handful of wooden stalls selling bananas and plastic holdalls. From the reaction of the locals to our arrival, it is not a place often visited by tourists. Eliza and Ana manage to find a guesthouse for the night—somewhat below their usual standard—and will catch the train to Mombasa tomorrow. We share a few awkward hugs and exchange addresses. I suggest Eliza gives the New York job the flick and sticks with the bronzed Brazilian. She hands Winjau an enormous tip, 'For all the extra hassle and driving to the lodges,' she says. 'Thanks.'

We wave them off and sleep the five hours back to Nairobi.

We are greeted by Kepher and Dana who are waiting at the hotel when we arrive. Being met by people we know, however superficially, is a treat, and coming back to the hotel—bed bugs and all—feels almost like coming home. Kepher has been keeping Dana company and looking out for her since we left. They have been to the Karen Blixen Museum, visited the market, done some shopping and seen two movies. 'How was the safarai?' Kepher asks.

'Absolutely fantastic,' I say without hesitation. 'We loved every minute.' He breaks into a big broad grin. 'Good,' he says. 'I am happy.'

'Seen Paul?' I slip in casually, 'our Mount Kenya guy?'

'Ah…he went home for Christmas and he is not back yet.'

Dana is full of tales of woe: there has been escalating election violence in Nairobi and up country. She met a group of Israeli boys who had just climbed Mount Kenya who said the weather was terrible, freezing rain and blustering winds, that it was exhausting and dangerous. And did we know a busload of people had been set alight just outside town? She has decided she cannot face climbing Mount Kenya, she is lonely and scared and has booked an early flight home. We check our guide-book for a western-style restaurant that doesn't serve bananas or fried eggs, or carrot and cabbage, where Dana can feel safe for a couple of hours. We find a tacky little trattoria and order pizza, which after the past two weeks, feels like the height of fine dining.

In the morning, Kepher is waiting for us outside the hotel to check if Paul has been in touch. He hasn't. Kepher says he will look for him and meet us later. We contemplate our options if Paul fails to show; the election is in three days and we don't want to be in town. Kepher appears at the café where we are having lunch, but has no news. By evening he is frantic; he has checked Paul's house, his friends, and every safari company in town, but no one has seen him for days. He escorts us back to the hotel, questions the touts hanging round the entrance and heads off to check a local bar.

At the desk we grab our valuables from the office safe and pick up our key. 'Message for you,' says the guy on duty, handing me a screwed up piece of paper. *Hope you had a lovely Christmas and a great safari. Will pick you up at 9.00 a.m. Regards, Paul.*

CHAPTER 4

'...BOTH OF WHICH CAN BE FATAL'

OUR FIVE-DAY Mount Kenya climb begins with a two-hour drive in a 'shared taxi' which reminds me of one of those competitions where you squeeze four hundred people into a telephone box. We arrive in Nanyuki with rather less feeling in our buttocks than we are accustomed to, and I have a detailed imprint of Sarah's boot stamped onto my right calf. We are dropped at the 'Riverside Hotel', though 'Petrol-station-side Hotel' might be a more accurate title. A young man, in blue plastic open-toed sandals, shuffles towards us. He grunts and jerks his head which I take as his way of saying 'Welcome to the Riverside. I hope you had a pleasant journey. Please follow me.' We are escorted to a dingy concrete room, where the beds appear to be bug free and where the toilet flushes, which makes this the best place we've stayed in so far.

Our climb begins tomorrow at 2900 metres and we ascend to 4985 over four days—about 350 metres below the height of Everest base camp. We spend the afternoon walking to the Equator just outside Nanyuki in order to acclimatise. There is a tacky, rusting sign showing a large map of Africa with a line running through it which announces 'You are now on the Equator.' Sarah and I stand beneath it and jump from one side to the other: 'Now we're in the Northern Hemisphere and now we're in the Southern Hemisphere. Northern. Southern. Northern. Southern.' We make Paul take a photograph of us in front of the sign and then—well, it's not everyday you get to stand on both sides of the world—make him take another with us on the other side.

Back at Petrol-station-side we meet a Swiss couple, Pascale and Uli, who are also attempting the climb. Uli spent a year in Kenya as an exchange student when he was sixteen and is an encyclopaedia of African tribal culture. He can differentiate between Masai, Kikuyu and Luo by sight and by certain linguistic characteristics. The Kikuyu, whose traditional tribal lands cover the Nanyuki area, mix up 'l' and 'r' which accounts for the 'lice' with our curry and the repeated references to the forthcoming 'erection'. Kikuyu and Masai often inter-marry because both tribes are circumcised, but neither tribe would marry a Luo, because they are not.

We are joined by David—Pascale and Uli's guide—Paul, and a group of porters who discuss their hopes for Mwai Kibaki in tomorrow's election. I garner opinion on the one female candidate, who according to newspaper reports, is becoming increasingly popular. Not here it seems. It doesn't matter how good she is, Kenya is not ready to be governed by a woman.

We are packed up and ready by ten in the morning, but there is no sign of Paul or our lift to the gate. At eleven, he arrives to explain that our driver is stuck in a queue at the polling station, and at twelve, he returns with the same news. We sit on our packs for the next two hours as guides, porters and unconnected interested parties try to find us a lift. 'We need a four-wheel drive,' Paul explains, 'a good one' and they are all being used to ferry people to and from polling stations. He manages, eventually, to secure a Toyota Land Cruiser and a driver who has generously offered to transport the other three groups currently stranded in Nanyuki. Nineteen people and their packs and five days camping and cooking gear are squeezed aboard. Sarah and I spot the two empty seats in the cab at the front. 'Shall we?' I say.

'Absolutely.'

We arrive at Sirimon Gate around 2.00 p.m., four hours later than planned, and off-load our gear onto a flat grassy plain. Paul hands us a pre-prepared lunch comprising two cucumber sandwiches and a banana, which does not augur well for the future. The temperature has dropped markedly and I pull out my fleece and gloves. Clouds roll into the valley below and I lose sight of Paul barely twenty metres from where I stand. The cold, the mist and the lateness of the day give the whole thing an edge, and as I throw my day-pack onto my shoulders, I feel a slight flutter in my stomach. My *frisson* is back.

We begin with a gentle climb taking deliberate steps 'pole pole' (pro-nounced poh-lay poh-lay), 'slowly slowly', to allow our bodies time to adjust to the altitude. Two young, keen Canadians and an Australian zoom off ahead of us laden with gear. Sarah has read and memorised the National Park brochure on 'How to recognise altitude related sickness', and tells me that ascending too quickly and over-exerting oneself is dangerous. She is checking us both for symptoms every five hundred metres.

We ascend via a broad, rocky track through dense bamboo and cedar trees, and tall native pines; a landscape quite unlike anything I have seen before. The path is littered with huge buffalo droppings and we can just make out herds gathering in the valley below. The walking is easy and the relaxed pace provides an opportunity to chat with our fellow trekkers. We discuss Switzerland's refusal to join the United Nations or the European Community, a result of what Uli sees as an outdated sense of neutrality. They would both like European

Community passports and the option of working in other countries, and they would like to be rid of the National Service. Uli trained for fifteen weeks when he was eighteen and has to serve for three weeks every year until he is forty. He has finagled his way into the army band so that he no longer has to spend his time rolling in mud. The government, he says, believes it could mobilise the army in twenty-four hours. He is less confident.

Far off in the distance we can see the Keeny Canadians who passed us at the beginning, storming up the mountain; they have no porters, are not stopping to drink and are climbing way too fast. Sarah and I shake our heads in smug agreement. 'Asking for trouble.'

We arrive at Old Moses camp in rapidly thickening cloud and bitter cold. I change into my thermals and hat and quickly erect the tent, unravelling the thick down bags and spreading them out across our thermarests. We can see snatches of the bamboo forest below and the foggy peaks across the valley. I huddle against Sarah pulling my collar close against the sharp night air. When I was fifteen I fell in love with the mountains on a school trip to North Wales and something from that time has stayed with me, like a talisman. Now, whenever I'm in the mountains, I get a rush. I feel a kind of exuberant confidence, an intense optimism—as if I'm young again and the world is mine and I can do, or be, anything I want. 'It's a magic spot, Doll. I love it,' I say.

'I love *you*,' says Sarah.

'Me too you,' I say.

The rest of our party is in the hut warming around a stove, but I linger outside somewhat reluctant to enter. I have read, in more than one guidebook, about the preponderance of Rodentia here. I have a slight mouse phobia, which I claim as genetic since it is shared by all members of my family. Paul insists there is nothing to worry about, but I know this is only because Sarah has told him to lie. It is dark and freezing, and we cannot spend the whole night outside. I send Sarah in to check the place out and stomp around loudly in what we privately refer to as her 'anti-mouse dance'. She gives me the all-clear and I step in hesitantly, perching on the bench by the door. As I sit, a fat, black rat wobbles out of the kitchen into the dining area, slinks along the wall and disappears into the bunk room. I watch, frozen and only through the exercise of an enormous degree of self-control do I not scream and stand on the table. Sarah sees it too and I catch her eye, 'So, no rodents then. Pleased about that. Excellent. Wouldn't want to have to rush through dinner or spend the evening with my feet on the table.'

We have finally caught up with the Keenies: Elana, a waste management expert working with Canada Crossroads, Martin, a tree-planter from Newfoundland and Damien, a medical student from Melbourne in his sixth year. They are climbing on a miniscule budget which accounts for the lack of porters and their eagerness to make it up and down in the shortest time possible. We share a dinner of packet onion soup, beef stew and rice, and as soon as I am done we leave the hut—and the fat black rat—and step into the sharp night air. It's bitterly cold and we make a dash for the tent, burrowing into our sleeping bags fully clothed. I pull the cords tight around my neck and shoulders, kiss Sarah goodnight, and drift into an easy sleep.

After an early fried egg breakfast we begin the nine hundred metre ascent to Shipton's Hut at 4200 metres. Paul estimates it will take approximately eight hours, allowing for lunch and frequent short drink stops. The vegetation thins out quickly as we start to climb past the timber line and the forest is replaced by squat, twisted St John's Wort trees. We cross a flat grassy plain, almost an alpine meadow, and head into the Mackenzie Valley. High rugged peaks protect one side and a shallow incline gently rises on the other. The lower slopes are sprinkled with lobelia, a low, bright green cabbage-like shrub that becomes taller as we climb until it eventually turns into a cabbage-like tree. The lobelia is interspersed with 'ostrich plume feathers', tall elongated plants with drooping, bluish leaves that stand out against the increasingly sparse and rugged backdrop. It is an eerie, other-worldly landscape.

Slowly, the snow-covered peak of Mount Kenya appears, dominated by the jagged Point Lenana. It is steep and icy, and I am not completely convinced by the idea of our pre-dawn ascent. I understand the desire to see the sun rise over the summit certainly, but I'm not great at 4.00 a.m. and, call me crazy, climbing up frozen scree in the dark in sub-zero temperatures is not my idea of a good time.

The walking is heavy going and we are all beginning to feel the effect of the altitude. We stop often to drink and each time I gently massage my temples with my fingertips. As we climb higher, the mountain comes into sharp view, the snow on the peak translucent under the clear, bright sky. I feel a slight pressure building in my forehead and check with the others; everyone has a headache which, according to Sarah's brochure, is normal at this height.

We are only an hour from the hut, but I stop more frequently to drink and catch my breath. The pressure in my head has turned to a throbbing, which goes away when I stop walking, and then begins again. Sarah is asking me to describe how I feel every five minutes. We take the last hundred metres *very* slowly and each time my foot hits the ground, a hammer hits my head.

We reach camp at about 4.00 p.m. The view is stunning, but raising my head to admire it hurts. The porters sift through our gear and prepare some packet tomato soup. I am not sure this is a great idea, but Paul is insistent. I sip, slowly bringing the spoon up to my lips, trying to keep my head perfectly still. I swallow a few mouthfuls and shove the bowl across the table. Sarah helps me onto my feet and to the tent, where I crawl into my sleeping bag, laying my head on the boulder that is my rolled up jacket.

When I awake an hour later I can barely move. Every headache I have ever had, every second of motion sickness, every episode of drunken vomiting, is all compressed into one. Sarah goes to find Paul, leaving me flat and rigid, my hand pressed against my forehead. I lie, absolutely still, and am overcome all of sudden with a violent shuddering nausea. I drag myself to the side of the tent and throw up the tomato soup.

Sarah returns with a cup of hot, sweet tea which Paul insists will make me feel better. While I hug the tea she checks her brochure for symptoms of high altitude pulmonary and cerebral edema. 'Who's the President of the United States,' she says.

'*What?*'

'Can you recite the alphabet?'

'I'd rather not just now.'

'I'm just checking you're not confused or disorientated.'

'Sweetheart, I know exactly where I am and what's happening. Though you might not be able to see him, a hippo is sitting on my head and any minute now, I am going to spew the entire contents of my stomach, and its lining, over the floor of this tent.'

She takes my pulse and listens to my breathing and as I don't have a *dry cough deteriorating to frothy sputum* or *audible gurgling from the chest area*, she is satisfied I'm not about to slip into a coma.

Paul arrives and hovers outside the tent with Sarah. There is a general consensus amongst everyone who is not throwing up that I should try to eat something. I assure them that, if I as much as lift my head, they will have to make a very rapid exit from the tent. I lose this battle, take a sip of tea and vomit violently over their boots.

It is dark and bitterly cold and it seems like a good idea to transfer to the warmth of the hut. Sarah helps me up and I bow my head supporting its weight with both hands. I shuffle, shaky and breathless, towards the door. As I enter the hut, I am vaguely aware of the presence of Uli and Pascale, the Keenies and numerous guides and porters. I sit on the bench, place my head on the table and hope that I will die soon. A plate of rice and another cup of tea are shoved in front of me. Great. Yes. Very clever. I can't stop vomiting, but hey, here's a good idea, why don't I eat more?

It's 7.00 p.m. and the temperature has dropped below freezing. I have been like this for three hours now and it is as much as I can do to sit rigidly still and breathe. I am vaguely conscious of a debate raging around me. Going down will involve a five-hour walk in the dark, across rough terrain, back to the hut at Old Moses where we started today. As I can barely make it to the door, this doesn't seem very realistic, but if the pressure in my head doesn't equalise, and we remain at this height, I am in danger of developing more acute symptoms. Sarah appears with Damien, the medical student from Melbourne, who is the nearest thing she can find to an expert opinion. He sits by my side, places his hand on my back and, almost imperceptibly rubs gently between my shoulder blades. It is a quiet gesture of such tenderness from a complete stranger and, in my current miserable state, makes me cry. He thinks we should descend.

Somewhere in the midst of all the commotion, it has occurred to Sarah that we have our tent with us and, therefore, do not have to trek all the way to Old Moses. We can descend a few hundred metres and sleep on the mountainside which, according to her now somewhat dog-eared brochure, should do the trick.

I sit with my head down, immobile, next to a plate of cold rice and listen to the flurry of activity and discussion in three different languages going on around me. Uli and Pascale are pumping water through a purifier and decanting it into our water bottles. The porters are digging through boxes for bread and biscuits and loading up Paul's pack, and the Canadians are organising sleeping bags and extra clothes. Sarah and Damien are packing up the tent.

We set off about an hour later, Paul with a huge pack carrying the tent, three sleeping bags, food and emergency equipment, and Sarah with two smaller packs, strapped to her front and back with spare clothes, eight litres of water and two packets of biscuits. There is only space for one person to walk on the track which forces Paul to clamber awkwardly across uneven ground while holding my hand and attempting to light my path with a torch. We stop every few minutes for me to drink the awful chlorinated water as per Damien's instructions. My stomach settles quickly, but my head is still severe.

After half an hour I begin to feel a slight release of pressure in my head which continues as we descend. It works like magic, and after forty minutes I ask Sarah if she's brought anything to eat. She smiles, a huge great smile, and gives me a hug.

We stop after an hour and erect the tent by the side of the track. My headache has lifted a little and I have stopped feeling nauseous, but I am completely done in. The three of us squeeze into our small two-person tent, Paul's head at one end, Sarah's and mine at the other. I am asleep in seconds and wake with the sunrise.

In the morning Sarah tells me she didn't sleep terribly well, and I must say, even without my glasses on, she looks dreadful. Paul, it seems, took his full allocation of space leaving Sarah desperately squashed between the two of us, and periodically dodging down-covered kicks to the head.

We breakfast on biscuits and bananas and I watch Paul and Sarah pack up the tent. I still have a severe headache and cannot bend down or make any sudden movements. I manage the trek back up, stepping slowly and deliberately and keeping my head as still as possible. When we enter the hut Pascale and Uli, Elana and Martin, the guides and porters clap and cheer and I exchange a quiet thumbs-up with Damien.

Paul makes tea and suggests we do a short walk close to the hut in preparation for our summit ascent in the early hours of tomorrow morning. It's about eight-hundred metres to the top and should take us two and a half hours. I catch Sarah's eye over the top of my steaming cup. Did I just miss something here? I thought I'd spent last night in an acute state of oxygen deprivation, throwing my guts up and barely able to put one foot in front of the other as a result of the very activity Paul is now proposing. 'I have another plan,' I say. 'Why don't we spend the day looking at the glorious view of Mount Kenya and drinking tea?'

This time, I win.

Over breakfast, we join Uli and Pascale at a table and listen while they de-brief from the Point Lenana ascent they've just attempted. They left at 3.00 a.m. rugged up in full thermal underwear, fleece, jacket, hat and gloves and scrambled up the ice covered scree. There was little light from the moon and they negotiated the rocks in the faint glow of a small fading torch carried by David. They walked at a ridiculous pace, not stopping to rest or drink. 'It's a very macho thing with our guide,' Pascale says 'reaching the top and doing it as quickly as possible.'

They climbed like this for two hours, repeatedly losing their footing and slipping on boulders. When they finally reached the steep, icy wall of rock near the summit Pascale burst into tears. Another group was on their way down and she decided to join them and descend. Uli pro-ceeded to the top with David, but was so exhausted, and so worried about Pascale he really didn't enjoy it.

This is not, I suspect, the story we want to hear. We have the rest of the day to decide if we will attempt the summit, but to be completely honest I am not terribly keen. In fact, as my friend Kate would say, I would rather stick pins in my eyes.

We spend the rest of the day drinking tea, and looking at the snow glistening on the peak. It is warm and sunny and clear and we park our-selves outside the hut, breath in the beautiful mountain air and doze.

In the early afternoon I spot a faint dark line moving towards us from the valley below. As it approaches I discern the individual shapes of middle-aged hikers wearing lederhosen and little pointy ski hats. They march, stocks in hand, up the valley and across the ridge, weaving in an out of the lobelia trees like a column of ants. They walk in a long, ordered line through the col, around a rocky outcrop and disappear into our hut.

They are a party of Germans and Austrians on an eighteen-day climbing tour of Mount Kenya and Kilimanjaro. We chat with Klaus, a software engineer who works long hours and travels all over Europe. He believes taking three weeks away from his job is terribly decadent and I get the impression he would consider half a year off almost immoral. 'But surely you will work?' he says.

'Well…no actually. Just travel.'

'*Just* travel? For six months. That is very strange. Very strange indeed.'

By evening the hut is crammed full. I count sixteen climbers dressed in smart casual outdoor gear, seated at two long tables. They have at least twenty porters with them, most of whom are spilling out of the cooking area at the opposite end of the hut. Sarah and I perch quietly on the end of a bench by ourselves. A clean blue cloth is placed on their table and laid with matching plates and mugs, cutlery and individual napkins. Three kerosene lanterns cast a gentle glow down the centre. As their cook brings out trays of what can only be described as 'hors d'oeuvres', a symphony of 'oohs' and 'aahs' fills the room.

Klaus catches my eye. I think we have been staring. He approaches and hovers by our table and I am suddenly aware of our single white candle and motley collection of plastic dinnerware. I suspect, too, that neither of us looks our best. 'We were wondering if you would like to join us for dinner,' he says. The hors d'oeuvres are tempting but I know our cook has been working on the packet asparagus soup for hours and it seems rude to change our dining arrangements at this late stage. 'Thank you,' I say. 'That's very kind, but our meal is coming…Really it is.'

Clearly, packet soup is a bit of a challenge for our guy, and while it arrives mostly green and runny, it is full of lumps of congealed powder that float around the bowl pretending they might be tasty little nuggets of asparagus. The main course is some kind of meat stew and rice and, as I chew through it, I try not to think about where the meat has been during the heat of the last two days.

Animated conversation drifts down from the Germans' table and after three courses and coffee someone produces a harmonica and they break into song. The cooking and the food and the talk have warmed up the hut and the atmosphere is cosy and congenial. I sit back listening to 'Oh Tannenbaum', trying to remember the words I learnt at school. Sarah puts her arm around me and we relax into the music and the flickering lanterns. One of the Germans fiddles with a radio, tuning in and out of Swahili, until he finds something he recognises. The hut is suddenly filled with the strains of the 'Blue Danube' and everyone laughs and claps. An older man stands and holds his hand out to his wife. She takes it, embraces him and they begin to waltz. Another couple joins them, swinging their arms high and sashaying round the benches. Gradually, they all pair up until the hut is filled with waltzing Germans gliding round the tables and spinning each other in elaborate turns. I raise my plastic cup to Sarah. 'Happy New Year,' I say.

'Happy New Year, Babe.'

And I can't remember a better one.

It's decision time about the summit. If we want to attempt the peak we must tell Paul and he will wake us at 3.00 a.m.—three hours from now—with tea and biscuits. We shall begin the ascent at 3.30 a.m. and reach the peak for sunrise at 6.00 a.m. To be honest, I think I made my decision when I threw up for the fourth time yesterday evening. I do not want to sully Mount Kenya's pristine peak with my vomit, and I certainly don't want the hammer to return to my head. Sarah is reluctant, but without excuse, though she is pretty exhausted and has developed bronchitis over the last couple of days. She would have to climb without me and, apart from anything else, Paul is not loquacious and it would be a grim, silent ascent.

We wake at three in the morning and poke our heads outside the tent. It's bleak and bitterly cold. 'Thank God we said "no",' I say, snuggling down into our bags. In the morning, when it's bright and warm and the peak glistens, we're not so sure.

By mid morning we are up on the ridge above the hut. The extra day at 4200 has helped me acclimatise, and though I still have a lingering headache, my appetite has returned and I have more energy. We climb to 4600, 385 metres below Point Lenana and though it is technically not the top, there are patches of snow and it feels incredibly high. There is no vegetation apart from the odd lichen which gives the rock a delicate green hue, and the view is spectacular. To the north-west we can just see down the Mackinder Valley and to the east, the steep scree slopes above Simba tarn. I stand atop a rocky outcrop in my 'Woman with Altitude' T-shirt—Sarah suggests I should paint the word 'sickness' on the end of it—posing for photographs. Paul and the guides are gathered round a pocket radio trying to find out the first election results; there is tribal violence in the Rift Valley and allegations of corruption and election tampering, but none of that's happening here.

We have a long walk ahead across the ridge to Minto's Hut with the Hinde Valley to our west and down to Chogoria gate at 2990 metres. We are told there are excellent views of the Gorges Valley and the glaciers beyond, but as we clamber up the scree and onto the ridge, the cloud rolls in and the gently undulating track takes us in and out of the mist. We stop for lunch around midday: some bread, an orange and a few digestive biscuits. 'We will have soup,' Paul explains, 'but we cannot cook until we reach the road. It is a little way off.'

We continue down the eastern side of the mountain, the sun periodically breaking through the clouds, revealing the sheer cliffs only a step away, and the valley hundreds of metres below. By 4.00 p.m. we are ravenous and the promised vegetable soup finally appears—warmish and pink, with crunchy bits I don't think are veg-etables. The temperature drops rapidly and we push on to our camp arriving just before sundown.

The site is swarming with English people and I stand amongst the closely erected tents and listen to the northern accents. I can see Tesco's Five Pints and Sainsbury's muesli bars and boxes of Readybrek. There must be at least fifteen people wandering around the site, organising Tupperware boxes, filtering water, packing and unpacking rucksacks.

They are part of a climbing club from Derbyshire and have just done the thirty-two kilometre walk from Chogoria to the gate. They are 'raight buggered' having arrived in Nairobi from London only the night before. 'Shockin' place that,' says John, a six-foot square Yorkshireman, 'Ah were scared bloody witless.'

Over coffee we regale them with details of our sorry adventure on the peak and they relay their I-had-a-friend-who-died-of-altitude-sickness anecdotes. By the end of the evening my story has spread around camp and I am a cautionary tale, each new club member emerging from his or her tent to ask, 'Were you lass wot got poorly up mountain?'

'Aye t'were me,' I say.

Our final day is a brisk thirty-two-kilometre walk down an old four-wheel drive track to Chogoria town—the route the climbers have just taken. We need to be there by midday so we can eat, and arrange transport to Meru and on to Nairobi. As far as I can determine, Meru is further away from Nairobi, but Paul is sketchy on the details of our return so I don't enquire further.

We say goodbye to the English and head off, walking quickly into the thick rainforest. The ground underfoot is extremely uneven and littered with potholes and puddles which makes looking up very difficult. After an hour I have shooting pains in my neck and begin to feel a strain in my knees. We discuss our plan to climb Kilimanjaro which, after the events of the past few days, seems a less attractive idea. Kilimanjaro is a six- or seven-day trip, ascending to a point four hundred metres higher than we reached on Mount Kenya. Altitude sickness, it seems, is completely random and the fact that I succumbed this time doesn't mean I will again, but just now that's not terribly comforting.

After three hours of non-stop power walking over rough ground we are both experiencing a range of pulls and twinges and have developed blisters on various parts of our feet. It appears that no rest or eating stops have been factored into our day and with sixteen kilometres still to go, we must push on. In an attempt to stop us focussing on our injuries we play a game: pick one thing from Africa you would like to take home, and one thing from home you would give to Africa. Sarah quite fancies the first of Eliza's lodges in exchange for high-style toilets or a regular water supply. I plump for Kilimanjaro, in return for either a greater range of vegetables or pedestrian crossings.

For the last two hours we give up trying to be positive and concentrate exclusively on our physical discomfort on the 'if-you-can't-beat-them-join-them' principle. We identify the degree of pain experienced in the various parts of our body on a scale of moderate, significant or severe. Sarah begins: left instep, moderate; both outer heels, severe; right Achilles tendon, significant; both calves and right thigh, significant; left groin area, severe and so on. When she is done I run through mine and we compare notes.

By the time we reach our lunch stop at the one restaurant in town we can barely walk. We are the only white people amongst a clientele of local businessmen and nurses from the adjacent hospital. We do not really blend in, but in case anyone hasn't already noticed us, we make our way from the door to the table like two old ladies who have lost their Zimmer frames. Sitting down is excruciating and is only achieved by supporting ourselves on the edge of the table and lowering slowly into the chairs. By the time we are seated all eyes are fixed on us and forks of food held in suspended animation between plates and mouths. A snigger begins in one corner and makes its way around the room like a Mexican wave. A waiter approaches and smiles, 'Mount Kenya?' he says.

'Aah! Mount Kenya,' whispers everyone else in unison.

From Chogoria we take a *matatu*, a fifteen-seater Nissan van carrying twenty-five passengers. Sarah and I share the back row with three other adults and a baby, which means that only one buttock at a time can ever come into contact with the seat. Our luggage is placed where, in other circumstances, our feet might go, so that our knees fit just under our chins. It is a little tricky to maintain this position when you are tilted at an angle, trying to hang on to your one buttock's worth of space and, at the same time, protect your head from the roof of the van—especially as everyone in your row, and in the three rows ahead of you, is trying to do the same thing. The only advantage to being squeezed in such a way is that we cannot see the breakneck speed at which the driver takes the hair-pin bends—we can only feel it.

After half an hour we reach Meru and I peel myself away from my neighbouring passengers, stomp out the pins and needles in my foot and attempt to re-circulate the blood in my bum. There is no shared taxi waiting as promised, nor any sign that one may arrive within the next week. Our only option for the three-hour trip back to Nairobi is another *matatu*. Paul assures me we will travel 'express', no stopping and only four people per seat instead of five. We have no choice but to squeeze back on.

It is late and dark when we arrive at the hotel and our muscles have completely seized. We step down slowly from the van and hobble into the reception where we are welcomed with amused looks and chuckles. 'Mount Kenya?' they say. 'You have just climbed Mount Kenya?'

'*Oh yes,*' we say. 'We have climbed Mount Kenya.'

CHAPTER 5

A TRAIN RIDE, A TOILET AND A HAIRCUT

THE RAILWAY STATION at Nairobi is littered with porters bent double under the weight of freshly laundered linen. Dozens of muscled young men swing huge bundles onto their backs, haul them across the platform and pile them high onto two-wheeled trolleys. When the trolleys are teetering they grab the handles, lower them carefully and manoeuvre through the crowd, nodding and smiling and muttering deferentially, 'Excuse me, Madam.' 'Thank you, Madam.'

Sarah and I sit at a wrought-iron table in front of a glass-fronted western-style café, and order drinks from a polite waiter in a crisp, starched uniform. He balances two china cups and saucers and a silver-plated teapot on a tray at shoulder height and flicks the crumbs off our table with a rolled-up cloth. Smiling, he slides the cups smoothly in front of us and gently deposits the tea, milk and sugar. 'Your drinks, Madam,' he says. 'Please enjoy, Madam.' We sit, awkwardly, like mem-sahibs, brushing up against Kenya's colonial history.

Behind us, the train extends the full length of the platform—at least ten carriages—each stamped with the Kenya Railways crest. It is clean, looks as if it has been painted in the last decade, and is in remarkably good condition for a country where nothing is maintained. There are dozens of people waiting to board: businessmen in dark suits, workers in blue overalls, a handful of scruffy backpackers and a smartly turned out Abercrombie & Kent couple. I pour more tea from the pot and we watch the pick-pockets watching us.

I leave Sarah guarding our packs and go in search of a toilet. At the end of the platform I find the 'Second Class Ladies', but the warm choking stench is somewhat uninviting, and I wonder if there is a 'First Class Ladies'. At the opposite end, I discover the 'Upper Class Waiting Room' which has proper stalls—no seats of course—and an old-fashioned chain flush, though I suspect it has not been cleaned since it was frequented by the aforementioned Upper Classes.

We check our names on the list posted outside the ticket office and wander up and down looking for our cabin. A small card stuck to the outside of the carriage reads *Ms Sarah Nichola* and *Mrs Jaqi Thomlin*. We climb up, squeezing our packs through the narrow corridor. There are four bunks in our cabin which we share with a pregnant woman, Grace, and Eva, her three-year-old daughter. Eva is excited to have *wazungu*—the Swahili term for 'white people'—so close to hand. She cannot take her eyes off us and keeps stroking Sarah's forearm. 'Mama, *wazungu*,' she says. '*Wazungu* Mama.' Grace quietly explains that she must call us *Sarah* and *Jacqui*; *wazungu* is not really polite.

The fourth bunk (children don't count for the purpose of allocating bunks or seats which is why there are usually so many of them) is occupied by a very large older lady referred to as 'Mama'—the much used term for any woman over twenty-five. Mama lies down on the bottom bunk explaining she is not well. She went on a crash diet for a funeral and it has left her weak and sick. Her husband, son and nephew attend her, depositing packets of crisps, biscuits, boxes of cakes and bars of chocolate at her side like the Three Wise Men.

We wedge our packs under the seat as securely as we can and leave Mama on guard while we explore. The corridor is only wide enough for one person to pass through so there is much to-ing and fro-ing and bobbing in and out of other people's cabins. The first class cabins don't look much better than ours—they only have to accommodate two people and are tiny and cramped. Third class is a different story: upright wooden benches with dozens of people crammed up against sacks of maize and baskets of fruit, and babies and children everywhere. On the way back we pass a 'high style' at the end of our corridor. It is in a tiny cubicle that looks like an old aeroplane toilet that's been stripped of its modicum of comfort. The smell is shocking already.

Within minutes of pulling away from the platform the guard rings a bell to indicate the first sitting for dinner. Mama says she cannot possibly move from her bunk and will make do with her supplies, so we join Grace and Eva and head for the dining car. Eva takes Sarah's hand and trots happily beside her. 'Look Mama, Sarah-*wazungu*,' she says. '*Wazungu*-Sarah, Mama.'

'Eva, it is not *wazungu*. It is just *Sarah*.'

'Yes Mama.'

The tables are laid with starched clothes and napkins, silver-plated cutlery and white crockery, but the lights aren't working and everything is in semi-darkness. We stumble to our seats and order drinks by the light of a single, flickering candle. The Abercrombie couple are seated at an adjacent table dressed in fresh, pressed khakis. The husband grabs our waiter as he passes, 'Can we do something about the lights, old chap? Bit grim eating dinner in darkness.'

'They are broken, Sir. Soon they will be fixed, Sir.'

In the half light they ponder the wine list, ordering something expensive and South African. The waiter fetches their wine and returns, steadying himself at the end of the table and pouring a drop into the husband's glass. 'Not bad,' he says, nodding to the waiter to fill both glasses. They order their main meal and settle back slowly sipping their wine. 'I say, Gerald, the Pinotage really is terribly good.'

'Hmm. Not bad, Deirdre.'

We order Cokes, select our main course and watch the waiter expertly ladle soup from a large silver tureen—not easily done in semi-darkness with the rough movement of the carriage. As we lift our spoons to eat, the train comes to a violent, sudden stop and the creamy vegetable soup splashes onto the table and our Cokes fall into our laps. A short high-pitched scream emanates from the table next door as the terribly good Pinotage is flung onto poor Deirdre's terribly well-pressed safari suit. She stands, grabs a napkin and tries to soak up the wine as it spreads across her lap in a deep crimson circle. 'Oh Gerald, what an *awful* mess.' Gerald is half standing, frantically wiping the soup from his right thigh and trying to lift the material of his trousers to avoid scalding his leg. 'Oh, Good God!' The waiter hovers next to them offering clean napkins and spooning the soup from the table-cloth to a side plate. 'What a bloody shambles!' says Gerald.

We drink our remaining inch of Coke and wipe the vegetable soup from the tablecloth. Sarah retrieves our Maglite from the cabin which provides just enough light for the main course. The train continues to jerk and jolt and Gerald and Deirdre continue to struggle—forkfuls of lamb masala periodically dropping into their laps and creamed potato plopping onto the seat between them.

The overhead light finally flickers on and the full extent of the damage can be seen—squashed broccoli spreads from beneath Gerald's brogues and two long green beans poke out of his trouser turn-up. Deirdre has an additional smudge down the side of her skirt where the mashed potato lingered before hitting the seat. The table is covered with orange and red stains and sprinkled with droplets of brown gravy, and the remaining Pinotage floats in the side plate with the scooped up soup. 'Oh good Lord,' mutters Gerald. 'Whoever suggested we take this trip should be shot!'

Our table is somehow less catastrophic, and we manage to finish our meal with only a little beef madras, and a few sprinklings of pappadum ending up in our laps.

When we return to our cabin the beds have been made up with clean sheets, pillows and a light blanket. Sarah and I clamber up to our bunks and affix the PVC webbing that is designed to ensure we don't fall out should there be more unexpected movement. I slip into a T-shirt and boxers and stretch out between the fresh sheets. It reminds me of a trip to the south coast of England as a child in one of the old country trains with the six people compartments. Listen to the rhythm of the train my mother had said: *penny a mile, penny a mile, penny a mile*. It's not pennies or miles anymore, of course, but the rhythm brings the same comfort.

Grace tucks Eva into the end of the bed and reads her a story. 'Say goodnight to our friends,' she says, closing the book. Eva pokes her head around the edge of the bunk and looks up. 'Goodnight Sarah-*waz*…Sarah-White-one,' she says. 'Goodnight Jacqui White-one.'

It is hot and paralysingly humid when we arrive in Mombasa. Grace's husband is there to meet her and offers us a lift to our accommodation, a YWCA rest house which bears an uncanny resemblance to a minimum security prison. We stand silently in the housekeeper's office as she looks us up and down, examining our boots, our muddy trousers and faded baggy T-shirts. Generally we try to look vaguely respectable when arriving in a new place, but with the lack of water and our limited wardrobe, it's not always possible. After an awkward few minutes she announces she has a room, but it's the last one and very small. I take this to mean that we pass inspection, but only just.

We thank her politely, smiling and nodding as she takes a key and marches out of the office. I step around an old woman scrubbing the floor on her hands and knees and pass another three people sweeping floors or mopping. We follow the housekeeper through a dry, dusty courtyard dotted with thin patches of grass and the occasional cactus carved with the initials of former residents. The yard is lined with square concrete boxes, each with a rusty iron grille on the door at head height like a cell. There are no women anywhere, just young single men hovering in doorways or loitering around the toilet conveniently located next to our room.

The housekeeper unlocks the door and steps aside for us to enter. There are two single beds with sagging squeaky springs and a mosquito net with gaping slashes. The walls are painted with dark blue gloss and a naked bulb hangs limply from the ceiling. 'Lovely,' I say, smiling to the housekeeper. 'Thank you. It's great.' There is a sink in one corner with a cold tap that dribbles muddied water, and a wardrobe in the other that I am reluctant to investigate. I sit on the edge of the bed and grab the guidebook—mostly it is very accurate but every now and again it is spectacularly wrong. 'Why did we choose this place?' I ask Sarah.

'It was in our price range and it's close to town,' she says. I flick through the book to the accommodation section and re-read. 'You're right, but I think what really clinched it was its *relaxed atmosphere and pleasant ambience.*'

We escape as soon as we can and head out for a walk along the sea front. It is a Sunday afternoon, hot and steamy and tropical and it couldn't feel more different from Nairobi. We stroll along the edge of the Pacific enjoying the slower pace, the absence of speeding *matatus* and pick-pockets high on glue. It is not without its own particular charm however, and in the course of an hour we are whistled and shouted at—'hello beautiful ladies'—interrogated about our marital status, followed by a car, a moped and a bicycle and offered a ride in a pick-up with four, very drunk but, otherwise, really terribly charming young men. We receive a total of five offers of marriage and six non-specific declarations of love.

We spend the afternoon touring the seventeenth century Fort Jesus, built by the Portuguese to maintain their trading stronghold on the East African coast. It has been impressively restored with steep spiral staircases leading up into the turrets and painted black cannons that poke through the narrow slots in the walls. From the top of one of the turrets we can see out across the Pacific, and facing the other direction, the roof-tops of the city. Down below, there appears to be a British television crew with cameras and sausage-shaped microphones covered in fluffy grey material. We race down and hover, but, to Sarah's great disappointment, see no-one famous and aren't asked to be extras.

On our way out, Sarah discovers that Fort Jesus has the best toilet in Africa so far, outside of the lodges of course: a high style in a separate lockable cubicle, with paper, a working flush system and, a first for this trip, a seat. After a longer than usual bathroom break we return to the 'Y', dine on bread and bananas and try to sleep through the humidity.

In the morning we join the other guests for breakfast in the dining area, a long thin room with tables in rows like a school cafeteria. There are no other tourists, just single men who sit alone and in silence. The Kenya 'Y' motto, 'By Love, Serve One Another'—and the local branch dictum, 'Loving, Caring, Sharing'—are carved into a plaque at the end of the room. Above them, is the ubiquitous picture of Daniel Moi, President now for another five years.

Breakfast is laid out underneath: a large pot of something lukewarm, runny and grey that looks like a much-diluted porridge, and which I suspect, though I have only ever read about it in Dickens, is gruel. There is a kettle, with something hot and brown, but I cannot determine whether it's tea or coffee or something completely different. We grab some bread and sit down, whispering to each other only when it's absolutely necessary.

A fifty-something Englishwoman of the 'jolly hockey sticks' variety plonks herself next to us. She, like most of the 'Y' residents, is a teacher who lives here during term time. She works at a local Ishmaeli school and spends most of her evenings at 'The Club'. She talks at us for ten minutes with barely a pause for breath and at the first opportunity we make our excuse to leave. 'Oh,' she says, 'but you haven't had breakfast—bit like gruel I know—but really terribly good.'

By the time we have picked up our day-packs and are ready to head out, all the guests have moved into a small adjacent room from which the strains of a Swahili prayer meeting emanate. A solitary man remains in the dining room re-mopping the floor and scrubbing the tables. 'It's next to Godliness,' I whisper to Sarah.

Despite the seediness of the 'Y' we have managed to end up in a rather affluent part of the city. The road into town is lined with huge two- and three-storey houses with balconies and courtyards, arches and statues, the homes of wealthy Asian merchants and businessmen. Each house is surrounded by a high brick wall topped with razor wire, and has a guard posted at the entrance gate. Groups of children, mostly Indian, some black and some white, march down the street in neat uniforms carrying backpacks and hockey sticks, and shiny four-wheel drives cruise up and down depositing kids at the school gate.

As we approach the centre of town the big brick houses turn into municipal concrete blocks, and the roads fill with cars and mopeds, and people heading to work. We walk under the famous, and very ugly, fake giant elephant tusks on Moi Avenue, pass an unusually high number of places professing to be driving schools, and half a dozen *Please Do Not Spit* signs.

Though it feels safer and much more laid-back than Nairobi, negotiating the roads is still a nightmare. Living in Australia for the past eight years has taken the edge off my jay-walking skills, and my recent experience has made me more anxious than usual. We manage to cross after waiting five minutes for a pause in the traffic, and only after making eye contact with each driver. What I don't anticipate is a speeding moped that shoots up between the two lines of traffic and heads straight for me. He swerves, but there is nowhere for him to go. His front wheel and bumper hit my leg and I stumble back onto the bonnet of a car. Sarah grabs my arm and pulls me onto the pavement dazed and shaky. 'Oh Babe, not again. You OK?'

'Yeah…I think so.'

The moped zooms off and a young man appears out of nowhere and asks if I am OK. 'I am *very* sorry about the Vespa,' he says. '*Very* sorry about the Vespa. You are welcome in Kenya. Welcome.'

I brush myself down and we head for the Old Town and the market quarter in an attempt to get away from the traffic. A labyrinth of narrow lanes is lined with small shops selling batiks and carvings, cheap children's clothes and washing powder. Tall wattle and daub houses block out the sun and cast the alleyways in shadow. Groups of boys sit on the stone steps playing cards and girls peer down from the overhanging balconies above. Local African women gather around the *kanga* stalls shaking out the brightly coloured cloth and draping it across their arms, while the men hack at coconut husks with huge curved knives, leaving piles of long thin leaves that clog up the path. The Indian women, in long black robes and hijab, bustle through the stalls and disappear into the houses. The men, wearing traditional Muslim dress with plastic rainbow sandals, gather in groups to talk and smoke. Periodically the muezzin calls everyone to prayer, the shutters come down on the shops and the men hurry to the mosque.

We stumble across a stall piled high with freshly cooked Indian delicacies: samosas, vegetable kofta, chaptis, pakora, puri and naan and a number of other enticing little pastry packages. It's been a while since I was excited by the sight of food and I linger at the stall in delightful anticipation. As I dig around my pocket for some change, Sarah sidles up to me and takes the money from my hand. 'Sorry Babe,' she says.

'What?'

'It's not a good idea to eat this stuff.'

'What do you mean? It looks fantastic.'

She pulls out a newspaper and thrusts the headline in front of me: *Cholera spreads through city slums.* 'But we're nowhere near the city slums,' I say.

'It doesn't matter. It's the *oral-faecal route* you need to worry about. Someone goes to the toilet, forgets to wash their hands, or washes them in contaminated water, and then they cook and the faecal matter on their hands...'

'Yes. Thank you. I get the message. Let's go find some faecal free...*bananas* then shall we?'

We head back via the supposedly thriving dhow harbour where a handful of decrepit boats flutter in the wind. A small, somewhat precarious dhow is being loaded up with barrels and hessian bags, and huge cardboard boxes tied with string. On the shore, a long line of people wait patiently to board. As each person steps onto the boat, the water level rises, until the edge of the wooden hull is only inches above the water. The man standing next to me explains that it is possible to take a dhow to Zanzibar, much cheaper than the hydrofoil and it only takes a week. There are no facilities on board—you take your own food and water and sleep on the deck. Sarah and I agree that ten years ago we might have thought this a jolly adventure. Now, it would be squalid and uncomfortable, and fun for about half an hour. 'Where is this boat going?' I ask.

'They drop off some people up the coast in Lamu,' he says, 'then sail to Bombay.'

On the way home we pass The Lotus cinema, and consider a night at the movies as an alternative to prayers at the 'Y'. It is a dark, scruffy building with about twenty or thirty men lounging around on the front steps. We suspect it is a long time since it was patronised by a couple of white girls but, not wholly deterred, we check the billing. Through the crowd we catch a glimpse of the poster advertising tonight's feature: a blood-spattered man holding a large glinting blade at the throat of a terrified woman, the words *Serial Killer* splashed across them both. 'I think we've been a little harsh on the "Y",' I say. 'Really, it's not that bad. In fact, I like the atmosphere. How about a quiet night in?'

On the way home, we pass the Odeon, a rather more respectable venue, where for a dollar we can sit through *Independence Day*. Not my first choice of movie, but somehow it has rather more appeal here than it did back in Oz.

There are a handful of other patrons inside—six youngish men all sitting by themselves, smoking and occasionally spitting into the aisle. The chairs are covered in a dark sticky vinyl with stuffing poking out around the edges. We plonk ourselves down, our forearms and thighs sticking to the chairs with the day's accumulated sweat. There is a stale, damp smell to the place and as I lean back in my chair I feel a slight, but definite, itch around my ankles and down the back of my neck. 'Do you think we might not be the only ones sitting in these chairs?' I ask Sarah.

The show begins with a newsreel that flickers onto the screen and jumps about to a slow and distorted soundtrack. President Moi's most recent good works are narrated in a classic 1950s BBC accent, like a *Pathe News* feature. The main item, which runs for twenty minutes, is a report on the World Ploughing Association Championships that have recently been held in Kenya. Representatives came from all over the world, including one female contestant from Sweden, and the reigning champion, from County Keogh in Ireland. A judge explains, in considerable detail, that each contestant must plough a designated area against the clock and is assessed on the straightness of his lines, the depth and evenness of his furrows and the neatness of his corners. We watch the ploughs in action, with close-ups of the furrows, and finally, President Moi pinning a ribbon on the proud winner.

The movie, which follows, is less interesting.

We have been fantasising about a few days on a tropical beach, a little swimming and sun bathing under gently swaying palm trees. The eleven-day safari, the Mt Kenya climb, Nairobi and the Mombasa humidity have left us feeling exhausted, and after four weeks of constant movement we need to be still. We book a bus up the coast to Watamu, a tiny village two hours north where there is a campsite run by the Seventh Day Adventists. According to our book, it has a superb view of a lagoon, a place to cook and good toilets and shower facilities.

Before we leave Mombasa we have one more thing to do. I need a haircut, unfortunately, and though there is nothing in Mombasa that even vaguely resembles a western-style hairdresser, there will be even less choice further up the coast.

We check out the numerous 'Hair Saloons' in town and select one at random, a small, dark shop with a handful of faded posters on the wall and a couple of cracked sinks. A stooping old woman approaches us as we hover in the doorway and beckons me to a seat. I am confident she has never been anywhere near a *mzungu* head of hair.

She places a towel around my shoulders and I explain what I want done. She smiles, nods energetically and picks up her scissors. There is no shampooing, no spraying with water from a bottle, no comb or brush, just the cool steel of the scissors scraping the back of my neck. She places them halfway down my crown at a right angle, in the way a child might, or how you imagine they teach you not to in your first week of beauty school. She begins to cut, slowly, methodically, labouring over each snip.

In the mirror I can see Sarah standing behind me, her eyes wide, her jaw slightly dropped, in an expression that encompasses both horror and pity. The old woman doesn't speak, doesn't look up, in fact doesn't move at all except to make deliberate, repeated cuts along a straight line from one ear to the other.

Periodically, I remove my glasses so she can work on the sides—my ears seem to be causing her some difficulty—but I am reluctant to keep them off for long. Sarah's shoulders gently shake and I can hear stifled laughter from behind the newspaper she is pretending to read. I have visions of a long session back at our hotel and Sarah fixing it up with the scissors of her Swiss army knife.

It is more than an hour before we are done and I sit forward gingerly, brushing the hair from my shoulders and arms. The front doesn't look too bad, though I suspect it may be bit lop-sided and if I tilt my head slightly it looks straighter. I nod and pay the old woman who beams back at me clearly delighted with her *mzungu* cut.

Outside, Sarah runs her fingers up the back of my head and I hear her sharp intake of breath. 'How is it?' I ask hesistantly.

'Well…it's…a bit…'

'A bit what?'

'Well…a bit…'

'*For Christ's sake is it OK or not?*'

'Er…not….Actually. No. It's not OK. Sorry.'

'What's *wrong* with it then?'

'Well…where shall I start?…The line across your crown is almost straight…in a couple of places…and there's a bit of a…bald patch around your right ear…and I can see the definite shape of the arm of your glasses around the left. But other than that…and the zig-zaggy hair line…'

Back at the 'Y' we brave the communal lounge which is separated from the dining room by a wrought-iron grille. Leftover crepe garlands and deflated balloons hang limply from the ceiling and a plastic Santa pokes his feet out from behind a brown vinyl settee. A handful of orange plastic chairs are set in a neat row against the wall, and the floor, of course, is freshly mopped.

In the centre of the room there is a television encased in iron lattice and affixed with two large padlocks. The locks and the ironwork obscure about a third of the screen and we have to bob up and down to follow the picture. We try to catch the evening news, but apart from the occasional CNN report it is entirely in Swahili. Sarah pokes her finger through the metal frame in an attempt to find a different channel, but there is only one. We sit back on the brown vinyl and watch, excited by the English snippets that appear every ten minutes or so, and otherwise rely heavily on the much-obscured visuals.

We've had better nights.

CHAPTER 6

A PASSION ON SARAH

IT IS A LONG hot traipse across town from the 'Y' to the bus station and I weave through the crowded market, carefully stepping over piles of chillies and tomatoes and cheap digital watches spread out on blue gingham tablecloths. It's difficult to avoid bumping into people and I shuffle along the pavement, stepping one way, then the other and angling myself through the crowd, 'Excuse me...please...would you mind...yes...sorry...thank you.' Sarah is way ahead and I can see her in the distance waiting for me to catch up. 'Babe. You have to be a little less English about this,' she says. 'Think North American.' She grabs my arm, hauls me across the road and drags me into the throng. In minutes we are at the bus station.

The coach to Watamu is old and battered with dints and paint chips down both sides. As usual, there are five seats across where there should be four, and about twice as many rows. The sun beats down through the window and we drip, sticking to the green plastic seats. A dozen sacks of maize and ten bags of assorted vegetables are passed up the aisle and wedged into the back of the bus. Four large crates of what look like used-car parts are stacked around them. Plastic holdalls stuffed with kitchenware and a variety of household appliances are squeezed on top, and two corrugated iron roofs are tucked nicely down the centre. A buxom Mama, loaded with shopping and children, hauls herself over the freight to her seat, and three or four young men clamber over the backs of the chairs to theirs. When everyone is seated, and the bus fully loaded, an extra twenty people climb aboard and stand in the centre aisle, balancing themselves precariously astride the sacks of cabbages and the corrugated roof.

We are only a few minutes out of town when the driver starts to shout in Swahili, waving his hand above his head. The people in the aisle duck down below the height of the seats, squatting over the roof or perching on the car parts. Everyone is suddenly still and silent. The bus slows to a stop at a road block where a young, armed police officer walks carefully around, examining tyres and dints and craning his neck to see inside. The people in the aisle look vaguely perturbed at the thought of being turfed off and having to schlep the contents of a small semi-detached all the way back to town.

The officer pokes his head through the driver's window and they chat leisurely, a few cigarettes changing hands. In the aisle, the passengers maintain their awkward positions, some clearly feeling the strain. An old guy shifts the sharp end of the roof from his backside and his son grabs a saucepan handle that's digging into his thigh.

The policeman finishes his smoke, and with a thump to the side of the bus, waves us on. Everyone remains crouched and silent until we round the next corner when the driver makes another announcement and they bob back up, dusting themselves off and massaging their limbs.

Before long we hit another road-block—three, in fact, before the end of the journey—and each time a policeman shares a smoke with the driver and pretends he doesn't notice that the inhabitants of a medium-sized town are secreted on board.

We transfer to a *matatu* a few kilometres out of Watamu and, using the information from our guidebook, describe the camp site to our driver—its excellent facilities, its proximity to a lagoon, its lovely view. He frowns and shakes his head, grabs our book and passes it around to the other passengers who are similarly perplexed. Clearly, our little tropical hideaway bears no resemblance to anything in or near Watamu. We are dropped at the end of a dirt track, the consensus being that there is a Seventh Day Adventist clinic up the hill and, maybe, a place to pitch our tent.

After a long hot walk we arrive at something that might once have been a camp site, a patch of dry dirt with the occasional clump of yellowing grass. In one corner there is a derelict concrete building surrounded by empty milk cartons, old banana skins and an assortment of general household waste. There is not a soul in sight.

We dump our packs and check out the view. There is a lagoon, edged with palm trees, but the tide is out and the beach a mass of thick, dark, seaweed. We change into our bathers and pick through the kelp until we reach the shallow water a hundred metres out. Under the fierce noon-day sun we squat in eight inches of tepid sea. 'No really,' I say to Sarah, 'Lovely spot. Just what I imagined. Great. Fabulous.'

A young man, pulling his shirt on as he runs, comes bounding towards us as we walk back up the beach. This is the camp site he explains, it's just that they haven't been very busy lately. There are toilets and showers, and a safe place to store our luggage if we want to visit the village. He shows us the amenities block which is brown and foul smelling both inside and out. There is a squat toilet, home to an extended family of flies that feed off the excrement that has somehow managed to creep up the walls. A cold, saltwater shower dribbles onto a couple of sleeping lizards when Sarah turns it on, and dries up before she has a chance to turn it off.

We erect the tent and pile our gear into the caretaker's back room, watching as he padlocks the door. The afternoon clouds have moved in and the humidity increased in anticipation of the coming storm. We head for the village along the main street which is lined with young men sitting in front of curio stalls. They make unenthusiastic attempts to encourage us to buy, gesturing vaguely towards rows of carved giraffes and painted masks. Women lean against barrows of tomatoes and onions and chat. It is a hot, hazy, slow afternoon, the grass hissing with crickets and the air thick and heavy. Tall coconut palms rustle as the wind picks up, and tiny white caps form on the distant waves. As the sky darkens, the stall holders pick up their crates and amble inside, and the women drag green tarpaulins across their barrows.

At the end of the village there are a handful of glass fronted shops advertising fishing trips and diving courses and, as the storm breaks, we hover in a doorway sheltering from the rain. We are ushered into an office by a well-dressed and politely spoken young man who introduces himself as Boniface. He used to be a teacher, he explains, but is now trying to make a better living organising trips for tourists. Business is bad, a combination of the protracted rains and the elections. Most overseas visitors to Watamu are older Europeans who stay at the expensive resorts on the beach front where everything is arranged for them.

We negotiate a price for a half day snorkelling trip. I explain that I will go along for the ride, but snorkelling is not my best thing given that once I remove my specs everything becomes rather vague. 'No problem,' says Boniface. 'We can give you an extra large mask that will cover your glasses.' I try to explain that in order for the mask to work properly it must be watertight and would therefore have to cover my ears as well. I don't recall ever having seen a snorkelling mask with extended ear flaps. Has he? He is unconvinced. He will come to our camp site in the morning and escort us to the boat, and he will find me a mask.

As the rain eases off, we head away from the village towards the 'supermarket'. We have been fantasising about cooking a meal—if we can rustle up enough ingredients that we recognise. In between the sacks of maize flour, gallon drums of oil and giant boxes of washing powder, we discover tins of Heinz baked beans, jars of Marmite and Lyons Golden Syrup, and an impressive selection of Kelloggs' breakfast cereals. I feel like we've stumbled into a sub branch of Sainsburys. 'Do you think there might be a few English around?' I ask. We buy a packet of McVities digestive biscuits and the makings for tuna pasta, about which we are unduly excited.

Back at the camp site we meet the owner in the derelict building that turns out to be his house. He suggests, rather than camping, we might be safer in one of the bandas, the round concrete and thatch huts dotted about the site. There are bars on the windows, he explains, and as long as we have a padlock for the door, we should be safe. I'm not quite sure who or what we are aiming to be safe from, but I don't inquire further. We collapse the tent and transfer our gear to the hut where we sit amidst six wooden mattress-less bunks under a naked light bulb. But at least we feel safe.

It has been a long and sticky day and my T-shirt, soaked with sweat since Mombasa, now clings like a wetsuit. We have discovered that washing our clothes with the small cakes of pale brown 'Fortune' soap provided by the 'Y' was an error. Everything looks vaguely clean, but smells as if it's been left in a washing machine for a few days before being hung out to dry. I am coated with layers of sunscreen and insect repellent, plus extra salt from our midday squat in the ocean. It is still intensely humid and I cannot begin to imagine how I will sleep. Sarah is sitting disconsolately under a bunk flicking through the accommodation section of the guidebook.

In an attempt to rescue a rather flat evening, I empty our shopping bag and prepare to cook pasta. I spread the onions and tomatoes out on a bottom bunk and dig around for my Swiss army knife. It's gone, along with the Maglite to which it was attached. I double check both packs and scramble around the floor, groping underneath the bunks in the fading light. 'I think the caretaker has taken care of my stuff,' I say, and head up to the house for a chat with the owner. I explain that certain items of mine seem to have gone astray and suggest that he might want to ask his caretaker if he knows anything about them. He gives me a long, silent stare which suggests he's not terribly keen on this idea. Alternatively, I could write to the publisher of the guidebook in which he is recommended and explain what a squalid little rip-off joint he is running.

I return to our tropical concrete *banda* and dig out the stove and fuel. We don't have the Shellite we normally use, which is clean and cooks beautifully, but kerosene, which is unreliable, smells, and leaves a layer of soot over everything. I struggle to light the stove which hisses and spits at me, and fizzes fuel all over my hand. I pause, wiping my palms on my trousers and try again. I turn the knob and flick the lighter, waving it gently across the hissing fumes. A huge, yellow flame suddenly shoots up, engulfing my hand and forearm and I jerk back. As I step, I hit the edge of the billy and send the chopped onions spinning across the room in a huge arc. Sarah looks up from her bunk, 'Oh Babe. Can I help?'

'Rescue the bloody onions, while I deal with this.'

I kick the stove towards the door of the *banda*, away from the ever-so-slightly combustible bunks and thatched roof, and wait for the flames to die down. Sarah scrapes up the onions, picking out the largest bits of dirt and grass and rubble and hands me the billy. I slide it quickly on top of the stove before the flames flare up again. I grip the handle onto the edge of the pot, and empty a tin of tomatoes and tuna, attempting to mix it all together. Periodically the flames shoot up, singeing my T-shirt and threatening to melt my glasses. I step back, and when they subside for a second, I dart in with my spoon for a quick stir. Sarah watches silently from the bunk, hands clutching a water bottle, ready to douse the whole lot if it gets out of hand.

I battle with the control knob, trying to get the bastard thing to move without burning off the tips of my fingers. It appears to work on only two settings: *Off* and *Pyrotechnic*, the latter resulting in great globules of pasta sauce bubbling up and pouring down the side of the pot.

By the time it is ready, I have small blisters emerging on both hands, large sooty smudges up my arms and, I am told, across my nose and left cheek. I present Sarah with her dinner which she assures me is absolutely the best tuna pasta she's ever had. She can't, in fact, think of a meal she's enjoyed more and can she do the dishes while I take a few deep breaths.

We sit on the *banda* step and watch the rain. The detritus of former travellers is littered about us and there is a strong smell of human waste. My level of personal, physical discomfort has reached new heights and every inch of my body is screaming for a shower. I strongly suspect we've been ripped off by the caretaker who, at this very moment, is probably preparing his midnight sortie into our belongings. 'We have to get out of here,' I say.

'I know Babe. First thing, I'll find a place in the village.'

We unroll our thermarests and try to work out a way of erecting the mosquito net. We have moved into malaria country and have started taking our chloroquine Paludrine combination, though Sarah forgets repeatedly, but a net is still essential. We push the bunks together and hook the net over a nail under the top bunk. I attempt to spread out the corners with a rolled up sleeping bag, the camera and first aid kit. It's hopeless, the tiniest movement leaving one side or the other hanging limp. We crawl on to our mats and lie still under the sagging net, the suffocating air closing in around our skin.

I drift in an out of sleep, waking at every noise, to adjust the net and massage the life back into my shoulders. I dream that I bump into an old friend who invites us to stay in her new flat which has a beautiful white bathroom and a king size bed with crisp, clean sheets.

We awake before dawn and are up with the sun.

Sarah has fifty-two mosquito bites—we count them—on and

around her left knee where it must have poked out of the net. By the time Boniface arrives we are packed up and ready to leave. On the way out I explain to the owner that if my stuff doesn't turn up by this afternoon I will have to go to the police. 'But the Kenyan police are very corrupt,' he says. 'They will come here and arrest me.' I assure him it is not my intention to have anyone arrested, but if he's that worried, he might talk to his caretaker.

We follow Boniface along a white sandy beach lined with high tropical palms. It is drizzling and I am sceptical that we will make it out today. When we arrive we discover the rest of the group with whom we are meant to share this tour have already left, paying extra to take a boat on their own. Our guy is reluctant to go out unless we pay more. Quite frankly I am more interested in getting us and our gear out of the Seventh Day Adventists' hell and finding somewhere I can shower. On top of feeling vaguely like a refugee, my period has started and I am desperate to find the Naprogesic. I tell the boatman to forget it; we will come back tomorrow when the weather might be better anyway.

Boniface escorts us back to camp and we discuss our stolen knife predicament. We are really not keen on a trip to the police station, but cannot claim insurance without a report. 'The Kenyan police are very corrupt,' he says.

'Yes. So we hear.'

'I will come with you,' he says. 'The police know me and respect me because I am an educated man.'

Whether it is because Boniface is with us, I don't really know, but we have a remarkably easy time. An officer records my complaint, sends us next door to buy a postal order for twenty-five shillings (50 cents) and, half an hour later, we are provided with an appropriately stamped and signed report. We agree to buy Boniface a beer after work as thanks, and he is clearly very chuffed at the prospect of spending the evening with us. We rescue our gear from the *banda* and, finally, check into a hotel in the village.

Our room at the Dante is small and dark and musty. It has a shower, clean sheets and a large functioning mosquito net. 'It's beautiful,' I declare to Sarah, dropping my pack and untying my boots. I strip off and am in the shower in seconds, luxuriating in the warm fresh water splashing across my body. I spread my arms, flattening my palms against the walls and let the water run down my neck and back and shoulders. With my head back in the jet, I cover myself in Imperial Leather and spin around. I cup my hands together, letting them fill and spill over, and throw the clean clear water at my face. I laugh out loud and wonder how such a simple thing as a shower ever got to feel quite so good. Wrapping a towel around my waist, I lie back on the bed under the fan. I love Africa and am uncommonly happy.

At 6.00 p.m. we meet Boniface who is positively jaunty, dressed in a fresh salmon pink shirt and scuttling around us like a small child. He takes us to a bar in the village which is empty when we arrive but fills up quickly with a stream of local young women. They hover at the door, glancing around the tables, then sit by themselves as if waiting to meet friends. A series of unaccompanied middle-aged European men enter, buy themselves a beer and sit down next to the women. The men are remarkably similar: overweight, balding, unshaven and dressed in too tight nylon shirts and cheap, ill-fitting jeans. 'Nice place,' I say to Boniface, on whom my irony is completely lost.

As we talk, he becomes increasingly focussed on Sarah, delighting in her stories and I begin to wonder if he's not rather keen. A pretty, young Kenyan man enters, pausing at the doorway to survey the scene. He is wearing designer label shorts and a tight, white vest clearly designed to show his highly toned physique to best effect. On his arm he escorts a somewhat less pretty, older German woman. I sneak a look at Boniface who is still drooling over Sarah. Ah...do I detect an ulterior motive?

Boniface is drinking quickly and arranging the rest of our evening. An old guy opposite is sliding his hand up and down the thigh of his companion, and in the corner a woman sits astride a fifty-something man who is having problems controlling his tongue. I try to convey 'time-for-us-to-go' messages to Sarah and we empty our drinks. Boniface is not happy—he doesn't want to leave. The beer has given him an aggressive edge and he insists we stay and eat. 'Eat what?' I whisper to Sarah, grabbing her arm and heading for the door. He downs his beer and follows us back to the hotel where he hovers persistently. We thank him for his help once again, and for the drink and attempt to say goodbye. The hotel security guard is watching and we finally persuade him to leave, but only after agreeing to have one last drink later in the week.

As promised, he is waiting the following morning to escort us to our snorkelling trip. He is sober and pleasant and chats about the weather. The tide is out and dozens of blue and red and yellow fishing boats are banked up on the beach. There are palm trees as far as the eye can see and low grassy cliffs that rise up from the still, blue water. The white sands slowly turn to flat barnacled rock submerged in three or four inches of sea, and we pick our way across to a headland where the water is much deeper, and where our boat awaits.

We clamber aboard and I try a couple of masks over my glasses and though they fit over the front they are still not watertight at the sides. It will be fine I assure them, I will see all the beautiful colours and shapes of the coral and fish, they will just be a little blurry. We head out to a series of reefs accompanied by a dozen dolphins who, as if on the boatman's payroll, entertain us with beautifully synchronised dives and jumps.

A few kilometres out, we slip over the edge of the boat into the deep, sparkling turquoise waters of Watamu National Marine Park. As I swim towards the reef, I glance back towards our boat to check I'll recognise it. There are a number of other identical boats, all ranged in a circle and, even close-up, there is no way I could identify ours without my glasses. Clambering over the side and hauling myself with a big splash into the wrong one, might be a little embarrassing. I grab Sarah who is wearing her bright pink bathers, bought expressly for ease of identification in these non-glasses wearing situations.

I can see the coral—large flat mushrooms in some places and huge round bubbles in others. The fish are clearly used to people and, fortunately for me, swim close. When we stop, they hover, swimming near our faces and nudging our masks—bright blue and yellow, deep orange and fluorescent green. A large flatfish, clothed in purple velvet with a pointed snout, circles repeatedly, and each time it disappears from view I feel a nipping on the back of my legs. Sarah points excitedly to something in the distance, but beyond a few metres it is all a blur. 'Did you see the huge black and white striped one at the edge of the coral?' she asks as we come up for air. I recall something faintly stripy in the distance, I say, but for all I know, it could have been a zebra.

Back on shore, Boniface is waiting and insists on accompanying us. He is breezy and talkative though we try to limit the conversation to the tourist trade, and walk as briskly as possible. He has a curious smirk, like someone preparing to reveal a piece of long awaited good news. Outside the hotel he stops and, smiling broadly, pulls out his wallet and produces a small package wrapped in tissue paper. 'I have a gift for Miss Sarah,' he says, thrusting the bundle towards her.

Sarah turns ever so slightly pale and we endure a seemingly endless, awkward moment before she manages to take it. She unwraps a beaded iron-ore necklace with a large butterfly attached and holds it limply in her hand. She is flummoxed, truly lost for words, and we stand hovering around a huge, embarrassing silence. 'That's lovely,' I say eventually, elbowing Sarah, who manages a mumbled 'Thank you'. He smiles, does a kind of little dance, clearly delighted with his latest move. We reluctantly confirm our drink the following night and leave him at the gate.

I wrap my arm around Sarah and we head for the hotel bar. 'I think young Boniface has designs,' I say. We order Cokes and work out a strategy for persuading him that no amount of beaded iron-ore jewellery, nor in fact any other trinket he might be able to rustle up, is likely to persuade Sarah to flash wads of cash or provide access to foreign citizenship in return for highly risky sexual favours.

As we talk, I note the bar is otherwise silent, despite the fact that there are a number of other couples. Looking around, I realise we have stumbled upon another pick-up place—the same unattractive, badly dressed men drooling over indifferent teenage girls, the same barely disguised under-the-table groping. Watamu, we have discovered, was a favourite destination for sex tours during the eighties when hundreds of European men, and a few women, came for a cheap bonk. The prevalence of AIDS has reduced their numbers, but clearly hasn't scared everyone away.

The atmosphere is thoroughly depressing and we drain our drinks and head for the door. On our way out, we pass an old man sitting alone with a half-eaten meal in front of him. His chin is resting on his chest and a long trickle of spittle dangles from the corner of his mouth. Both arms hang limply at his side and I'm sure he hasn't moved a muscle in twenty minutes. 'Do you think he's OK?' says Sarah.

'No. I think he's dead.'

In the morning we hire a couple of bikes and plan a day out of the village in the hope that our absence might make Boniface rethink his wedding plans. It is a scorching day and I pull out my sunglasses, Tilley hat and red bandanna which I tie around my neck boy-scout style. Sarah leans on her bike and smiles, 'What?' I say defensively.

'Nothing.'

'You're not suggesting my standard of dress is slipping are you?'

'Wouldn't dream of it, my love.'

My bicycle is about the same size as the one I received for my tenth birthday. There are no gears, of course, and the right-hand pedal doesn't rotate properly and flicks my foot off at every third turn. I force it down and strain up the hill, head bobbing and knees hitting my chin. A group of women and children walking crocodile fashion along the road pause and point, and as we ride past I see the baskets of bananas carried on their heads wobbling gently as they laugh.

We head towards the Gedi ruins, the remains of a thirteenth century Arab-Swahili community that is something of a mystery to archaeologists and historians. The site covers about five acres, set back amidst dense forest, and is believed to have once been home to two and a half thousand people. There is evidence of a sophisticated and well-organised society and the discovery of Ming porcelain and glass from Persia suggests there was trading with overseas merchants. Yet, despite there being much written about the other towns in the area during this period, this settlement is not mentioned anywhere.

The ruins are quite beautiful and, like pretty much everything else at the moment, we have them to ourselves. A waist-high wall sur-rounds the main complex which houses decorated pillars, elaborately carved arches and ancient tombs and, because the forest has encroached, everything is covered in a soft green hue. A sunken court, where the ruling men entertained, is filled with long grasses and a pair of grooming baboons. Low walls, still intact, divide the building into rooms like an estate agent's floor plan. We take a long, slow walk around the perimeter and, when the sky suddenly changes from blue to black, shelter in the 'museum', a long thin room with a leaky ceil-ing and some unlabelled broken pottery in grubby glass cabinets.

By the time we leave, the track back to the main road is four inches deep in water and we are just able to pedal through as long as we can maintain momentum and don't have to slow down. I hadn't really noticed how hilly it was on our way in, and as I pedal around a corner, my front wheel disappears completely into what is now a fully-fledged river. I jump off and am standing knee-deep in a great brown torrent.

Up-stream a donkey pees into the water and a collection of general village waste drifts down and gathers between my legs. 'Cholera, anyone?' I ask.

As quickly as the sky turned black it is blue again and, by the time we hit the main road, we are both hissing steam. On the way back to the village we pass a number of very expensive looking resorts set back amongst the trees. Sarah is intrigued and hatches a plan. We climb off our bikes and walk down a manicured path towards the entrance of the Turtle Bay Beach Club. After an exchange of smiles and pleasantries with the security guard, he takes our bikes and waves us through to reception. 'My parents are planning a trip to Kenya and this resort has been recommended,' says Sarah, tossing back her ponytail. 'I'm wondering if we might have a look around?'

'It would be our pleasure,' says the nice young man behind the desk.

We are escorted through the cocktail lounge and past the Sugar and Spice shop, where a range of English brand-name biscuits and chocolate are displayed. A sign encourages guests to try 'Big-game fishing' at two hundred pounds a pop, and laminated pictures of luxury tents and baby elephants advertise fly-in safaris. Waiters in crisp uniforms slide about the room carrying tall pink glasses overflowing with pineapple slices and miniature umbrellas.

As the lounge opens out onto the beach I am stunned by the sight of so many white people. Not only are they white, but they are all English, so they are *actually* white, apart from random splotches of red where they have failed to apply their sunscreen properly. In the whole time we have been on the coast we've barely seen any Westerners, and now there are hundreds of them—spread along the beach or lounging around the pool—all secreted away in this private resort. 'It's one of these "all inclusive" places,' explains Sarah. 'You pay a set amount which covers all your food and drink and activities.' On our way out she picks up a tariff sheet and as her finger runs down the columns I see a sparkle in her eye. 'You can come for a day,' she says.

Back at the hotel we are regretting our commitment to a drink with Boniface. We decide we'll have one beer and leave after an hour. We head back to the sleazy pick-up joint where we met the first time—there are few bars to chose from and at least we know the way back to the hotel from this one. Boniface has brought a friend, Derek, who is young, very pretty and dripping gold. He buys drinks all round. I ask him what he does for a living. He is evasive and I joke that perhaps he has a rich Western wife who keeps him. Boniface is concentrating his attentions on Sarah who is yawning a lot; it's been a long hot day, can't stay long, very tired. We divert questions about boyfriends and professions and discuss whether trade might pick up now the election is over. The bar fills up with the same sad, mismatched couples, hands wandering and tongues venturing into places they shouldn't.

Suddenly, I feel Sarah's fingers squeeze mine tightly under the table, and when I turn towards her, she is staring fixedly at me, her eyes wide, eyebrows raised. I try to interpret her look. Boniface is sitting opposite with a curious smile, but I have witnessed nothing untoward. I cough a 'what's going on?' into my hand.

'Later,' she whispers into her beer.

Derek takes his leave and Boniface explains that he has a Kenyan wife and a two-year-old son in Mombasa, but spends most of his time in Watamu, servicing the needs of a wealthy older Italian lady. Boniface, clearly, has plans to service the needs of a wealthy older Canadian lady.

The hour is up. I have had enough of the company and the atmosphere and declare the evening over. Boniface is adamant that we will eat together and drink more. We tell him, rather more assertively than before, that we are not interested and make our way back to the hotel. He follows, sidling up to Sarah as we walk, placing his hand on her arm and whispering in her ear. At the entrance to our hotel Sarah takes me aside and gives me our room key, 'I need a minute with lover boy,' she says.

'Oh I don't think so,' I say.

'It's OK. I'll be fine. Trust me.'

I hover reluctantly until she mouths a determined 'Go!' and I head off in the direction of our room. A few metres away I duck into a bush from where I can see them both clearly. Boniface is gesturing wildly, placing his hand across his heart and shaking his head. Sarah stands a few feet away, remonstrating through a strained smile. They continue for four or five minutes, Boniface looking more and more desperate. He takes a step towards Sarah and I am about to jump out from behind my bush when they shake hands and he shuffles off down the road.

'Pssst!' I say, emerging from the frangipani, 'What the fuck's going on?'

'He gave me this in the bar,' she says, handing me a crumpled piece of paper. I unravel the corner of a page of newspaper and read: *Sarah, I have strong passion and feeling on you. You are on holiday, but spare some hours or day for me. Love Boniface.*

'He proposed,' she says. 'Said he loved me, that I obviously liked him, that he was an educated man and we would make a good match.'

'Oh dear.'

'It's OK. I told him, in the nicest possible way of course, that although I secretly longed to give up my career, relationship and life and become a Sugar Mommy in an obscure African village, I really couldn't manage it this week.'

We are done with Watamu. The not so undercurrent of sex for sale is becoming irksome, and the almost dead guy we saw in the hotel bar has been laid out to bake in the sun right in front of our room. We are rested and ready to head back to Mombasa and on to Zanzibar, and mainland Tanzania but Sarah has just one more thing she wants to do before we leave.

The nice young man behind the desk snips off the end of our plastic bracelets and smiles, 'Enjoy your day,' he says.

'Oh, I'm sure we will,' replies Sarah.

We grab our day-pack and wander through the cocktail lounge, past Sugar and Spice, and along a low board-walk that weaves through beautifully landscaped tropical gardens. Sheltered amongst the giant ferns and wild orchids are the shuttered guestrooms with their 'Beach view', or 'Garden view'. We emerge into an informal style café by the pool—shaded by a high thatched roof—and next to it, a more formal, à la carte, dining room.

We find a couple of vacant banana lounges close to the café and settle in. We have eight hours to eat and drink as much as we can, and we start with a series of non-alcoholic cocktails: two 'Tropical Waves', a 'Cinderella' and a couple of banana smoothies, which we down in half an hour. After six weeks of bottled water and Coke, fresh juice and milk is a real treat.

We head for the dining room which, like everything else, is exquis-itely designed: high-backed, dark wooden chairs, deep green cotton tablecloths and highly polished floors. Lunch is a buffet of fish in meunière sauce, pork medallions with onions and red peppers, pont-neuf potatoes, stuffed Chinese cabbage leaves, pilau rice, three or four different salads and a range of dressings, two choices of home-made soup and a huge selection of fresh bread and rolls. There are many things we haven't seen since we left Australia: mushrooms, zucchini, broccoli, lettuce. It is all beautifully laid out on large silver platters, in deep tureens and huge terracotta bowls. We stand in front of the long tables not quite sure how to begin. 'We need a plan,' I say.

'We could put a little bit of everything on our plate to start with and then come back for more of what we really liked.'

'Or we could assess what we think we're going to like most and load up with that.'

We do both, grabbing a separate bowl for salad and bread and soup and piling up our main plate. After three trips back and forth to our table we are ready, and as I slide a piece of pork medallion onto my fork, I realise that six weeks doesn't seem a long time to live without good food, until you actually live for six weeks without good food.

We wobble back to the pool and park ourselves in the lounge chairs next to the windsurfers and sea kayaks. I feel quite at home amidst the plethora of English accents—a strange mix of middle class southerners and northerners made good. I eye up the numerous copies of the *International Daily Express* that lie across bulging white bellies and listen to a discussion on the various embarrassing ways conservative MPs have killed themselves recently. Beside me, an older gentleman sunbathes in baggy, misshapen trunks and grey nylon socks, and as I glance around the resort, I am reminded once again that on the whole, the English are not a fashionable people.

We reject calls for beach volleyball, water polo and windsurfing and steadfastly remain doing nothing at the poolside. A couple of big game fishermen arrive proudly dragging a very large dead fish which they plonk down by the bar. 'What do they actually *do* with it once they've caught it?' I ask Sarah.

Joseph, one of the ubiquitous, overly attentive waiters, keeps us well-stocked with 'Caribbean Ladies' and fresh passionfruit and pineapple juice. Sarah, though she is not in the least bit hungry, but just because she can, orders a beef-burger and chips from the all-day snack bar. At 3.00 p.m. afternoon tea is served and Joseph brings a tray of freshly baked doughnuts and a pot of English breakfast. We read, relax and occasionally take a turn about the pool in an attempt to make some space for our evening meal.

By 6.00 p.m. the beach begins to clear and we head to the washrooms to shower and change. I am not as hungry as I would like, but feel confident we are up to the challenge of dinner. We order cocktails, a vodka and pineapple combination, and take our seats. Dinner is roast stuffed leg of lamb, pampettes of sea-fish with a hollandaise sauce, vegetable and nut stroganoff, gratinated spinach and potato parcels, steamed basmati rice, Lyonnaise potatoes and an assortment of sautéed vegetables. I limit myself to one portion of everything in the hope that I will be able to sample the dozen different desserts. We toast Sarah's parents who, though they don't know it yet, have just treated us to 'dinner somewhere nice for Christmas'. We wash down the main course with an excellent South African red, and finish with bananas in chocolate sauce, fruit salad, chocolate profiteroles and a crème caramel.

We walk back to the village—a beautifully balmy tropical night with a slow breeze whispering through the palm trees. We feel wholly satisfied with our splurge and are ready to move on.

CHAPTER 7

'...CONSULT A DOCTOR IMMEDIATELY'

WE ARE FIFTEEN minutes into the seven-hour trip to Zanzibar when I remember that I don't travel terribly well on boats. After another five minutes I am in the toilet, where I remain for some time. Sarah hovers outside the door handing me tissues and platitudes while craning her neck to watch the TV monitors in the main cabin—there is a BBC wildlife documentary playing which, I suspect, is somewhat more entertaining than I am. Every so often, I am able to stand long enough to discover how the elephant-nosed fish uses sonar, and why goldfish can see a greater range of colours than people, though how anyone can possibly know this is beyond me.

From what I could see in the few minutes before I ended up in the toilet, the boat is surprisingly modern and well-maintained and captained by a hearty German. With the less than one hundred per cent safety record of Third World ferries, I find this reassuring. The chairs look comfortable, are well-spaced with tables in between, and there is a kiosk selling snacks and cold drinks. It is clean and, astonishingly for a mode of public transport in this part of the world, there is virtually no one on board.

A chirpy English crewman passes me in the toilet and suggests I go out on deck for some fresh air. I grab Sarah's arm, stumbling up the stairs with my head down and my palm flat against my stomach, as if this might somehow stop me throwing up again. Outside it's raining heavily, not a crisp cool refreshing rain, but a sticky humid downpour. We shelter beneath a stairwell where the warm air mixes with diesel fumes and the undulating horizon makes my head spin. With every sudden lurch of the boat, we are flung against the stairs and doused by streams from the upper deck. I lean against Sarah, resting my head on her shoulder, 'I think I liked the toilet better,' I say. Soaked and shivering we climb back down and I settle in over the bowl.

Sarah lingers by the door, snatching glimpses of the TV announcer who is introducing a movie—a proper Western one. She looks at me, looks longingly at the empty cabin with its rows of comfy seats. 'Go and watch,' I say.

'Are you sure Babe?'

'Yeah. I'm fine here. Really. The toilet's great. Just lovely.'

By the time we reach Zanzibar our boat is packed full of young European and Australian backpackers and a handful of locals, whom we have picked up from Pemba Island and a few coastal towns south of Mombasa. The port is teeming with people and it is a shock to see such a great wave of Westerners again.

We are ushered through the port by efficient and charming customs officials who check and stamp our passports and hand us a batch of 'Where to eat' and 'What to do' brochures. 'Welcome to Zanzibar,' they say, smiling. As we leave the dock we are approached by a young man who introduces himself and politely explains that he is employed by the government to act as our guide. Can he recommend a hotel and escort us there? Are we familiar with everything Zanzibar has to offer? Wow! Sarah and I exchange glances—tourist information and customer service. What a treat! 'That would be lovely,' we say. 'Thank you.'

We follow Abdul to the Malindi Guest House, a large two-storey old building with ornamental iron latticework and painted wooden shutters. The interior is pristine: a clean flagstone floor and white-washed walls enlivened with Tinga Tinga paintings, batiks and sisal baskets. A giant banana tree fills the downstairs courtyard, rising up through the open roof. At the top of the stairs, rush matting covers the floor of a large open square, and long bolsters line the walls. In the centre, is a huge Zanzibari chest, elaborately carved and patterned with shining brass studs, an ancient Arabian coffee pot sitting on top. The whole place is light and airy and has *atmosphere*, something we have not previously encountered in our accommodation in Africa.

We off-load our packs and lie under the fan enjoying the luxury of a clean, firm mattress and fresh sheets. The humidity is still unbearable—if anything, worse than Mombasa—and we still cannot bear to touch each another. I have to say, low budget African travel does not lend itself to intimacy: bedbugs, mosquito bites, inadequate showers, clothes that smell and skin caked with sunscreen, sweat and insect repellent tend to dampen any romantic inclinations. We shower, dress in our lightest, coolest clothes, and are dripping with sweat in seconds.

On our way out we meet some of the other Malindi residents: two Rachels—one English, one American—who picked each other up in Zimbabwe and have not stopped arguing since, and Mark, a youth hostel manager from Yorkshire and his girlfriend, Mandy, who works in a horse and donkey sanctuary. They are on a quest to see as many endangered species as they can: the silver-backed gorillas in Uganda, the chimpanzees at Gombe Stream, and next year, the orang-utans in Borneo.

The waterfront is littered with tourists, not just backpackers, but couples who look like they've flown in from London or Paris for a winter getaway. The low sea wall is lined with people watching the ancient dhows drift between the smart modern yachts, and the shady cafés are full of well-dressed Europeans sipping tall glasses of fresh juice. Groups of Zanzibari men lie under the trees and chat or play bao—in the intense midday heat, no one does anything quickly.

A line of historical buildings in various states of renovation face the water. The original Old Dispensary has been beautifully restored and is now the Stone Town Cultural Centre. Inside, long staircases and carved banisters have been stripped and polished, and the windows re-fitted with stained glass in bright geometric patterns. From the wrought-iron balcony on the second floor we can see across to the Beitel-Ajaib, the 'House of Wonders', the Sultan's Palace built in 1883. Its four-storey edifice is chipped and cracked, the masonry crumbling and paint peeling from the woodwork, though you can still imagine its earlier grace and splendour. The British almost destroyed it in 1896, bombarding it with cannons from the sea in an attempt to oust the Sultan.

There are roadworks everywhere—young men, glistening with sweat, heaving picks and excavating huge holes. A new sewerage and drainage system is being installed and, once it's complete, the main roads linking the various parts of the town will be repaired and sealed. I'm not quite sure why, but the money for the building renovations and for the infrastructure, is being provided by the European Community. After Kenya, where everything is in such an appalling state of decay, it is striking to see such development.

Small dusty shop fronts and offices advertise scuba diving courses, spice tours, boat trips, four-wheel drive hire and fishing trips. Everyone is friendly, and while they are keen to book us on a tour, they are not pushy or aggressive. Maybe because there are so many more tourists here than Kenya, or maybe because everyone seems a little better off, the pleas to buy are much less urgent. The young men chat easily, asking where we're from and how we like Zanzibar. The sense of pride in the island is striking—there are lots of people wearing T-shirts with Zanzibari motifs, rather than the 'Mike Tyson' or 'Chicago Bulls' we saw so often in Kenya. Even though they are now part of Tanzania, the Zanzibari maintain a strong separate identity and, if you travel from the mainland, you are still required to show your passport and clear immigration.

We walk back along the waterfront to the seventeenth century Portuguese Fort. Behind its high crenellated walls is a modern café serving fresh fruit cocktails, salads, garlic bread and a selection of home-made cakes. I pore over the menu with its long list of drinks and varied dishes. No fried eggs. No carrot and cabbage combo. No steak of goat. We order fresh fish in a coconut sauce with a green salad, followed by apple pie and ice-cream, and take a very long time to eat it.

In the afternoon we head into Stone Town, the labyrinthine old quarter, much like Old Town in Mombasa, though rather more sprawling. The narrow alleyways are full of traditional houses with overhanging balconies and beautifully carved front doors. A line of dark, shady shops display studded chests, *kangas* and *kikoi*, carvings, pendants and paintings. The men loll in the doorways nodding and smiling, and the women and children laugh and shout hellos as we pass.

Around every corner there is a mosque—Zanzibar is ninety-five per cent Muslim—though we also stumble across the one Hindu temple and the one Catholic church. It is Ramadan which explains why everyone is tired and lethargic—no one has eaten since before sunrise. A notice in the hotel asked us to dress 'modestly' and avoid eating and drinking in public. As the muezzin calls, the shutters are pulled across the shop fronts, the women and girls disappear inside the houses, and the men and boys hurry to pray.

As we stroll back towards the Malindi we are approached by a young man selling spice tours and explain that we have already booked everything. 'Sorry,' I say 'we're organised.'

'You must not be sorry,' he replies. 'It makes me happy that you see so much of Zanzibar.'

We have booked our spice tour with the locally famous Mr Mitu, who developed the concept in the early sixties, and has been successfully running tours ever since—he even has his own website. We pile into an open van with two long benches down either side and drive out along one of the few roads on Zanzibar. We share the bus with an eclectic mix: a German primary school teacher sent by God eight years ago, a middle-aged Irish man interested only in what plants can be used to brew alcohol, and an English couple on their second honeymoon.

I sit next to Tara, a rather plump, buxom American woman who tells me she works as an entertainer. I speculate perhaps she is a singer, could be an actress. 'I am a dancer,' she explains. Given that she is taking up three times the space of anyone else on the bus, I wonder if she might not have some difficulty squeezing into a tutu or persuading her ample bosom into a leotard. She is not a *Swan Lake* kind of a girl, nor can I see high kicks and twirls, rumbas or mambos. 'I am a top professional belly dancer,' she says. Ah!…That makes sense.

She is currently working in Kuwait, though she has trained with all the best belly dancers in Lebanon, Egypt and Saudi Arabia. 'If you put a paper bag over the head of any dancer in the world and had them perform for me, I could pinpoint exactly where they were from,' she says.

'Really,' I say. 'Remarkable.'

Belly dancing, in the Middle East at least, is a lucrative business, but was especially good during the Gulf War, when Tara was paid by money shower. At the end of a performance members of her audience would take a wad of bills and flick them like a pack of cards over her. These days there are fewer showers and she charges a set fee up-front. 'I have been dancing for seven years now,' she says, 'and I'm ready to retire. I'll head back to the US and be the Grand Diva for a while, do a lecture circuit and perhaps a few master classes.'

We stop at the ruins of the Maruhubi Palace, a series of courtyards and sunken baths surrounded by mango trees. It was built by Sultan Barghash to accommodate his harem of ninety-nine concubines who, it seems, spent most of their time in a vast steam bath massaging each other in oil. I'm sure there were worse jobs.

Mitu explains a little of the Island's history, its importance as a trading centre for spices and slaves, the arrival of merchants from Egypt, Indian, China and Persia, the settlement and rule of the Omani Arabs, and the colonial struggles of the Dutch, Portuguese and English.

We pile back into the van, driving along a dirt track until we are herded out again into the middle of a small village. Huge clumps of breadfruit hang from the trees, with giant avocados and grapefruits and bunches of bananas. Mitu takes his knife to a tree and cuts off a hunk of bark which he passes around inviting us to sniff. I place it under my nose and take a deep breath. 'Cinnamon. Wow! I didn't know that's where it came from. Here Doll. Smell. It's cinnamon.'

'Yes Jac. It's cinnamon.'

He cuts a small pod from a tree, chops it in two and holds it in the palm of his hand for us to look at. 'Nutmeg,' he explains, 'and the red plastic looking substance here is mace.'

'Sarah look! Nutmeg and mace. I never knew what they looked like in real life.'

'Yup. Nutmeg and mace, Jac.'

Mitu forages amongst the plants on the ground and pulls out a root, slicing off the bottom to reveal a bright orange circle. 'Turmeric,' he announces. Perhaps I am the only one of our group brought up in the city, or perhaps I am just easily impressed, but I am unduly excited by this revelation. As far as I was concerned, turmeric came in small plastic packets from Safeways. I grab the root and its little coloured circle. 'Look Hon. It's turmeric, it grows as a root in the ground.'

'Yes Jac,' says Sarah trying to back into the crowd.

'That's so cool.'

'Uh...huh.'

'Hey Doll, take a picture,' I nod, 'of me with the turmeric.'

Lunch is prepared by the women of the village using many of the spices and vegetables we see on the tour. We sit cross-legged on reed mats under a thatched roof as a series of hot, fragrant dishes are deposited in front of us: a mild fish curry with cassava spinach and egg-plant, a large bowl of highly spiced rice and a huge pile of chapattis.

We linger after eating, lying back on the mats and enjoying the light afternoon breeze. A young girl paints Sarah's hand with black hair dye in the elaborate swirling designs used for brides on their wedding day—though so far we have only seen them on tourists. The German primary school teacher digs out a book from her bag and starts testing the children to see if they can read. She suspects they are not attend-ing school, though there is one close by and it's free. She questions their parents who nod sheepishly and scurry off.

Mitu rounds us up and we head to the beach, a quiet, empty bay of white sand, palm trees and still turquoise water. We change into our bathers and wade in—Tara remains on the beach and hauls what looks like a small tent out of her bag. She grapples with the bright yellow material, attempting to bring it under control against the sea breeze. From the water we try not to stare as she disappears beneath it and begins to wrestle, the material flapping wildly and making loud cracking noises as it picks up the wind. Eventually, her head emerges through a small opening—though the rest of her body remains hidden—rather like someone wearing a large, old-fashioned bicycle cape. We assume the rustling and fidgeting that follows is her changing into her bathers—she remains upright, her head still and her body jin-gling about from the shoulders down, not unlike belly-dancing, in fact. After a few moments she casts off the great billowing canopy and emerges in her bright, floral tasselled swimming costume. Our entire group is pretending not to watch and I can't help thinking that if she was aiming for discretion, a beach towel might have done the trick.

In the evening we head to Africa House where the *wazungu* go *en masse* to watch the sun go down over the ocean—Mark and Mandy are there, the Rachels and every other backpacker in town. As soon as it's dark the place empties as quickly as it filled, and everyone heads down to the Forodhani Gardens for dinner. 'Gardens' is perhaps a little generous for the scruffy patch of green between the Old Fort and the ocean, but there are a handful of trees, and at night you can't see much anyway.

A narrow, dirt path leads through a mass of wooden stalls each lit by a single kerosene lantern. An uneven glow falls across a line of boys threading meat onto bamboo sticks, or dangling leather necklaces from their arms. 'Good evening Madam. Welcome to Zanzibar. A necklace for you? A bracelet?'

The place is packed with Westerners, and we shuffle though the crowd, elbowing our way to the front of the stalls. Huge piles of skewered beef, chicken and prawns bedeck the tables, with three or four different varieties of naan, vegetable patties, deep fried fish sticks, roasted sweet corn and fried chicken. Samosas hiss and splutter as they are dropped into hot oil, and a huge machete thumps down onto a wooden block, splitting a pineapple in two—the sweet scent of fruit mixing with the fragrant smells of the *bhajis*.

A young man grabs a tall stick of sugar cane, hacking it into foot long sections and feeding them into a rough wooden press, like a dry-cleaner's iron. He pushes down, the juice running into a plastic jug filled with ice cubes. I pause to watch. There can't be any danger drinking sugar cane surely? 'I'll try some,' I say.

He grabs a cup from the ground and sloshes it around a bowl of warm water filled with other cups. He throws in some more ice, pours in the juice and hands it to me. I have a moment's hesitation—I'm sure Sarah could find something in the health section of the guidebook about this. I grab the cup and drink—it's cold and refreshing and I offer Sarah a taste. 'Ah...no thanks darling. No dysentery for me.'

We grab a paper plate, make our selection and watch the boys drop handfuls of skewers onto hot coals. We pile up tomatoes and lettuce and edge back through the crowd towards the sea wall, where the locals play bao by moonlight, and the tourists eat.

We spot Mark and Mandy and park ourselves next to them. They are planning to head east, as we are, up to Mwanza in the north, over to Lake Victoria and down to Gombe Stream. They have heard nightmare stories about the rains which have caused massive flooding in Kenya and Tanzania over the past week, particularly around Lake Victoria where towns are completely submerged and villages are being evacuated. The main road from Nairobi to Mombasa is impassable and Isiolo, where we spent the night in the hotel on safari, is now under water. Vans are getting stuck for hours on Masai Mara and tourists are being robbed by bandits. President Moi has declared a state of emergency. In Tanzania, the train from Dar es Salaam is out, the track under water and a major bridge down. The tenuous infrastructure in the north and centre is literally collapsing, and it's taking days to cover even the shortest distances.

'What do you think,' I ask Sarah as we head back to the hotel, 'about going to Gombe?'

'Sounds pretty grim—floods, bridges collapsing, bandits. It's a bloody long way to see a few chimps.'

'Shall we go then?'

'Sure.'

Back at the Malindi the power has failed and the path to our room is lit by candles. We can manage with torches, but no electricity means no fan and no showers. As a rule, we've been showering three or four times a day in Zanzibar, and though the fans aren't great, sleeping without them is impossible. We wander around the room trying to put off the inevitable—I can't bear the thought of another night like the few we had in Kenya.

Reluctantly, I crawl under the net and lie on my bed and, though I remain perfectly still, I sweat profusely. I shuffle around, trying to find patches of the sheet not soaked in sweat, and will myself to fall asleep.

I awake at 4.00 a.m. feeling light-headed and nauseous. At six, I wake again, sticky and sweating, and drag myself to the bathroom. I spend the next twenty minutes with my head over the toilet. Well joy oh joy, it's been…let's see…all of two days since I was doing this.

I return to our room feeling disorientated and with another headache from hell. Sugar cane juice? Lettuce washed in dirty water? King prawns? After five minutes I am back in the bathroom, this time with diarrhoea as well. I have never experienced both at the same time and I'm not quite sure exactly how to manage it. I am up and down and turning around like someone doing a frenzied aerobics routine… and down…hold for a few seconds…good…and up and around… face the back wall…leaning over…pause…good and up…few deep breaths…around and down.

I crawl back to the room and Sarah takes my temperature, checking it against the 'Fever facts' leaflet that came with the thermometer. 'Oh dear,' she says. 'This is not good.'

'What is it?' I groan.

'Forty,' she says. 'It's in the "consult a doctor immediately" category.'

I dash back to the toilets, repeat my routine, return and lie down, and in minutes, rush back again. It takes four hours and a dozen more trips to completely empty my system and, when I am done, I collapse utterly exhausted on the bed. I am desperately thirsty and fantasise about gulping down great drafts of iced water, but the smallest sip ends up in the bucket by my bed. Sarah has re-read the health section and is checking me for a scattered blotchy rash, sensitivity to light and stiffness in the neck. As I pass on all three, she rules out meningococcal meningitis which is handy, because otherwise I'd be dead by lunchtime.

There is no way I can manage to walk to a doctor and I don't fancy my chances of a home visit. I lie on the bed and sleep, waking periodically to find the thermometer sticking out the corner of my mouth and Sarah hovering with more questions. 'Have you got aching joints?' she asks. 'Do you feel like you have flu?'

'I haven't got malaria.'

'You don't know.'

'I'm not having malaria unless we move to an air-conditioned hotel with an en suite bathroom.'

Sarah leaves me sweating in bed and trots off to the reception, though I'm not sure what kind of assistance she expects to find there. She returns minutes later with news that the sugar cane sellers in town have been barred from the food markets because their ice-cubes contained cholera. We check the book and discover my symptoms are not hugely dissimilar to those described. We agree to let me sleep, monitor my temperature and attempt to find a doctor if it hasn't dropped by morning.

I wake every hour or so through the night and make feeble attempts to wipe my body with a cold face cloth—the sheet is sodden, my skin is white and clammy and I fancy myself a consumptive in a Dickens novel.

By morning my temperature is down marginally, though I still have a severe headache and can't bear the thought of food. By midday I can manage a glass of water and summon enough energy for a game of cards, but after the exertion, I sleep until evening. My temperature continues to drop to safer levels and I can at least prop myself up against a pillow and talk with Sarah. After another review of the guidebook, we decide on 'severe gastroenteritis' for which I have the exact symptoms.

Sarah has been sitting by my bed for hours and I persuade her to join the Rachels for a drink at Africa House. It is our first separate activity in almost eight weeks and I think she is quite excited by the prospect of an independent conversation. I am quite excited by the prospect of ten minutes without having a thermometer shoved in my mouth.

Some time in the early hours of the following morning I awake to see Sarah rushing to the bathroom. She returns twenty minutes later, one hand clasped across her forehead, the other on her stomach, and falls onto the bed. I dig out the thermometer and place it under her tongue. 'Uh oh. Your turn, Doll.' We spend the next two days doing exactly the same as we've done for the last two, only the other way around.

We prescribe ourselves a day at the beach to convalesce and take a boat out to the tiny Chenguu Island a few kilometres off the coast. The island was bought in the nineteenth century by an Arab trader who used it to house recalcitrant slaves, and later it was taken over by the British. The landing area is dominated by a crumbling mansion which has been turned into a very basic café with a few rooms for rent. Apart from the two park officials, and a young man serving Cokes, there are only six of us on the island.

At the front of the old house there are four giant tortoises who lumber across the grass, pausing to sniff rocks and munch leaves. Their shells are about four feet long and inches thick and their long scaly necks periodically emerge like ET. There is a sign saying 'Please do not sit on the tortoise' which suggests that some people actually do. Sarah is still weak and I leave her resting under a tree and take a turn about the island. A forested track skirts the edge leading to rocky outcrops that jut into the ocean. I poke around some ruins and park myself on a tree trunk looking over the water and enjoy a rare moment of solitude.

It takes just over an hour to circle the island and when I return Sarah is watching a large group of Italians who have just been dropped off. They have obviously dressed for Ramadan—bikinis and speedos in a range of fluorescent colours—and they talk as if they are at a party with too loud music. They knock the shells of the tortoise with their knuckles, poke their soft underbellies with sticks and try to lift them up.

A woman in a pink two-piece sits astride one while her husband snaps photographs. We watch as she dismounts and the next person climbs on and poses. 'Do you know the Italian for "What the fuck do you think are you doing?"' I ask Sarah. Fortunately, before we feel obliged to act, their guide calls them and they strut back to their boat.

I drag Sarah up and we stroll through the woods to one of the isolated bays. The water is exquisite, the sand soft and warm and a single palm tree rustles in the breeze like an advertisement for tropical rum. We strip off and dive in, feeling fresh and cool for the first time in days. We cannot see or hear anyone else, and we remind ourselves that we are swimming in the beautiful turquoise waters of the Indian Ocean, off the coast of a small island, off the coast of Zanzibar, off the coast of East Africa, and we are completely alone.

CHAPTER 8

NOT POACHING
BUT PEEING

DAR ES SALAAM is dirty, crowded and ugly and, after Zanzibar, soulless. We walk directly from the port straight through the grey streets of the town centre to the bus station on the other side. Familiar, battered old coaches sit on the potholed tarmac surrounded by crowds of people buying tickets and squeezing oversize bags through too small doors. As we approach, we are spotted by a group of men who immediately dash towards us, bumping waiting passengers, upsetting piles of boxes and sending cases sliding into the dirt.

Within seconds, we are surrounded by twenty or thirty touts waving tickets and shouting prices in our faces. Sharp, dark eyes and neat moustaches hover inches from my nose and I have to back away to avoid projectile spittle as they bark their questions. As one man is shoved aside, another pushes in until he is elbowed away by yet another who fills his place. They are everywhere, completely encircling us, grabbing our shoulders and arms and trying to wrest our packs from our backs.

I feel a hand grip my arm and am gradually separated from Sarah who disappears into a crowd of screaming faces. In an instant she is completely obscured from view by six men towering over her. I step back trying to shake them off and attempt to restore order in my best teacher's voice, 'One at a time *please*!' They do not, as I had hoped, instantly fall silent and await my next instruction, but continue to jostle and, if anything, shout louder.

I crane my neck trying to locate Sarah, and catch sight of her yellow sleeve disappearing into the mêlée. I take a deep breath, throw my arms in the air and try a new approach, 'SHUT THE FUCK UP!' I scream.

It has absolutely no affect, whatsoever.

I pick one man at random, brushing the others aside and trying to focus on him.

'How much and what time?' I shout.

'Eight thousand, five hundred shillings. Half an hour.'

'We'll take it.'

I manage to extricate Sarah from the throng and we follow the young man to his bus. 'It is luxury coach,' he says, throwing our packs on top and gesturing for us to board.

Our 'luxury' coach has only two seats either side of the aisle which appear to accommodate only two people and there is room for legs and luggage. There are no goats and only one chicken, and it appears we will not be travelling with the addition of a football team secreted down the centre. As we bump our way out of the station, a man runs alongside thrusting a flyer through our window. 'Tell me your name,' he shouts. 'I will pick you up in Arusha. You can stay at my hotel— look on the flyer. What is your name?'

'Sarah,' shouts Sarah, as he disappears into the crowd.

The road out of town is sealed with only occasional potholes and, much to my surprise, we proceed at a safe-ish speed. Three weeks ago, we discover, two buses from rival companies spun out of control as they raced each other around a bend and twenty-five people were killed. As a result, dozens of buses have been taken off the road and, for the time being at least, the drivers are being slightly more cautious.

We are provided with 'in-flight' entertainment in the form of videos from the 'Adventure Film Production Company' and, given that we are subjected to four in a row, they are clearly very popular. They bear some resemblance to the very worst, low budget action movie you've ever seen, but are not nearly as good. Each features a blonde muscled American hero wearing army trousers and a cut off T-shirt and his not terribly bright female companion who follows him around the jungle in high heels and a skimpy low cut dress out of which her large breasts repeatedly bounce and fall. The action involves said hero machine-gunning, stabbing, garotting, drowning and karate chopping several hundred Central American, maybe Middle Eastern—but definitely dark with shifty eyes and dodgy accents—bad guys. Said bimbette dashes from tree to tree behind him, sweating and panting profusely and thrusting her heaving bosom in his face asking *literally*, 'Oh Mike how did you get to be so brave?'

Fortunately, the view out the window is more engaging. Wattle and daub villages form distant interlocking circles on the gentle green slopes, and as we approach the foothills of the Usambara Mountains, the huts creep closer to the road and settle beneath giant banana palms. We stop every so often, the villagers gathering around the bus and thrusting items for sale through the window: bunches of tiny finger bananas, plastic bags of hot chips, bottles of shampoo, bright red and orange frozen triangles and cheap digital watches.

Sarah pokes her head out and stumbles through a transaction in her fledgling Swahili, negotiating what seems a very low price for a very large pineapple. She leans out and grabs it by the pointy leaves, attempting to pull it through the window, but it is somehow caught. Beneath it, tied with string, are three more very large pineapples that clearly make a set. She gathers them up in her arms, hauls them through the window and pops them in the middle of her lap. 'Oop la,' she says. '*Four* pineapples!'

Better work on those numbers.

We pull into a pitch-black station at Arusha—there are no food stalls, no cabs, no cafés, no light, not a kerosene lantern anywhere. We have no idea how far we are from the centre of town, or where any of the hotels are, or how we'll reach them. At the front of the coach I can just make out a large group of touts vying for position—we are the only *wazungu* on board and I brace myself for another onslaught. 'Just hang-on to our stuff,' I say to Sarah, 'and don't let them separate us.'

As we gather up our day-packs, water bottles and half of Coles' fruit and veg department, we hear a muffled, but urgent call from the darkness, 'Sarah...here...Sarah.' The guy from Dar es Salaam is waving from the back of the crowd and pointing to an awaiting vehicle. We hug our bags, lower our heads and step down from the bus, into a tightly packed group of men. We elbow our way towards the voice of the Dar es Salaam guy, who is shoving people aside in his attempt to reach us. We meet somewhere in the middle of the crowd, and he grabs our packs and leads us out of the throng to his four-wheel drive. We hop up, slam the doors, and are delivered, in minutes, to the hotel.

Meru Inn does not have quite the same ambience as the Malindi Guest House—in fact it has as much ambience as a run down block of flats, which is actually what it is. The office and reception are situated underneath a stairwell on the first floor and the dining area is spread out along a small stretch of concrete at the top of the stairs and along two sides of a narrow balcony that overlooks the parking garage. The tables and chairs are laid out in a single row and as soon as one person sits, the table behind is completely blocked off. There is a strong smell of diesel rising from below, which mingles with the stench of stale urine emanating from the men's toilets. We are shown to our room which is basic, but clean, though the perfume of the garage dining area pervades. It will do for a few nights.

Arusha is our first post-restante address and we are at the post office at 8.00 a.m. collecting nine pieces of mail: eight letters and a postcard. It is almost eight weeks since we've had any contact with home and we examine each letter eagerly, establishing who it is from, the approximate date it was sent and alternately commending and berating friends and family who have or haven't written. We allow ourselves to read the postcard on the walk back to the hotel, but save the letters until we are seated for breakfast.

We lay each one on the table, shuffling plates, cutlery and salt and pepper to make room. Two of the letters are addressed to us individually and we begin with these, reading each in turn, slowly and aloud. Some law school friends of Sarah's are now living in Singapore and we speculate how we might fit in a visit. My old friend Kate is wading through a mass of essays for her last year at the London School of Economics and thinks she is beginning to understand what 'post-modernism' means. Perhaps she can explain it to me some time.

Over omelettes we argue about who gets to read the letters that are jointly addressed and in what order—shall we read the most exciting ones first or save them until last? We divide them up and Sarah begins, taking a deep breath and clearing her throat. 'Dear Jac and Sarah...' I let her read, uninterrupted, enjoying every detail of every description and, when she is finished, I make her read the whole letter again. This time, she pauses and we discuss items of news and linger over stories: the first family Christmas where our friend Leigh's girlfriend was invited to dinner, her anxieties over starting a new job and the excesses of an ultimate frisbee drinking game. We pause for tea and toast. 'Would love to have been a fly on the wall for Christmas.'

'I know. Can you imagine?'

'She'll do brilliantly in the new job.'

'Of course she will. This is Leigh we're talking about—you know how she stresses.'

My turn, and I take a fat airmail from Perth and slide my knife carefully under the seal. There is a page from my brother who writes as regularly as Halley's comet, and letters from my sister-in-law, nieces and nephew. Kassia sends drawings of crocodiles, toucans and springboks and eager questions. 'How close did you get to the animals? Are they really scary? Do you get to, like, pat any zebras and stuff?'

Oh Kassia you'd love it. The animals are fantastic, they're kind of scary, but when you see them you don't really think about it. The lions, the elephants—it would blow you away! In my dreams, you know, I bundle you all into a safari van, Lydia and Matt, Cara and Stefan, Mick and Lauren and we head off together on a huge Enid Blyton adventure!

We alternate reading the rest, poring over the pages and squeezing out every drop of information and gossip: a hectic semester for Lee with a group of first-years who know astonishingly little about anything; Maria and Jacki now proud owners of their new tent bought expressly for Africa and erected in the living room for general viewing; and Tamara's office Christmas party where she got to play Santa and kiss all the girls.

We order more tea and shuffle paper and envelopes to make space. It's a delight to hear from so many people, though I can't decide whether it makes me feel closer to them or more distant—perhaps both at the same time. Here it is again though, wanting to be in Melbourne and London and Perth and Toronto, all at the same time—a perpetual tugging in different directions. I feel like my life is spread out across this breakfast table, and I wonder how I'll keep all these people close, when they are so far apart.

We pack away our treasures and focus on the day. We have no idea how the rains have affected access to the parks or the distribution of animals, and we need to find a reputable safari company. We chat with an American couple who booked a seven-day trip, at a cost of one hundred US dollars a day, per person, and returned after only two days because their vehicle broke down. They are in dispute with the company—the brother of our hotel owner—but as yet have received no refund. A group of young Australians, just returned from a five-day trip with another company, relate stories of inadequate food, a day spent waiting for spare parts to arrive for their van, and a restriction on the number of miles the driver was authorised to travel once in the parks.

On the positive side, the rain appears to have subsided over the past few days making the roads passable and the animals plentiful. It has, in fact, altered the migration pattern of the wildebeest who are migrating across the Serengeti, not in their hundreds of thousands as they do in the famous August migration, but in big enough numbers to provide a spectacle.

Somewhat wary, we check out the various companies in town, all of whom promise a wonderful safari experience from anything between—and this is for a 'budget' safari—eighty US dollars per person, per day, to one hundred and eighty. After chatting with as many other travellers as possible, and asking lots of questions, we book a five-day trip to Lake Manyara, the Ngorongoro Crater and the Serengeti. A guide will pick us up at the hotel in the morning where we should be ready to leave by 9.00 a.m. On the way home we check out a few souvenir shops, but Arusha is not a pretty or interesting town, and we return to our parking garage to write postcards.

Our guide is at the reception desk when we come down for breakfast in the morning. There is a problem. The Swedish couple who are accompanying us on safari are both sick. Do we mind waiting another day? Well we'd love to hang out in the hotel breathing in diesel fumes and listening to other traveller's tales of woe, but unfortunately we can't. 'Yes we do mind,' I say. 'Let's talk to the Swedes and see if we can sort something out.' He is not keen on this idea, explaining they have diarrhoea and vomiting and really are unfit to travel. The company won't go out with so few people and we must wait until tomorrow. We agree reluctantly and, rather than spend the day in town, arrange a trip into Arusha National Park.

The park is smaller and much less famous than its neighbouring Serengeti, but beautiful. Mount Meru rises steeply at its western end and overlooks the Momela Lakes that dot the wet grassy plain. The lakes formed in a depression of mud and lava deposited when Meru blew away most of its eastern flank, about two hundred and fifty thousand years ago. Flamingos, egrets, ibis, plover and other waders potter about in the shallow alkaline waters, and herds of buffalo, bush and waterbuck graze along their shores.

We drive slowly around the lakes and surrounding swamp towards the Ngurdoto Crater, which marks the eastern edge of the park. The round flat caldera, surrounded by a forest of wild mango and African olive trees, is rather like a miniature Ngorongoro, though the surface is inaccessible to vehicles.

Above us, a troop of black and white colobus monkeys performs an aerobatics routine in the tree-tops, their deep guttural barks letting us know where they are. Further off, a family of warthogs wallow through the water-logged grass and pairs of dik dik munch on the thick low vegetation. To the west of the crater is Ngdogo, or 'Little Serengeti,' an open plain where herds of Burchell's zebra roam. We stop at an observation point, hack into one of our pineapples and sit for an hour watching the animals drift across the grass below.

The next day we learn that the Swedes have cancelled, apparently, but lucky for us, some other people have booked into our tour so we can proceed as planned. Our safari van is a little classier than Savuka's—which wouldn't be difficult—the chairs are upholstered and appear to have both springs and padding. It is a little smaller, but provides just enough space for our party: Gavin, a white Zimbabwean computer geek, and his somewhat younger American girlfriend Megan—she works for an organisation in San Francisco arranging cultural exchanges in southern Africa; Jennifer, a Canadian micro-biologist working as a security guard; Linus our guide and driver, and Aristide our cook. Sarah jumps in the back and starts Canada-bonding with Jennifer, and I chat with Gavin and Megan in the front.

We know very little about our first stop, Lake Manyara National Park, except that, for some reason, there are lions who often climb and sleep in the trees. The park entrance looks new; a freshly painted building with clean toilets and an office, and even a 'museum' which suggests that maybe some of the enormous fees—twenty-five US dollars per day to enter the park, and an additional twenty-five to camp, are actually being reinvested. We proceed through the entrance which is guarded, as all the parks are, by armed anti-poaching per-sonnel in military fatigues.

The road is covered with literally hundreds of olive baboons that spill out from the trees on either side of the road. Adult pairs sit comb-ing through each other's hair, plucking out fleas and flicking them into the air. There are dozens of tiny young, hanging on to their mothers, or swinging from the lower branches, and a pair of red and wrinkly babies who look barely a few days old.

We edge our way along the road—the baboons scampering into the bushes—and drive deeper into the park. As the vegetation thins out, the bright pink surface of the lake appears, the algae sparkling in the sun-light. Low trees, with long spreading branches, surround the lake, and beyond, gentle green hillocks edge one side of the park, a steep, scarp slope rising on the other. Linus pauses frequently and stares off into the distance and, though we follow his gaze, we see nothing. Our guide-book is not optimistic about the possibility of seeing the lions, and we have met a few groups who spent the day here and saw nothing.

We drive further into the park, watching the wading birds skirt the edge of the lake through our binoculars. Linus takes us off road, down a rough track, across a tiny stream and stops alongside a sprawling tree. We look up astonished to see five female lions stretched out along the branches, barely ten metres from our van; if they wanted, they could jump onto our roof in a stride.

We pull our heads inside the van and watch them dangle their giant paws over the branches and flick flies with their tails. The folds of skin over their haunches are scarred, and their ears and noses marked with scratches and nicks. Each time one looks up and approaches us, Sarah falls back into the middle of the van, the lions' gestures magnified by the telephoto lens.

They are curious, pacing up and down the branch, making eye contact, then striding away, and returning a few moments later. The longer we watch, the more agitated they become and, after twenty minutes, they begin to get a little restless. They step from one branch to another and stare rather more intently. Linus decides it's time to move on and we don't argue.

Back at camp, dinner is on the table, a hot, tasty and plentiful fish curry and rice. Our tents are already erected and, as everyone is exhausted and the mossies are bad, we are happy to crawl into our sleeping bags, and leave Linus and Aristide sitting around the fire.

We are breakfasted and packed and on the road shortly after sunrise, and arrive at our camp site on the rim of the Ngorongoro Crater by lunch. The crater, just south of the Serengeti, is the largest intact caldera in the world, formed when a volcanic cone collapsed inwardly, leaving a six-hundred metre high rim surrounding a flat plain.

We pile out of the van and head towards an observation point over-looking the crater floor. The view from the top is stunning—a vast, green circle dotted with swamps and trees, and the shimmering Lake Makat in the centre. Below us, some five hundred metres, are the yellow-barked acacias of the Lerai forest, and the Gorigor Swamp, where herds of elephant and buffalo roam. In the distance, we can see the flat-topped Olmoti Crater and the trio of volcanoes, Lolmalasin, Losirua and Empakaai. Along the rim of the crater, huge cumulostratus clouds gather, pouring down the caldera walls like a slow moving avalanche.

We drive down the steep southern slope, the road winding sharply and displaying the magnificence of the crater at every turn. It is a self-sustaining ecosystem, the underground springs nourishing the pasture, and ensuring many animals never leave. As we drive down through the forest and out onto the crater floor, the clouds in the west and north lift, leaving a bright blue sky dotted with tufts of white. Linus stops the van and turns off the engine. We are dwarfed by the steep green slopes that rise on all sides, by the giant empty plain that spreads out behind and ahead of us. We pause for a moment in the silence, in this huge beautiful, natural bowl, in the gentle light of afternoon. I slip my hand into Sarah's. I can recall few places as beautiful, and truly, I feel blessed to be here.

It is a chilly night, but fresh and clear, and I snuggle into my bag and am asleep in minutes. I awake in the darkness before dawn to a chirpy Sarah bouncing about the tent. 'What *are* you doing, Doll?' I groan.

'Get some clothes on,' she says. 'We're going out.'

'It's still night.'

'Up,' she says, 'and don't whinge.'

Barely awake, I pull on my thermals, find my glasses and crawl out of the tent. 'Come,' she says, holding her hand out for me. We stumble across the rough uneven ground to the edge of the crater, the forest and swamp blanketed in darkness below. Beyond the steep wall, the trees are in silhouette, and above them, splashes of stratus cloud in purple, pink and orange spread out along the rim. I slide my arms around Sarah's waist, resting my chin on her shoulder, and watch as the sun edges above the crater and the deep red mackerel sky slowly clears and brightens to a bright warm blue. 'Glad you came?' she says.

'Nah. Rather have a mortgage.'

It is an exquisite day for our trip into the Serengeti—warm and clear—and as we bump along in our bus I feel utterly content, as if there is nowhere in the world I would rather be than this magnificent place. 'Nice spot, eh Doll?'

'Yeah. Nice spot.'

At the park gate, Linus jumps out to complete the necessary paperwork, while we smile sweetly at the anti-poaching guys leaning on their rifles. As we pass through the entrance, the great Serengeti spreads out before us, vast and flat, occasionally edged by low hills, occasionally edged by nothing. It is really a featureless plain, no termite mounds, no acacias, lakes or swamps, just an endless expanse of low scrub, but it is undeniably beautiful—the sense of space, of openness, of an ancient place still only inhabited by its original tribal people and the animals they once hunted.

Herds of wildebeest in their hundreds mingle with zebra heading slowly south. They blanket the road—separating as our vehicle approaches—and the further we drive, the more there are, until tens of thousands stretch out towards the horizon. Linus drives off-road again, and we creep into the middle of a herd and stop the van. Sarah and I climb onto the roof and look out over miles of untouched natural vegetation. I love the sense of space and knowing this land has always been like this. In Britain there's nothing that's always been there, and even when you venture into the countryside you are never more than a few miles from a pub or farmhouse. Perhaps it's the ancientness of this place that makes it so special, that makes you feel a connection with something bigger than yourself. Perhaps that's why I love the Australian bush so much, too.

Linus calls us back into the van and we leave the wildebeest snorting and shuffling and kicking up the dust. In his characteristic style he finds the only clump of trees for a hundred square kilometres and we head towards the shade for lunch. We pause some ten metres from a low spreading acacia, Linus checking out some movement in the grass. 'Look,' he says, 'beneath the tree.' We peer through the open window of the van at what appears to be the ears of a whole pride of lions. The heads of two females and six juveniles bob up and down and, as Linus inches forward they emerge fully, sitting upright and panting heavily. 'They have just returned from the hunt,' Linus explains, 'which is why they are out of breath.'

The two older lions flop down onto the grass, while the juveniles stand, leaning up against each other, still alert and searching. A sound in the distance startles them and all eight turn and snarl in unison. Slowly they begin to relax, and the younger ones nudge each other playfully, whacking each other's noses with their huge flopping paws, and flicking away flies with their tails.

We unpack our sandwiches, thickly spread margarine and grated carrot which are particularly unpleasant, but with this view—really, who cares?

After lunch, we head for Olduvai Gorge, a fifty-kilometre canyon carved into the southern Serengeti Plain. It is the site of the famous 1959 discovery by Mary Leakey of the skull of an early hominid, *Zinjanthropus*, or *Australopithecus boisei*, which led scientists to radically change their beliefs about the date of the origin of humans.

We are ushered into a wooden shelter overlooking the gorge by Thomas, the curator of the site. The view is stunning: a huge ochre rock face with the multi-layered deposits that preserved the fossils as clear as any diagram in a geology text book. Behind, the gentle Mount Makarut rises with wild sisal, the 'oldupai', sprinkled down its flanks.

Thomas waits for us to take in the view and begins by asking what we have studied. 'Science,' Jennifer says.

'Law.'

'Humanities.'

'Social science.'

'Literature.'

Thomas nods and smiles and we feel vaguely embarrassed, caught out almost, not really a bunch of budget travellers on a cheap safari after all. I wrap my arms around my knees and sit back as Thomas tells the story of our beginning.

For nearly two million years volcanic deposits were laid down here, one on top of the other, with little or no disturbance. Caught in these layers of mud and ash and lava were the well-preserved remains of our ancestors. Long after the deposits had settled, the area was tilted as a result of seismic activity, the layers were exposed, and archaeologists began to excavate. Mary Leakey discovered 'Zinj', and close by at Laetoli, unearthed a line of footprints, evidence of early hominids walking upright, three and half million years ago. 'This place,' Thomas tells us, 'this beautiful, quiet, precious place is the cradle of humanity.'

By the time we arrive back at camp it is 6.30 p.m. and I cannot believe we have been out for twelve hours. We plonk ourselves on the stools and let Aristide serve us packet soup and vegetable curry while we recount the highlights of a spectacular day. As we finish dinner another group arrives, piling out of their van with long faces. They gather around their guide, thrusting a piece of paper in his face and arguing loudly. It seems they spent the day skirting the edge of the park, never actually entering the Ngorongoro Conservation Area. The guide insists they haven't paid the park fees, and when we check their itinerary, the wording is all very vague, saying something about the Ngorongoro 'region'. 'We already lost two days of our trip,' says one man, 'because a Swedish couple who were supposed to be with our party got sick.'

Ah…yes…sick Swedes. Sounds familiar. 'Did they recover?' I ask.

'No, they found someone else to fill their place, but if I'd have known there was going to be a delay, I would have booked with some-one else.'

I leave Sarah offering advice and prepare for bed. The toilets at the site are 'low style' and, the last time I looked, their entire contents were floating around the stalls. I make an executive decision to pee in the bushes and disappear into a clump of trees a few metres behind our tent. The stars are spectacular—the Southern Cross is far brighter than it ever is in Australia—and I can see the Milky Way splashed from one end of the crater to the other. A sudden rustle of leaves interrupts my star gazing and I freeze, caught between wanting to pull up my trousers and not wanting to attract attention. There it is again, a short, but definite rustle, as if something is moving, stopping, then moving again.

I remain squatting, balancing on the balls of my feet, and try to pull my pants and trousers up over my bended knees and thighs. As I struggle with this somewhat tricky balancing act—attempting to avoid any rustling of my own—I hear another, quite different sound, nothing that a lion or cheetah might make, but something rather more human...a hand hitting a metal object perhaps?

Before I have time to contemplate further, a dark figure steps out from behind a tree and moves slowly, but deliberately towards me. I am frozen—trousers up, thank God—but frozen. Through the darkness I discern the distinctive shape of a khaki clad man holding a large rattling rifle that he wields high above his shoulder. I am still squatting and, though he and his rifle are probably only regulation size, they tower above me like something out of an Arnold Schwarzenegger movie. He starts to shout, blurting sentences in Swahili that mean absolutely nothing to me.

Oh God, I think, there is nothing under 'Dangers and Annoyances' that covers this. Sarah is over the other side of the camp site still talking, Linus and Aristide are chatting happily around the fire, and I am hanging out in the bushes with an over-excited, highly agitated and probably very poorly trained armed ranger who doesn't speak a word of English.

Tricky.

I realise I am not in a great position here, actually as well as figuratively, and slowly and as gently as I can, I raise myself up, arms held loosely in front of me in as non-threatening and subservient a gesture as I can muster. He continues to shout and gesticulate, his rifle, which has now taken on monolithic proportions, filling the space between us.

I sense he is asking me questions, wanting some explanation. 'I went to pee in the bushes,' I say. 'Toilet…you know…er…peeing…um…weeing.' Oh God. This is not going to work. He shakes his head and continues to splutter, using his rifle to point in different directions. Please, *don't* jab your rifle like that. Shouting I can deal with, but the rifle thing is not good. I'm sure, after all, this is just a misunderstanding that we can sort out quite amicably, and that we'll both sit down and laugh about later.

I try a different approach, opening my arms in an expansive gesture and adopting a pleading, desperate tone. 'Sorry,' I say. 'I really am very sorry…I apologise…please forgive me…an error…a mistake…sorry.' He is unmoved and in desperation I trawl the depths of my brain for something he might understand. '*Pardonnez-moi?*…er…*Entschuldigen Sie?*…*Scusi?*' Fuck. This is ridiculous. I know it's a long shot, but Swahili O-level wasn't big in Borehamwood in the mid-seventies.

He steps forward, grabs my arm with his rifle-free hand and hauls me in the direction of our camp. Linus and Aristide look up from the fire as I trot alongside the ranger like a small child. A heated exchange follows between my guy and Linus while I stand, stepping from one foot to another, wondering what the hell is going on. 'He wants to know what you were doing in the bushes,' says Linus.

'I was going to the toilet,' I say, relieved at last to have communication back on-line. Linus translates. 'He wants to know why you didn't use the toilets.'

Because they are completely disgusting and I can't go near them without heaving my guts up, is what I want to say, but it doesn't seem the most appropriate response under the circumstances. 'I was in a hurry,' I say. 'Traveller's tummy.'

Linus turns back to the ranger and then back to me. 'You must never enter the bush after dark. If the guard sees you, he will assume you are a poacher and will shoot you.'

Great. I'll remember that. Thank you. Please convey my apologies to the guard. I shall avoid peeing in his bushes in future, though I do think mistaking a tourist for a poacher and shooting them with their pants down might not be terribly good for his career in the ranger service or the Tanzanian tourist trade.

We have a slow morning, the peeing-not-poaching story relayed as a cautionary tale to the members of my group and sundry hangers-on, curious about the preceding night's commotion. Around mid-morning, we head out for a last drive through the crater and persuade Linus to drop us at the Serena Lodge for afternoon tea. 'Remember,' he says, 'you must be back *before* it is dark.'

'No problem,' we say. 'It is only a few kilometres. We'll be back before dark. We promise.'

The Serena, like all the lodges, is exquisite—lots of wood and thatch and white tablecloths and charming, smartly dressed staff. We find a table on the balcony overlooking the two hundred dollars-a-night view of the crater, and order fresh home-made scones and jam and fruit juice from the not very bright trainee waiter. While we wait for our order, I check out the rather more salubrious restrooms and take the opportunity to have a long, relaxing pee unmolested by military personnel wielding fire-arms.

Our waiter brings coffees and cake, which we haven't ordered, and on his return to the kitchen, slips up the stairs sending his tray and its contents crashing into the bar. It is some time before he emerges again with our scones which are light and fresh and served with real butter and cream. We head out just before the sun comes down, eager not to disappoint Linus and to avoid any more close encounters with AK47s.

The low green hills are dotted with spots of red as the Masai herd their cattle into kraals, and a steady stream of Land Rovers trundle up the track, returning from their evening game drives. We are about fifteen minutes away from the lodge when we notice someone running behind us, shouting and waving his arms. 'Oh God not again…but I'm not doing anything wrong!'

It is our waiter who, after catching his breath, explains that we must return to pay our bill. We assure him we have paid it, in full, to the man at the reception desk. 'No, no, no,' he says. 'You *must* please return. I will walk with you. You must *please*.' He is extremely agitated and so insistent that we reluctantly turn around and schlep back up the hill to the lodge.

It is sorted in seconds, the concierge confirming we have paid and the young waiter apologising profusely. By the time we are on the track again it is almost dark, the last Land Rover having returned and the Masai long since settled into their huts. We walk briskly, stepping into a jog every so often, as we catch sight of our camp site some way off in the distance.

Our circle of tents gradually emerges, dark and shady as the sun drops below the horizon. About a kilometre away from home we hear a familiar agitated shouting from behind and wonder what on earth could possibly be wrong now. We turn to see two figures approaching us at a trot. Oh God. Please no. Not again. It is our friendly camp guard and one of his buddies, their now all too familiar rifles slung across their shoulders. 'Madam!...Stop!…Now!…Madam!'

I haven't been anywhere near the bushes, honestly! In fact, it will be years before I can pee behind a tree again. We turn and wait for them to approach, rifles bouncing up and down with every step, 'You should be at your tent now,' says the buddy. 'It is very dangerous. I will walk with you and my rifle.' I look at Sarah who clearly has no more idea what is going on than I do. The only danger I am aware of, is an overzealous ranger who has a tendency to mistake me for a poacher.

We are escorted back to our site and are spotted by Linus as we approach the tents. I remind myself that I am a grown-up, despite feeling remarkably like a teenager summoned to the Headmaster's office. They talk in Swahili while Sarah and I stand awkwardly in silence. 'You were meant to be back here before dark,' says Linus.

'I know. We did try. It's just that...'

'I told you for a reason.'

'It wasn't my fault honestly, it was the waiter...'

'Do you realise quite how dangerous it is at this time of night?'

'I didn't go anywhere near the bushes...honestly.'

'On the track. It is dangerous to be on the track.'

'But...why?'

'Because of the leopards. At dusk there are leopards—they come out of the bushes and prepare to hunt. You do not want to be there when that happens.'

'No you're right...We don't...Yes...Leopards...Sorry.'

CHAPTER 9

PICK ME UP ON THE WAY DOWN

WHEN WE PLANNED our trip, the one thing I was determined to do was climb Kilimanjaro. Now we're actually here, I'm not so sure. We've met lots of people who failed to make it to the top, and everyone who did was sick on the way. The track is wide and well-worn and at any given time there are dozens of groups snaking their way up. Reaching the summit involves wading through the detritus of earlier trekkers and stepping over piles of regurgitated packet soup and vegetable curry. It is also expensive: twelve hundred US dollars for the two of us for six days, and, I confess, I am mildly concerned about the opportunities for violent headaches and unrelieved nausea. Theoretically, I am no more likely to experience altitude sickness than Sarah or anyone else, but—call me crazy—I am not terribly excited by the thought of another night puking my guts over Sarah's boots while hippos party on my head.

As a compromise, we decide to climb Mount Meru which, at 4566 metres, is slightly lower than Mount Kenya and only a three-day trek—if I do get altitude sickness, it shouldn't be too great a drama to descend. It's much cheaper and there should be far fewer people. Unlike Kilimanjaro, you can only ascend Meru accompanied by an armed National Parks Ranger, and the number of climbers on the mountain at any one time is restricted. Despite my recent diarrhoea, vomiting, fever and general all round gastro experiences, I feel surprisingly fit and am not really worried about the climb. I've checked out the route in our book—it's steep, but looks fairly straightforward with relatively few hours walking each day. Details of the early morning summit attempt on day three are a little sketchy, but it's only three or four hours.

Really, how hard can it be?

We assemble at Momela Gate, the Park headquarters, with Gavin and Megan from our safari, and our guide, Fred. We have four porters who each grab one of our packs, attaching their own bedding and clothes to the outside. They balance large baskets overflowing with food and cooking utensils on their heads. The guide with my pack also carries a bulging plastic bag, and has two dozen eggs in a cardboard carton tucked neatly under his arm. I shuffle around, trying to make my daypack look heavy and my camera bag more cumbersome.

By mid-morning we have sorted the park fees and paperwork and head out from the gate, filing across the boulder-strewn Ngare-Nanyuki riverbed and into a boggy grove of yellow-barked fever trees. As we walk, Fred explains there are buffalo, lion and elephant on the lower reaches of the mountain—we should stick close to him and not go wandering off into the bushes. I raise my eyebrows at Sarah. Yes, I think we've learnt that lesson.

Away from the riverbed the ground becomes drier underfoot and we trek gently upward, leaving the warthogs grazing in the undergrowth. The porters quickly disappear, walking at twice our pace, despite their burden. It's warm and sunny and not too humid and we settle into an easy and relaxed rhythm. The track opens out onto a plateau like an alpine meadow—bright green grasses littered with the purple flowers of the vernonia shrub and deep orange 'Black-eyed Susans'. We pause for a drink and to catch our breath, puffed even at this low altitude. Gavin is struggling already with a sore knee and a headache—he has read somewhere that altitude sickness affects men more than women. We nod and smile politely.

Through a clearing in the trees we can see across to the Momela Lakes below and trace our drive around Arusha National Park. Little Serengeti and the Ngurdoto Crater are easily identifiable off to the south and east, and in between them, a string of lakes and swamps that reflect the sunlight like tiny mirrors. Above us, we can see the tall African olive trees that mark the start of the lower montane forest at about 2000 metres.

The track weaves into the forest and we follow Fred at a slow, steady pace, enjoying the cool of the shade and watching the birds swoop between the trees. Suddenly, he stops, raising his hand and grabbing his rifle. We are immediately still and silent and focussed on the sound of snapping branches a few metres ahead. The trees are low and thick and all we can see are leaves being shaken violently from one side to another. A branch is torn from its trunk and dragged back into the undergrowth. 'Elephant,' says Fred, shooting the bolt of his rifle.

We stand, poised in a line behind him, watching the rustling bushes as another branch is wrenched with a loud crack. Fred raises his rifle and points to the sky and we brace ourselves for the shot. I squint into the bushes and can just see patches of dark grey between the foliage. I'm assuming that when Fred fires the elephant will run off in the *opposite* direction, though as far as I can see it could just as easily stumble our way.

The four of us are frozen like a still from an action movie, Sarah with one hand caught brushing loose hairs from her face. I take shallow breaths, as if the sound of my breathing might attract the elephant's attention. I look at Fred again who is concentrating intently on the moving undergrowth, his finger taut on the trigger. No one speaks. No one moves.

Slowly, the rustling begins to subside, the branches fall still and the heavy thud of elephant footsteps disappears on the other side of the trees. Fred drops his rifle and nods, gesturing for us to fall in close behind. 'Come. It is safe now,' he whispers 'but stay close—there may be more.'

I try to recall whether we covered elephants in Winjau's what-to-do-if-confronted-by-African-wildlife lecture. Try as I can, I cannot imagine any action—running, dodging, tree climbing, diving into water, asking nicely—that would protect us from a charging elephant. I walk a little closer to Fred and his rifle and attempt to stay calm when a guineafowl appears out of nowhere and darts across the track.

We head into the higher levels of the forest where juniper and African yellow-wood trees dominate. Olive pigeons feed off the berries and flocks of noisy red-fronted parrots swoop down close above our heads then disappear into the canopy. The track narrows as we proceed, guiding us up a sharp lengthy incline which I suspect is a hint of what's to come. My legs feel strong though, my head is clear, and I am hopeful for an uneventful climb.

We find a spot for lunch where we can see down the mountain and admire how much height we've gained. I retrieve our sandwiches from the depths of our pack, Sarah having placed a full litre and a half water bottle carefully on top. I lay the somewhat mangled package on the grass—two thin slices of processed white bread glued together with a thick layer of cheap margarine and, buried somewhere beneath them, a wafer thin slice of tomato and cucumber. Sarah looks at it from a distance, screws up her nose and hoes into the emergency packet of Hobnob biscuits we found in an ex-pat shop in Arusha. I pull off the crusts around the circular indent made by the water bottle, and leave the tomato to fossilise beneath the layers of margarine.

It's a short, but steep, climb up to Miriakamba Hut after lunch and we take it slowly, stopping frequently to drink. My lungs feel good, and lunch—what there was of it—remains happily settled in my stomach.

Gradually, Meru's summit emerges. Before 1874 when it erupted, Meru was the highest peak in Africa; now, only half the crater remains, forming a huge horseshoe with a steep back wall that rises 1500 metres to the summit—one of the tallest cliff faces in the world. Where there used to be a lake there is now a flat circular plain with a perfect ash cone at its centre.

The last hour to the hut is like walking up steep stairs and my calf and thigh muscles begin to pull with each step. Though we have only been walking for a few hours, it is a relief to reach Miriakamba, and the hut is a pleasant surprise—a long wooden bunkhouse that looks recently painted on the outside and swept clean on the inside. Beds—with clean and comfortable mattresses—line the walls, and there is a separate dining room with tables and bench seats. More exciting still, there is no evidence of Rodentia. Outside, there are two fire extinguishers, some hanging lanterns, a kerosene tank, rubbish bins and even a stall selling very expensive beer. It is the first sign of real management we have seen in any of the parks.

We drop our bags and sit on the dry grassy slope in front of the hut. Far off in the distance the flat-topped peak of Kilimanjaro emerges through the clouds, pristine and beautiful, and we rest a while, drinking tea and eating fresh warm popcorn.

The hut is situated on the edge of Meru Crater and after our break we head up a narrow track to explore. The crater floor is littered with rocks formed from solidified lava, like giant pumice stones. I place my foot on the edge of the nearest one and it rolls away from me, the chalky dust leaving smudges on my boot. I hoist a rock above my head in a circus strong man impression and Gavin balances one on the palm of his hand. We take it in turns to snap a few shots of us looking terribly butch. Sarah is somewhat less impressed by the lightweight rocks and the photo opportunities they present, but it's not easy to pretend you don't know someone half way up an African mountain.

We head further into the crater towards clumps of squat trees with gnarled trunks and off-white flowers, and low St John's Wort that sprouts up from the old lava flows. The trees are covered with 'old man's beard', a light, feathery moss that hangs from their branches like cobwebs creating an eerie, out-of-the-wardrobe-and-into-Narnia atmosphere.

By the time we return to the hut everyone is weary and eager for dinner—packet soup and something introduced as chicken masala which is hot and vaguely edible, unlike the oil-soaked banana fritters that follow. At 9.00 p.m. we prepare for bed in an attempt to adjust our body clocks—I have just discovered that on our third day we will be awoken at 1.30 a.m. to begin the summit ascent at 2.00 a.m. Not only that, but we then have to descend the whole mountain and reach the gate by sundown—a walk of about another ten hours. Like the guide-book, Fred is thin on detail, and when I ask him to describe the ascent, he shakes his head and mutters earnestly, 'You must not listen to all those terrible stories.'

We begin day two with fried eggs and a pep talk from Fred. We have a 1000-metre climb ahead of us up to Saddle Hut which we should complete in three or four hours, then a further one and a half hour ascent to Little Meru. It's pretty steep and we must walk close together and maintain a steady pace. I estimate we'll cover the same height as day two on Mount Kenya, but in half the time. If I am going to get altitude sickness, today's the day.

Above Miriakamba Hut the vegetation quickly thins out and the beautiful alpine meadows are replaced by squat trees, scrub and rocky outcrops. The elephants and buffalo don't venture this high, and instead, klipspringers—with their funny shaped hooves—bounce from one outcrop to another. Across the valley, there is nothing between us and the upper reaches of Kilimanjaro except clouds, and as we walk, even they are burnt off by the morning sun, leaving beautiful clear views. It is a *very* steep climb and everyone is beginning to feel the strain. Sarah's knees click and crunch with each step and Gavin is already dragging his left leg. We are all breathing slowly and heavily, and dripping sweat even when we stand still.

We plod, one step in front of the other, trying to keep up with Fred but not wanting to pace ourselves too quickly. Every now and again I look across from my feet, at the grey heath enlivened with 'red-hot poker' flowers and bright green mosses and lichens that coat the rocks. Occasionally, Fred points out a wild orchid nestled in the low branches of the trees. We pause every half an hour or so to drink— everyone concentrating intently on the climb and reluctant to waste breath on incidental activities like talking.

The last hour up to Saddle Hut is the worst, an almost vertical slog up rough ground, and I force myself to focus on the track, placing one foot higher than the other in a slow and laboured rhythm. Sarah is ahead with Megan and I can see poor Gavin way down below. It's not like I haven't done tough ascents before, but perhaps nothing quite so steep, and certainly not at altitude.

I have often wondered about the appeal of climbing mountains. I understand, of course, the buzz of reaching the top, but let's be honest here, the getting there really isn't so much fun and, if you think about it, that's ninety per cent of the activity. Perhaps, at this stage anyway, it's just a matter of pride. A girl really doesn't like to think she's being left behind. I muster all the energy I can for the final half hour, and haul myself up the track.

I admit, I am a teeny bit anxious about tomorrow's summit ascent.

We have a short and inadequate break for Milo and peanuts before heading up to Little Meru, the mini peak at 3820 metres. We are way above the clouds, their shadows drifting across the valley below, the crisp white cirrus so close I feel I could step out onto them. It is another steep schlep to the top and I drag myself up, taking the last hundred metres on all fours, and collapse on the summit with the others.

While we rest and drink, Fred runs though the plan for tomorrow—rather, for later tonight. 'The walk is in three stages,' he explains. 'The first hour is a brisk walk and a steep climb up to Rhino Point…'

Well at least we get the steep part over at the beginning when we'll be fresh and strong. It's easier that way, rather than having to do all the hard work at the end when you're exhausted.

'…The next two hours is a very steep climb up to the crater rim…'

Ah…*Very steep* climb…OK…two hours of that. Well that shouldn't be too bad. We'll be warmed up by then and into the rhythm of things and, at least once that's over, we can enjoy the walk up to the summit.

'…Then an *extremely* steep climb to the top for sunrise.'

Hmm…*extremely steep*…that must be about an hour-and-a-half to two hours that bit. Yup. Could be hard work, but then at least we're almost there and the promise of a beautiful sunrise will help us up the last stretch. Should be fine. Really.

An awkward silence descends upon our group as we each sit staring at our boots. 'But everyone who starts the climb makes it up don't they?' I ask, in as upbeat a tone as I can muster.

'Yes,' he replies dourly, 'but it is not easy and you must strive.' 'Strive…ah…OK…Yup…I can do strive…I'm up to a strive…Doll? OK for a strive?'

As we descend through the clouds the peak of Mount Meru and tonight's route becomes visible: the steep, the very steep and the extremely steep.

We are in bed by 8.00 p.m., willing ourselves to sleep in preparation for the 1.00 a.m. wake-up call. I lie in the darkness listening to the wind whip around the hut—it's cold out there, but not nearly as cold as it's going to be in six hours' time. I wonder—five hours of climbing in the

A GIRL'S OWN ADVENTURE

freezing darkness all so we can see a sunrise which yes, will probably be lovely, but, I suspect, the summit is just as lovely around about mid-day and we could see that after a pleasant morning's walk on a full night's sleep. But hey, where's the challenge in that? No. Much rather slog my guts out for two days, fortify myself with a handful of peanuts and the edge of a sandwich, and crawl up an icy scree slope in the dead of night. Much more rewarding.

What seems like only an hour later, I hear Fred's tap on the door and open my eyes to the darkness with a vague sense of dread. I poke my arm out of my sleeping bag to test the air and snatch it back before the cold seeps in. I love my sleeping bag, its great lofting cushions of down that envelop me and keep out even the most penetrating cold. Perhaps, if I lie very still and quiet Sarah might forget I'm here and accidentally go without me.

A rustling above suggests this will not be the case. Sarah pokes her head around the bunk and even in the dark I know she is bursting. I will her not to be cheery. 'Hi darling,' she says in that breezy isn't-life-great-and-aren't-you-happy-to-be-alive kind of a way. 'Let's get up and go eh?'

No. Let's not get up and go eh. Let's stay in this nice warm sleeping bag and wait until morning. Remember morning? That's when normal people get up. Normal people who might spend the day staying exactly where they are, admiring the pretty view and tucking into a packet of Hobnobs if their girlfriend hadn't already eaten them.

'Hi Doll,' I grunt. 'Forgot to tell you—last night, tripped over a rock and broke my ankle. Bugger really, 'cause I was really looking forward to the climb.'

I peel off my sleeping bag, step onto the cold floor and hop from one foot to another trying to find my socks. Silently, I pull my clothes on and head to the dining room for a cup of tea and a handful of dry biscuits. It is, as anticipated, freezing, though Fred assures us it is not quite down to zero—maybe when we are up on Rhino Point.

152

Great. Something to look forward to.

Sarah is psyched and hopping around the hut ready to leave; Megan and Gavin, fortunately, are behaving somewhere closer to normal, quietly sipping tea and adjusting the laces on their boots. I wander through the hut taking deep breaths, trying to quell the fluttering in my stomach and suppress the memory of my fourth driving test—long story—the last time I experienced this kind of palpable anxiety.

At 2.00 a.m. we recheck our gear: thermal underwear, water, head-light, food, fleece and camera. Fred has advised us not to put our thermals on until we reach Rhino Point because we will get too hot on the lower reaches. I am somewhat sceptical, huddled as I am in my jacket blowing desperately into my cupped hands for warmth, but he is insistent.

He places me immediately behind him, which suggests he may have picked up something of my commitment to this expedition, then Gavin, Megan, and Sarah at the back, who is totally smug because she thinks this means she's the fittest.

As we begin, I look down at Fred's boots in front of me and try not to think about the four, or five or six hours it might take us to reach the summit.

The only way to do this is one step at a time.

The start of the track is fairly well-worn and we step easily around large scattered boulders, though my head-torch is flickering and fading already. There is no view, of course, to distract our attention and nobody feels much like talking. As we approach the 'steep climb' the temperature begins to drop and I pull my jacket closer. I am totally focussed on Fred—matching him step for step—and am only vaguely aware of the others behind me. Though it's a group activity it feels like a very solitary pursuit. I ponder Fred's description of the climb and wonder whether he may have exaggerated its difficulty so that when we actually do it, it is easier than we expect. Unfortunately, I think not.

Rhino Point, as promised, is freezing and we hover on its exposed crag, icy winds whipping around the rock and piercing my fleece. In order to put our thermal underwear on we, of course, have to strip off the layers we are already wearing and expose bare skin to the elements. I stomp my feet and wrap my arms around my body, reluctant to remove anything.

The longer I stall the more difficult it becomes—I am waiting for a lull in the wind which I eventually concede is not coming. I take off my head-light and glasses, unbutton my shirt and pull on my thermal top as another icy blast slices through my torso. I replace everything as fast as I can and zip my fleece up to the chin. I undo my boots and stand in my socks, attempting to poke each foot into my thermal bottoms. The quicker I try to do this, the more difficult it becomes and I hop backwards and forwards desperately shoving my foot into the leg until it finally appears at the other end. I dig through my pack for my woollen hat and gloves and when I am finished dressing, feel like an Arctic explorer, the only part of me left exposed being my nose—not quite what I expected from Africa.

Above Rhino Point the ground is rocky and uneven and I struggle to maintain my footing in the fading light of my torch. The moon is high and pops out from the clouds every so often but provides little light, and the sun feels a long way off. After a tricky clamber around a rock-fall we reach the bottom of the 'very steep' which, in addition to being almost sheer, is made up of volcanic ash. In a reversal of usual mountain climbing philosophy, I tell myself, 'Don't look up—whatever you do, just keep looking down.'

I manage to drag myself up the firmer ash near the bottom of the incline, but once on the slope proper I flounder. With each step up, I slide most of a step down, like climbing a steep shifting sand dune. Not only is the ash unsteady, but it's littered with shards of sharp rock that poke into the soft part of my calves and wedge themselves under my kneecaps.

After fifteen minutes my chest heaves with the explosive banging of my heart desperately trying to keep up with the frenetic demands of my body. The muscles in my legs launch into full-blown spasms that leave me shaky and stumbling. I haul myself up slipping and sliding and, despite expending huge amounts of energy, ascend barely a few metres. Sarah and Gavin and Megan are struggling too, but have at least mastered the art of staying upright.

After forty-five minutes I am weak and wobbling all over the place, the light from my torch fading to a dull glow on the ash. I hear a distant call from Sarah below. 'Are you OK, Babe?'

I pause for a moment trying to find some breath with which to reply. 'Remember when I threw up on Mount Kenya and someone was playing football with my head?'

'Yeah.'

'That was "okay". This is something else entirely.'

Sarah manages to find some extra energy and in a few bounds is standing next to me. 'Try taking smaller steps or maybe increasing the angle of your feet.' I try both, but despite repeated efforts, continue to slip and fall. I crawl up the last hundred metres until I lose my footing completely and end up spread-eagled across the mountain—my face in the dirt, ash gathering on the inside of my spectacles, dust sticking to my lips. I spit out a mouthful of volcano and, defeated, lay my cheek against the soft cool ground. Prostrate and perfectly still, I find a moment's peace. 'I'm taking a nap,' I announce. 'Pick me up on the way down.'

I reach the three-quarter mark exhausted, but with some minor sense of achievement—though we still have 'extremely steep' to deal with—and then have to descend all the way down to Momela Gate where we started two-and-a-half days ago. We pause for water and chocolate and speculate where Kilimanjaro hides in the dark, but at 4200 metres and sub-zero temperatures we don't linger for long. I have no signs of altitude sickness which is perhaps the only vaguely positive thing in this whole ugly experience.

Despite my fumblings on the ash we have made reasonably good time, but everyone is weary and we proceed slowly and silently. Fred tells us to stick close to the path—there's a bit of a drop on either side which we can't see. We trudge towards the summit, seeing a faint glow in the east at about five-thirty, which provides just enough light to illuminate the huge buttress ahead. We pause at the bottom, psyching ourselves up for the final ascent—an almost vertical climb up a sharp icy wall. 'Really,' I ask myself, 'what the fuck am I doing?'

We begin to scramble, the wind raw and piercing, and I search frantically for decent foot and hand-holds, hauling myself up by my fingertips. With every step my muscles threaten to snap and every breath of rarefied air tears at my lungs. I drag myself up on my knees and elbows and clamber over one ledge after another. The last few hundred metres are interminable—I manage barely four or five steps before I pause and every time I look up, the summit seems no closer.

It is a monumental exercise of will that gets me up the final crag and onto the summit—Fred, Sarah and Megan are already there, and Gavin follows a little way behind. I collapse onto a rock and lay my head between my knees, panting desperately, my eyes watering, my chest heaving. I take long, deep breaths as every muscle in my legs and arms and neck twitches and pops. Thank God, I mutter to myself, this hideous ordeal is finally over.

After a few moments I look up. The peak is awash in a warm rose-pink light—though it is still bitterly cold. I stand, breathing in the scrubbed clean air, and spin around three hundred and sixty degrees. Below us, in every direction, is a thick layer of bright cumulostratus cloud and, in the distance, a single peak breaking through, like a mountain in a fairytale where a giant might sit.

Above us, the sun edges over a high eastern ridge, streaks of pink and purple littering the sky, which warms to a bright blue, the colour of cornflowers. As the light brightens I see the faces of my fellow climbers, strained and exhausted, each sitting in silent contemplation. Sarah clambers over the rocks and stands behind me, wrapping her arms around my waist. I grab her hands and slide them into my jacket pockets—her head resting on my shoulder. It is a cold, lonely and desperately beautiful view. I can't say I ever want to do another climb like that, but then again…how often are we blessed with moments like this?

Despite the sunrise it is still freezing—and we have a ten-hour descent ahead of us. We snap a few pictures of the peak and begin the long slog down towards the promise of tea and pancakes at the hut. The scramble just beneath the summit is less tiring, but more dangerous, to descend than it was to climb. In the thick damp mist that envelops us we move painfully slowly, inching our way down the sheer face. It's a long drop down and already my legs have taken on that characteristic wobble that accompanies a steep descent.

Below the rocks, we pick up the pace and as we hit the top of the 'very steep'—the ash slope where I paused for a nap—the cloud clears and provides our first view of the ascent and the surrounding terrain. Everything is a dark, charcoal grey: the mountains in the distance, the valleys between them, the rock beneath my feet. There is no grass, not even the green hint of moss or lichen, just a huge barren moonscape pitted with craters, and the perfectly formed ash cone which sits on the old lake bed, like a diagram in a geometry textbook.

We look across to the track we just climbed in the pitch black and discover Fred's 'bit of a drop'—a knife-edge ridge that falls away sharply on both sides. We pause for a moment somewhat perturbed at the sight of our thin winding path perched atop a razor-back. I contemplate the notion that in the event of a sudden gust of wind, or a slight loss of footing—neither of which would have been unremarkable—the chances of one of us falling away sharply would have been remarkably high.

We arrive at the hut at 9.00 a.m. after almost eight hours of climbing, and fall onto the grass, loosening our boots and gently massaging our feet. Our cook has made tea which is steaming, and a pile of pancakes which are not. I grab one from the top of the pile which is not only stone cold, but, in the two hours it has been sitting here, has meta-morphasised into a frisbee and become about as palatable. We pool our collection of dry biscuits and day old popcorn and munch silently.

I lie back on the grass, enjoying the warmth of the sun on my body and am vaguely aware of Sarah resting her head in my lap. It's a relief to have the summit over and I am desperately thankful there is no more climbing, though we still have the huge descent. It's dry at the moment, but the weather below looks unsettled and I fear we could be in for a very damp trek.

Fred is leaning over me, shaking my shoulder. 'No sleeping,' he shouts. 'Up. Up. Up. Must not sleep.' I half open my eyes to see him hovering over us and wonder whether we might arrange to have him fall away sharply. He wanders into the hut and Gavin and Megan emerge looking dazed and disorientated. 'Must go,' he says. 'Many hours still.'

We've been on our feet now for eight hours, after virtually no sleep and very little sustenance. We are weary and sore, and really not in the mood for Fred's chivvying. We begrudgingly grab our day-packs and begin the rest of the descent like a line of automatons. Gavin winces with every step and is ordered to the front, which slows our pace considerably. Am I enjoying this now? I ask myself. Now the hard upward slog is over, and it's just fun, fun, fun all the way down.

We bow our heads and plod in silence.

The track is much wetter than on our ascent and I slip repeatedly, ending up in deep brown puddles. Thick roots protrude from the rocky path and I trip, alternately twisting first my left, then my right ankle. Behind me, Sarah groans as pain shoots around her kneecaps and Megan steps awkwardly trying to avoid pressure on her blistered toes. I wouldn't have imagined anything could have been worse than the ascent, but it takes us three hours—an hour-and-a-half longer than it should—to reach Miriakamba Hut. We arrive, finally, and drop onto the grass, wet, miserable and exhausted.

After only five minutes, Fred starts to chivvy us along and none of us has the energy to object. We pull ourselves up and begin the final descent as the rain starts to fall—a light drizzle at first, then a heavy soaking downpour that turns the track into a stream. I can barely stay upright, and tear my hands repeatedly on the sharp acacia branches as I desperately try to keep my balance.

By the time we enter the lower montane forest my boots have gathered great clumps of mud and each step is like lifting concrete. I am covered completely in splatters of dirt and soaked through to my underwear. I have nothing clean or dry with which to wipe my glasses and look out at a big grey blur. I stagger down the track, utterly indifferent to anyone's pain but mine. I have no idea where Gavin is, and frankly I really don't care. I want this to be over. I want a bath, clean clothes, and a long sleep, and I never, ever, want to do anything like this again.

Through the drizzle, I can just make out the gate below the trees. I shuffle down the last few hundred metres, sliding through ankle deep sludge. I squeeze out my very last ounce of energy and finally, after fourteen hours of trekking on two water biscuits and a cup of cocoa, collapse, filthy and shattered, at the park gate.

CHAPTER 10

FIRST CLASS TO KIGOMA

BACK AT MERU Inn we spend a day sleeping and avoiding physical activity. We struggle with the short walk to the bathroom and the two steps to the toilet. Sarah's knees crunch audibly as she hobbles about the room and, every time I venture up, my muscles scream to be allowed back to bed. I tend the myriad cuts and bruises unearthed when I finally shower away the layers of Mount Meru caked to my skin, and dress the blisters sprouting on my heels and toes.

We spend much of the morning staring at the ceiling and comparing notes on our respective ailments. Slowly, we begin to relive the climb: the excruciating cold at Rhino Point, the agony of the ash slope, the darkness and bitter cold and, finally, the exhilaration of reaching the top. But, somehow, now we are clean and warm and fed, the hideousness of the whole experience has started to fade, and the memory of our rose-tinted morning on the summit is taking over. Soon, it will just have been a tough walk with a few steep patches. Really. Not bad at all. The ash cone? *Fine*. No problem. And then, of course, we will do it all again somewhere else.

We are not, however, planning another climb any time soon and as we spread out our map, we note with some delight that the terrain between here and Gombe Stream is remarkably flat. We have heard that the train to Mwanza on the edge of Lake Victoria is no longer running; the track is flooded and bridges are down. Bukoba, on the lake's western shore, is under water, and in the past week, hundreds of people have been made homeless. The only other way to Gombe Stream is to head south through the Masai Steppe to Dodoma, take the train to Tabora in the isolated rural west and on to Kigoma on the shores of Lake Tanganyika. No-one can tell us if the train is running beyond Tabora and everyone is telling us that Kigoma is full of Rwandan and Burundi refugees and not a nice place to be. It's not a short trip—I reckon about 1800 kilometres—but it will take us off the backpacker circuit and into country where *wazungu* mostly fear to tread.

Alas, the bus to Dodoma has no video and we sadly miss the next instalment of marauding Mike and his busty bimbette. Instead, we are entertained by not quite tuned-in Swahili radio which crackles out at the decibel level of a small rock concert. We leave the bus station roughly on time and make a few quick stops on the edge of town, the driver ushering people on and off with some urgency.

After the exertions of the past few days we are not unhappy to just sit, despite the fact that our bus has all the characteristic features of African travel. A sack of green oranges has been plonked on my feet, and the knees of two Masai men behind poke through the skinny seat into my lower back. A large woman, her enormous breasts sitting on the belt of her pink floral smock, stands next to me in the aisle, alternately thrusting her ample backside and bosom into my face as she turns to chat with her neighbour. She has a plastic bucket hoicked over one shoulder that I have to duck to avoid every time her conversation becomes animated.

We make ourselves as comfortable as we can and work through the crossword puzzles and end-of-year quizzes that Maria sent to Arusha.

As we head away from the mountains, the landscape flattens to a low grassy scrub and the small towns peter into villages. We play magnetic Scrabble and, as the pink lady's bucket swings around for a fifth time, contemplate the different notions of personal space we have encountered in Africa.

Mid journey, I start to feel shivery and break into a cold sweat. 'Oh God! Not again,' I mutter. In an instant I am bent double with a sudden violent gnawing in my stomach—pain shooting from one side of my gut to the other. I feel an urgent need for a toilet, or a least a small patch of grass behind a tree. I suspect our driver will not be happy about an unscheduled stop, but the message I am receiving from down below cannot be ignored, and I head up to the front of the bus. With my hand on my stomach I grimace at the driver who reluctantly pulls over by an adjacent field. There is of course not a tree, not a low shrub, not the skinniest twig for miles, just occasional patches of thin yellow grass. I scout around quickly trying to find the tallest bit furthest from the bus and hunker down with some relief.

As I look up I see a line of heads poking out the windows of the bus, smiling and pointing as if they've just spotted an interesting animal on safari. A woman near the front waves, actually *waves*, to me, like I'm her next-door neighbour hanging out the washing. At the back of the bus two guys chat and point, their earnest expressions suggesting they're having some kind of serious discussion. I can only begin to imagine. 'Terrible problem the lack of toilet facilities on these routes.'

'I know. Look at this poor girl having to go in front of a whole bus. How humiliating.'

The driver beeps his horn. Yes Buddy, I can assure you I want this to be over just as much as you do, but there are some things in life that one cannot hurry. When I do not return to the bus immediately, he lets out a long loud blast, just in case any of the passengers—or anyone else who might happen to be within a five mile radius—didn't know exactly what was happening. 'BEEP!...BEEP! Hey everyone, come check out this white chick with her pants down.'

The gnawing abates somewhat and I clamber up the steps, the people in the aisle seats who didn't get a look out of the window, craning their necks to see me. A general titter makes its way from front to back as I shuffle around the pink lady and flop down. Sarah makes an unsuccessful attempt to keep a straight face. 'Oh...I'm sorry Doll...it's awful really...in the grass with everyone watching and...'

Within minutes I am doubled over with cramps again—I clutch my side and thrash about in the seat, trying to take deep breaths and willing the pain to stop. I give up, shove my bag of oranges into the aisle and elbow my way to the front. The driver lets out a long sigh and shakes his head, but senses he has no choice. I run down the steps and into a field, the grass so painfully short I can only begin to contemplate the degree of humiliation I am about to experience. I squat, ignoring the long loud blasts on the horn and beckoning gestures from the bus. I keep my head down, face to the ground in a desperate attempt to avoid eye contact. I focus on the grass and imagine one of those women's magazine articles: 'Tell us your most embarrassing moment...'

Back on board my stomach settles momentarily, but in a few minutes the rumblings begin again. '*Oh Doll. I just want it to stop! What am I going to do?*' I lean forward, resting my head on the seat in front and watch my legs and arms erupt in goose pimples. Breathing slowly, I try desperately to ride it out, but my stomach continues to churn and I drag myself to the front once again.

We pull into a small village alongside a concrete café where the driver calls a ten-minute drink stop in recognition of my predicament. I dash past the group of smokers sitting at the plastic tables and shoot around the back. Aah...there it is, a foetid little 'low style' with a vile overbearing stench and crap crawling up the walls, *but* it has a door that shuts. I cover my mouth and nose with my bandanna and balance precariously over the hole, thanking God for strong calf muscles. It is possibly *the* most unpleasant place I have ever spent twenty minutes, but quite frankly, I'd have hung out there all day if it meant avoiding doing my business in front of the bus load of paparazzi with whom I am travelling.

It is a relief to reach Dodoma, to smile goodbye to my fellow passengers, and take a gentle stroll around town, stopping randomly at toilets whenever I feel inclined. Dodoma is the political capital of Tanzania though there is no sign of anything resembling a parliament or even a municipal building—all the embassies and diplomatic residences are meant to be moving up from Dar es Salaam, but clearly this has not happened. As awful as Dar was, at least it was busy and happening, which cannot be said for Dodoma which has the air of a place that would be thrown into confusion if something ever did happen.

The roads are unsealed and covered in vast puddles from the recent rains. A few battered old cars splutter along the wide main drag, soaking the two hawkers hanging-out on the roadside. A large scruffy patch of grass about the size of a football field links the street to the railway and a dozen women, all with babies on their backs, bend low scything the grass in long sweeping movements. We pass the tumble-down railway station, a scruffy looking Christian Conference Centre and a handful of rickety kiosks selling bananas and vegetables. There are very few *wazungu* and the high level of interest in us suggests not many pass through. It feels safe though; a quiet, unremarkable African town.

We find the biggest shop in the street, a dark dusty 'supermarket' filled with boxes of washing powder and plastic buckets. We grab a couple of bottles of water and look around for anything we recognise that we could buy for our up-coming train journey. The owner is a thirty-ish Indian man, polite and chatty who tells us he has just returned from a holiday in Toronto where he lived with his wife for ten years in the eighties. He and Sarah talk about Ontario and she asks why he returned to Dodoma, given that he obviously has access to

Canadian residency. 'We have small children,' he explains. 'We did not want them growing up with drugs and shootings. Perhaps we will return when they are older, but for now they are safer and better off in Dodoma.' Poor Sarah is utterly appalled and I can almost hear her frantic thought processes: how could anyone choose to live in a dusty, undeveloped Third World back-water when they could settle in her beloved Canada? And, heaven forbid, because they are *safer and better off* here. 'I...see,' she says. 'I...hadn't thought of it like that before.'

'Well there's a notion,' I say, as we walk back down the wide dusty street. 'Dodoma over Toronto as a place to bring up kids—not everyone in Africa thinks life is better in North America after all.'

We had been warned that buying a train ticket to Kigoma might be difficult and had attempted to book from the tourist office in Arusha. First class, we had been told, was full, only second class tickets were available and they involved sharing with four other people, plus children, and the ubiquitous livestock and assorted garden produce. Given the complete lack of *wazungu*—apart from businessmen, normally the only occupiers of first class—it is difficult to believe that tickets aren't available. 'First class,' of course, doesn't mean there'll be complimentary eau de toilette in our bathroom, or a chocolate mint on our pillow at bedtime, only that we should have a door—hopefully one which locks—and can decide for ourselves which foodstuffs and small farmyard animals, if any, will accompany us.

When we arrive at the station in the morning there are already a few hundred people waiting on the platform with the aforementioned items distributed around them.

The ticket counter is a tiny square cut into a brick wall covered by a rusty iron grille. Twenty or so people are pressed tightly up against it. We position ourselves at the back of the group and, in true British style, begin to queue. Two young men appear from the other side of the track and squeeze themselves in front of us, and another saunters up to the pack and hangs-out at the side.

As the guy at the front finishes his transaction and attempts to extricate himself, a tussle begins. The crowd surges forward as each person pushes up against the body in front, the people on the edges trying to force their way into the main pack. Sarah and I, oblivious to these manoeuvres, find ourselves elbowed out and shoved to the back of a now somewhat larger pack.

When the next man leaves we are more prepared, and I throw my whole bodyweight against Sarah who lunges forward, elbows rigid to repel any advances from the sides. I maintain the pressure from the rear, pushing up against Sarah with my shoulder, like a TV cop about to break down a door. She is crushed against the guy in front, her face tucked neatly into an armpit. I continue to apply the pressure, any relaxation on my part leaving space for someone else to squeeze in between us.

Another transaction is completed and we shift forward, holding our position as two frail and skinny old ladies are bounced to the back. We manage to propel our way towards the centre of the pack, using our elbows to create space, and exploiting the advantage offered by large, heavy boots in a predominantly open-toed sandal environment. Whichever way I turn, there are shoulders and chests and underarms hot and sweating in my face and, above my head, arms extended with fists wrapped around wads of grubby shilling notes. We are perhaps two feet from the grille, but there are still five or six people squeezed between the counter and us, and we stand firm, preparing for the final push.

One more person done and we lunge forward, successfully resisting any further incursions from the flanks. We are closing in on the grille, Sarah only one person from success, when a six-foot figure appears from nowhere, moving in over the top and waving a bunch of notes. We bow to experience and superior tactical skill, but as he moves away, Sarah thrusts her money forward shouting 'First class! Two tickets for first class.'

She shoves the cash through the grille, flattening herself against it so no one else can get close. Ten minutes later she squeezes out of the crowd and raises her hand. She is victorious: two tickets for a first class cabin to Kigoma.

The train is scheduled to depart at 3.00 p.m. and we are advised to arrive by two, which we do. The platform is packed: hawkers selling black and brown polyester trousers, ladies' sandals with feather straps in pastel pink and blue, and children's notebooks, painted with flowers in lurid colours. A parade of foodstuffs passes by: boiled eggs with tiny packets of salt, chapattis, corn on the cob, mandazi and samosas. The volume of people has tripled since this morning and we tiptoe around children, over sacks of maize and vegetables, over laundry bags and cheap suitcases, and pots of bubbling *ugali*—the lumpy, porridge-like staple of the region.

We find ourselves a spot on the platform, sit on our packs and settle in amongst the crowd, the now familiar smell of stale urine wafting past with unpleasant regularity from the 'choo' up wind.

At 4.00 p.m. I wander into the office of the 'stationmaster' where a dozen or so men hover unoccupied—half of them ignoring me completely, the other half looking me up and down and comparing notes in Swahili. They tell me there will be a two-hour delay, though I get the distinct impression this figure has been plucked from the air to placate the *wazungu*.

We dig out postcards and a writing pad and, as we are the only *wazungu* on the platform, provide free entertainment for all the kids who hover at a safe distance, jumping into their mother's arms each time we make eye contact. When they get bored we watch the boiled eggs go up and down the platform. A young man hovers close by and hunkers down and we chat. He is a student, he explains, from the

Ngorongoro Health Centre, in his third and final year of training. He will soon graduate with a Diploma of Medical Practice which will qualify him to work as a doctor anywhere in Tanzania. I place a hand on my stomach recalling the sharp pains I have been experiencing since my little upset on the bus and thank God for the medical evacuation clause in our insurance.

At 6.00 p.m. I check with the stationmaster again and am told there will be a further two-hour delay for reasons we cannot ascertain. The sun is going down, the platform is packed with milling people and I suspect we may be heading for one of those 'dangerous situations to avoid' described in our guidebook. No one seems to know what time the train is coming, or indeed if it is coming at all, and most people appear not to be the slightest bit bothered.

We spot two *wazungu* at the end of the platform weaving their way through the crowd towards us. They are thirty-something guys, one of whom looks incredibly fit, sinewy and agile and steps lightly over bags and dozing children. The other is overweight and lumbering, and struggles with an enormous, unwieldy pack. We shuffle our gear around to make room for them and introduce ourselves. Navid is an Iranian born doctor living in California, and Rick, a Canadian police officer from Edmonton who works as a sniper for the Tactical Response Team. They are also trying to get to Kigoma and on to Gombe Stream. As darkness falls, and every mugger in central Tanzania rocks up for a little late-night shopping, Sarah and I squeeze ourselves between them—it's handy sometimes, having a couple of boys around.

We share bananas and draw on our knowledge of American police shows to ask Rick a number of questions about his work. 'Do you…like…wear all that black gear and scuttle across roof tops trying to find the best spot to take out a crazed gunman who's like…taken hostages and is threatening to kill one every hour unless his demands are met?'

'Er…Well…It's not quite…'

'And have you like…been faced with an armed man who is really an OK bloke, but just lost his job after twenty-five years, and you like, talk to him and persuade him to hand over his weapon without firing a shot?'

He has been in…vaguely similar situations, but is far more likely to be called out to a house where gunshots have been reported or spend hours in a car, stalking a suspect. The 'TRT', he explains, is the most exciting section of the Police Department, but actual shooting is only a small part of the job.

Navid does locum work in intensive care, and we switch our frame of reference to 'ER'. He works for six months at a time, putting in long hours and earning a ton of money so he can spend the next six months travelling. He met Rick last year in India and they caught up again for this trip.

A long announcement in Swahili is met with a collective groan, which we presume means a further wait of an indeterminate period. We sit in the pitch-black swatting mosquitoes and discussing the pros and cons of the different malaria medication—Sarah is still struggling to remember her daily dose of Paludrine.

At 8.00 p.m., only five hours late, we hear the distant rumbling of the train and the platform comes alive as a couple of thousand people gather up vast quantities of luggage and prepare to board. Rick and Navid are in second class, and we head off in opposite directions, agreeing to catch up in the morning.

There are people everywhere, shoving bags and babies through windows, dragging huge sacks along the platform and crawling under carriages. The din drowns my attempts to communicate with Sarah only a few feet ahead. We barge through the heaving crowd, knocking people with our packs and kicking aside boxes and bags that get in our way. I have abandoned my polite—but as demonstrated in Mombasa, not terribly effective—forms of courtesy, exchanging 'excuse me's' and 'after you's' for the less civilised, but more efficacious, 'Outta my way here!'

After wandering up and down the dozen carriages we locate first-class and haul ourselves aboard through the tight corridor. Our cabin is lined throughout with a dull orange formica and lit by a flickering twenty-watt fluorescent bulb. If I stand in the middle with my arms outstretched I can touch both walls, and if I turn through ninety degrees, I am a few inches short of the window and door. A small, filthy stainless steel sink occupies one corner, and two bunks in maroon vinyl take up the rest of the space. There is a fan, a window that opens and a lock on the door. We wedge our packs into the tiny space between the sink and the bunks and begin to unpack our sleeping bags and toiletries.

A constant stream of people shuffles up and down the corridor outside our cabin, shouting and hauling bags and clambering over piled-up suitcases. After an hour there is still no sign of the activity abating, or of the train leaving, and Sarah nips out to investigate, leap-frogging a stack of hessian sacks and flattening herself behind what appears to have once been someone's front door leaning up against the window. She returns somewhat flustered. 'There's a slight technical hitch,' she says.

'Not another wait?'

'No...actually the opposite.' I shake my head, confused. 'What do you mean?'

'Well, strictly speaking, we aren't actually attached to the train any more, so if it does leave we won't.' As if to emphasise her point, the carriage jolts sharply sending us sprawling on to the lower bunk. We grab our packs and shove everything in as quickly as we can, and climb down onto the platform. An Indian businessman, from the cabin next-door, gestures for us to follow and we step across the tracks, crunching along the gravel, the carriages shunting back and forth in the darkness. Doors start to slam and a line of people on the platform shove last-minute luggage though windows and step back to wave.

Our businessman starts to run and we break into a jog behind him, packs bouncing back and front. Somewhere in the distance a whistle blows, a shout echoes down the platform and we jump up onto our carriage as it moves away.

Excellent! A few thousand locals manage to board the train without incident, but somehow, we manage not to. And, after a six-hour wait, we almost miss the bloody thing completely.

Our new cabin is identical to our last in every respect, except the fan doesn't work and the sink is a little dirtier. Handy for us though, it is situated at the very end of a carriage next to the unisex choo and the 'restaurant'—a smoke-, men- and greasy rice-filled formica dining room. It is already packed and the queue for the next sitting—and the one after that, and the one after that—stretches right past our door. The blinds on our windows provide some privacy, but do not, alas, protect us from an evening of loud, pre-dinner Swahili chit-chat.

We pull off our boots and prepare for bed, looking fondly at the tap in the sink which, I suspect, is only teasing with the promise of water. I turn it slowly, as far as it will go, and, despite the fact that half the country is flooded after a week of record rainfall, not a drop emerges. I pour some of our Glacier mineral water on to the edge of a towel and attempt to scrape away the day's dust and sunscreen. Finally, though I have been putting it off, I brave the choo.

I squeeze though the line of men in the corridor, smiling and nodding, and shuffle towards the end of the carriage. My arrival does not go unnoticed by the forty or so men supping Coke at the formica tables. I open the door to the choo and lock it behind me. Oh Lord, can it get any worse? A hole in the floor is surrounded by a stainless steel plate with a space for feet either side. There are splashes of urine *everywhere* and faeces around the edge of the hole. There is no sink or tap and the smell is indescribably awful. I am in and out as quickly as is humanly possible and back in the cabin taking deep breaths of fresh air. 'How was it?' Sarah asks tentatively. 'Wear shoes,' I say. 'Try not to breathe, and don't put your hands *anywhere*.'

I climb up onto the bunk, close my eyes and contemplate the possibility of sleep. Immediately outside our cabin a debating team are preparing for their next big gig, trying out a few of their more contentious arguments on each other. I tie the sleeve of my jacket around my ears and bury my head in my sleeping bag. I suspect popping my head out the door and saying: 'How about it chaps…can we keep the noise down a little?' won't have the desired effect.

Some time later we are awoken by loud and repeated banging on our door and I grope around for my glasses and torch, wondering what on earth might warrant waking us up in the dead of night. Sarah pokes her head up from the bottom bunk. 'What's happening? Do you think the track's flooded again, or maybe a bridge is down?'

'I don't know. Perhaps we have to get off for some reason.' I slide my glasses on and open the door. 'What's the problem?' I say.

'Tickets,' he says, utterly deadpan. You are joking of course…No, you're not joking, because you're just checking tickets and you started at one end of the train a while ago and now you're at this end of the train and that makes perfect sense, even if it is the middle of the night and everyone is asleep. 'You want to see our tickets?' I say.

'Tickets,' he replies. I rummage through my jacket pockets and extricate a crumpled piece of paper, shoving it through the door. He clips it, hands it back and disappears down the corridor. I fall back onto my bunk and check the time: it's 3.00 a.m.

As the sun rises I am vaguely aware of reaching Saranda Station where the train sits for an hour and a half before lurching back into motion and taking us out towards central Tanzania. At 8.00 a.m. we sit up and look out to a flat green landscape, broken infrequently by village huts and swamps, the water periodically rising to the edge of the tracks.

We attempt ablutions with another dribble of Glacier on the corner of last night's grubby towel, and munch through a breakfast of yesterday's bread and a banana. We have some food left for lunch, but hopefully we'll be in Tabora by midday and Kigoma by late evening where at least we might be able to grab a shower and a meal.

We prop ourselves on the bunks; Sarah grabs a book and I start a letter to our friends Maria and Jacki. It's a little difficult to know how to begin. 'Hi girls...Can't wait to see you in Harare. Having a great time, apart from the food, the accommodation, the transport, the lack of water and the threat of developing any number of unpleasant and potentially life-threatening diseases...' I throw down my pad and wander over to the window and see Rick and Navid shuffling up the corridor. 'Hi girls. No problems getting on then?'

'Er...no. Very smooth. How's second class?'

'Apart from the spitting competition and world chain-smoking-in-a-confined-space record attempt, it's delightful.'

We roll into Tabora at 1.30 p.m.—a wide dusty platform crowded with hawkers selling the same shiny sling-backs and seventies polyester slacks. Teenage girls with babies mind chapatti stalls in the sidings, and young men strut about in stars and stripes bandannas. We lean out of our window and watch the people passing, chatting with the women through smiles and gestures and the odd word of Swahili. After an hour or so the crowds begin to dissipate and, as there are no signs of movement, a few passengers alight and stretch their legs. After two hours we are still there, and after three. 'What was that they said in Arusha, about the train not running past Tabora?' I say.

We bump into our Indian businessman in the corridor who tells us there is water on the track further up which is causing the delay—he will let us know when another announcement is made. We flop back down in our cabin, attempting to create some breeze with a folded map and discuss the possible implications of an extended stay at a food-less, water-less, hygiene-less railway station, in the middle of absolutely nowhere. It's not that I'm not enjoying myself, really, and we did want to get off the backpacker track, but…we could be here for days.

Our cabin can only be locked from the inside so we cannot both go out at the same time. I leave Sarah watching from the window and step down on to the hot, ochre platform. A couple of hundred people are dotted about the station, women crouching around blackened cooking pots and young men idling by a Coke stand. Around the gate, there are a handful of beggars and some boys sucking on bright orange ices—as in Dodoma, nobody seems very bothered about the delay.

I am clearly the most interesting thing that's happened in Tabora today, my amble along the track being met with frequent smiles and hellos. I nod and wave like the Queen on walkabout. I buy a couple of bottles of warm water, at what I suspect is quadruple the price paid by locals, and look around for something to eat, hoping to surprise Sarah with a treat—a samosa perhaps or some fresh pineapple. I loiter by the one temporary shack that looks like it may sell foodstuffs, but fear a nice scoop of dried maize or a tasty unidentifiable root vegetable will not quite do the trick. Back on board, we break into the last of our sup-plies—a small tin of tuna and hunk of stale bread—and contemplate the chances of reaching anywhere civilised any time soon.

At about 7.00 p.m. a muffled message splutters out over the station's ancient loudspeaker and a few minutes later our neighbour appears. 'Very sorry,' he says. 'There will be twelve-hour delay.'

'*Twelve* hours!?'

'Yes, twelve hours. Very sorry.'

We flop down onto the bunk and stare at the filthy floor in silence. Was this really the plan? To be holed up in some grotty cabin for days on end, with no way of knowing when, or even if, we're going to get out. 'We've got no food left,' Sarah mutters.

'I know. Perhaps the purser will drop by with some coupons for a complimentary evening meal at that restaurant in town…'

'…Oh yeah, and while we're out they'll clean the cabins, give the corridors a quick sweep and disinfect the toilets.'

We relinquish all hope of a shower or a decent meal and prepare ourselves for a quiet night in—or should I say, a night in. We write some postcards, play a few rounds of gin rummy and argue over Scrabble. The debating team reconvenes outside our door and settles in for the night. Starving, we contemplate popping into the all male, all smoking, all drinking, all terribly-interested-in-the-*wazungu* restaurant for a spot of greasy rice. 'How hungry are you?' I ask Sarah.

'Funny. Thought I was for a moment there, but really still full from that slither of tuna I had an eon ago.'

We wake, hungry, sticky and smelling to news that we will not be leaving until after lunch. I know I said we wanted to see a different part of Africa, but not *exactly the same part* for days on end. I lean over the end of my bunk, poke my face out of the window and pour half a bottle of Glacier over my head, catching the dripping water in my towel which I then use to wash the rest of my body. I tie my bandanna around my nose and mouth and head for the toilet which now slops with the urine of an entire train load of men. When I return to the cabin the smell lingers, carried on my dress and hair.

We are totally out of food and the restaurant appears not to serve breakfast which I suspect is a blessing in disguise. I grab some money, step down onto the platform and am immediately accosted by the stench from down wind. Barely three metres away is the other side of our toilet—the outside—which, as we know, is not actually a toilet, but a hole in the floor, but which has, of course, continued to function as a toilet the whole time we have been stationary. A great shimmering pile of human waste spills over the track sending little typhoidal messages through the air saying, 'Catch me! Catch me!' I avert my eyes and cover my mouth and nose, but not quick enough to forestall a series of eye-watering dry retches.

The platform is now packed, most of the second and third class passengers choosing the more comfortable option of sleeping on the dirt.

I weave my way around dozing bodies and charcoal stoves and head for the station exit. I'm not exactly sure what Tabora railway serves—there must be a village somewhere, but all I can see are a few trees and a lot of swamp. Around the corner is a bar of sorts—scattered tables under a rough corrugated iron roof with groups of men smoking and drinking. I wander over to a low makeshift counter and check out the breakfast options. An old man is deep frying chunks of potatoes in what looks like a cut down oil drum. As there is nothing else I can see, or know how to order, I ask for a bag and wait.

As I hover by the counter, heads turn towards me and chairs slide closer. More men gather around the periphery of the bar until it is two deep in people craning their necks for a look.

I shuffle awkwardly, staring at my feet, and willing my chips to fry. The conversations become more animated and, though I have no idea what they are saying, I have the teeniest suspicion of what it might be about: 'blah…blah…*wazungu*…blah blah…*wazungu*.' I grab my bag of chips, angling it slightly to let the grease drip onto the floor, and with a fixed smile head back to the train.

I lay down my small offering at the side of the sink and peel away the dirty brown paper in which it is wrapped. Each chip floats in its own pool of grease and has at least one unidentifiable black nugget some-where along its length. I look at Sarah, whose capacity for dodgy food isn't good at the best of times—it isn't quite what I'd hoped to return with. 'Would Madam require freshly squeezed orange juice with that,' I ask, 'or can I bring a pot of tea?'

At midday, a group of men in orange jackets appears at the station gate and wanders up the line, apparently to check the tracks. They return at 2.30 p.m., nodding and smiling, and the platform dwellers pack up their stoves and climb aboard—after a twenty-five hour delay we trundle out of Tabora Station.

If the train manages to keep moving, we should be in Kigoma by the early hours of the morning. The idea of arriving half asleep, in the dead of night when everything is closed doesn't excite me, and we attempt to ascertain whether we can stay on the train until after sunrise. The guy in the restaurant assures us we can, the guy behind the bar says we definitely can't.

We check in with Rick and Navid who are wandering the corridors to escape the smoky fog that has settled in their cabin. Whatever happens at Kigoma we will wait for each other on the platform and try to find some accommodation together. We return to our cabin, read a bit, play cards a bit, chat a bit and wander up and down the corridor watching the endless, swampy, tsetse-fly-infested emptiness that is southern Tanzania. You can understand why the British, or anyone else for that matter, didn't want to colonise it. I think it's safe to say, we made it off the beaten track and, though it isn't quite what we imagined, there's something about being here that's pretty special, something that, though it shouldn't be, is really quite fun.

By evening we are starving, that huge cooked breakfast we had this morning at Tabora finally having gone down. We catch the eye of the young guy who works in the restaurant and ask if we can have meals brought to our cabin. Our options are beef and rice, chicken and rice, or *ugali*. *Ugali*—let's not beat about the bush here—looks like something a small child might bring up after an afternoon at the fairground. We have seen neither chickens, nor cows, nor refrigeration for days and, quite frankly, I wonder how and where the cooks wash their hands. We plump for the beef, on the not terribly scientific basis that bad poultry can do more serious damage than bad steak. In the end, it doesn't actually matter because, though the rice is just edible—greasy and crunchy, but edible—the beef is not. Think hooves, ankle joints, think sweepings from an (African) butcher's floor. We substitute the meat with a can of warm Fanta and watch the waiter scrape our plates clean out of the window.

As night falls, we linger in the corridor watching the darkness pass by. We pull up to a small isolated platform which sparkles with

flickering candles and lighters. The flames illuminate trays of cigarettes and toothpaste and chapattis carried by small boys, like cinema
ushers with ice cream. A passenger next to us loses his watch, snatched
from his wrist as he leans over to buy chewing gum. As the train pulls
out, the rows of flickering lights drift back along narrow paths to the
village, and the station is dark and silent once more. I put my arm
around Sarah's waist and pull her close—it is pitch-black and we know
there is absolutely nothing out there. 'You can't get much further away
from it all than this,' I say.

'I know. It's magic. And, secretly, I do feel like I'm in a Famous Five
adventure. It's just…I'd like to get away from it all, *and* have some
KFC.'

Sarah is up every time the train slow or stops, checking for stations and
ready to launch us into action should we have to vacate suddenly.
As we haven't done anything suddenly since we reached Africa I am
less worried.

It is 3.00 a.m. and raining when we pull into Kigoma and I announce
my intention of staying exactly where I am. Sarah bounces around the
corridor looking for someone vaguely official and approaches one of
the waiters. 'Do we have to get off now?' she asks.

'Yes. Yes,' he says, nodding assuredly. She swings open the cabin
door. He said we have to get off.

'No he didn't. Ask him if we can stay on still morning.'

'*What?*'

'Just ask him if we can stay on 'till morning.' She pops back out.
'Can we stay on 'till morning?'

'Yes. Yes,' he says, nodding assuredly.

CHAPTER 11

MEETING FRODO

KIGOMA'S MAIN DIRT road is dotted with cheap guesthouses, cafés, and stalls selling bananas, pineapples and corn on the cob. From the station we walk up the empty street four abreast, our every move scrutinised by groups of young men hunched over up-turned Coke crates. A handful of weary women shuffle through the dust, dragging thin plastic bags crammed with vegetables, and a few boys idle under an avenue of mango trees that might once have been grand. Beggars loiter outside the restaurant, old men slump wearily in the dirt and children dart through the door to snatch leftovers.

At the end of the street there is a one-pump Caltex, with a newish looking Land Cruiser, and an Air Tanzania office which, like the vehicle, seem strangely out of place—I can't imagine anyone flying off to Dar es Salaam for a weekend getaway. There is no sign of the hordes of refugees we were warned about; if anything, the place feels almost abandoned.

We check into the Lake View Hotel which, if they built a second storey or moved it half a kilometre west, might command a view of the lake, but as it is, looks onto some broken plastic tables and chairs in a concrete courtyard. Our room, which continues the concrete motif, has two hardboard beds with a threadbare sheet flung over each mattress. I perch on the edge testing for comfort. 'Hmm…I have an idea,' I say. 'If we lay our woollen walking socks on the top of the mattress we could double its thickness.'

The door locks, at least, and if we pull the curtain across our window, we can partially obscure the excellent view of our room afforded to passers-by. The bathroom—a tiny windowless box at the end of the corridor—has a shower and a 'low style' in such close proximity that, in reaching one, there is a danger of falling down the other. As is now the custom, we are the only women residents and the only *wazungu*, Rick and Navid having checked into a similar place opposite.

As we head out to explore, I realise we have not been approached by anyone trying to sell us a trip to Gombe Stream, or a Tanganyika Tour, or hawking carvings or batiks, or asking if we need to change money or hire a taxi. In fact, apart from some benign stares, we have received remarkably little attention. The streets are unusually quiet, and there appear to be no other travellers. Prior to the war in Rwanda and Burundi there was a steady flow of backpackers travelling south down the lake, but these days it seems few tourists pass through, and those who do, clearly evoke little interest. I suspect Kigoma has more important things to worry about.

We head towards the lake where a makeshift shelter has been erected along the shoreline—huge blue tarpaulins stamped with 'United Nations High Commission for Refugees' are stretched over a series of wooden poles. The flag of 'Caritas', a Catholic aid agency, flaps limply above it. This is the reception for incoming refugees from Rwanda, Burundi and the former Zaire. People's names and family details are recorded and they are given fresh water and biscuits before being bussed to a camp on the other side of Kigoma. The flow of people has abated over the past year, but every week a new boatload arrives fleeing hunger or violence somewhere. Today it is quiet—just a few boys flicking stones into the water, and a lone worker skirting the edge of the camp.

We take a circuitous route back to our hotel, passing evidence of a plethora of aid agencies: the Red Cross office, an International Rescue Corporation truck, four-wheel drives belonging to the Austrian Development Committee—and other organisations whose acronyms I don't recognise. UNICEF and UNHCR logos are on everything from cardboard boxes to bus shelters. It might explain the brand new Land Cruiser at the Caltex and the Air Tanzania office.

Back in the main street we meet up with Rick and Navid and check out our lunch options. There is not a great range and we opt for the one place that has a few white people inside. The menu promises beef and rice, chicken and rice, fish and rice and plantains—except there is no beef or chicken at the moment. But, the fish is excellent and the plantains, though they look exactly like cooked bananas, taste just like potato.

We sit next to an older couple—Baptist missionaries from Alaska—who spend a few months here every year, the woman teaching at the local hospital, her husband fixing up the building and doing odd jobs. There are a lot of missionaries in Kigoma, she explains, living in the ex-pat complex and working with the local people and the refugees. Sitting on our other side are two fresh-faced and clean-cut young men from the States. They look barely eighteen and I can't imagine they know much about anything, though they claim to be 'teaching' at the seminary. Clearly I'm out of touch—I thought the whole missionary thing was a little passé.

After lunch we head for the bank and attempt to withdraw money using our VISA card. In Arusha we were told this would not be a problem, but really…we should know better by now. The bank manager looks at us blankly, as if we're asking to take out a home loan or buy rubles. He explains that we can do a 'telegraphic transaction' which involves phoning our branch in Australia—that may not be easy but if we persist we should eventually get through—instructing them to transfer money to Dar es Salaam, who will then instruct Kigoma to issue the money. He doesn't do it all the time, but it should work and will only take about a week. I thank him kindly for his assistance and assure him that I would rather stick pins in my eyes than spend a week in Kigoma. We report our sorry situation to the boys and Navid—who really doesn't know us from a bar of soap—agrees to lend us a few hundred dollars until we can access some cash.

In the morning we meet the boys again and, while they haggle for a taxi to Kibelezi where the boats leave for Gombe, I attempt to buy some food for our stay. As far as I can detect the 'supermarket' sells only Omo and maize, but I manage to buy some rice, corn on the cob, and a few pineapples from the stalls outside. Hopefully we can find something else at the shop in the National Park.

We squeeze onto the foam and spring-less seats of the cab, Rick hanging on to the back door which flings open every time we turn a corner. Unlike in town, there are several hundred people spread along the water's edge when we reach Kibelezi, and half a dozen brightly painted wooden boats bobbing around forty metres from the shore. There are no docks or jetties from which to board or disembark—getting off involves hoicking up your *kanga*, popping your basket and bag on your head, clambering down the ladder and wading through thigh-high water to dry land. Once the people are off, the cargo—children, timber, chickens, wooden crates and hessian sacks—is passed along a line of young men from the boat to the shore.

We squat on our packs by a Coke stall while Rick goes off to investigate—he has spotted a guy in uniform and does cop-bonding in broken English and Swahili. They wander off together towards the boat owners, the policeman asking questions and gesticulating in our direction. After a long chat he and Rick amble back to us, smiling at each other and shaking hands like old buddies. Rick proudly announces that a boat leaves in three hours and his good friend Stephen will ensure we have a place on it.

We sit on a concrete step watched by twenty or so men and a bunch of raggedy, pot-bellied children who slowly inch their way towards us. None of them speaks any English, but we manage to communicate names, ages, countries of origin and establish who has brothers or sisters. An older boy, better dressed and less sickly, hovers at the edge of our crowd. He is from Burundi and speaks French, and he and Sarah fall into easy conversation. He explains that he is here with his family, but that most of these children are orphans—from his country and from Rwanda—who survive by stealing or scrounging whatever food they can. He is hoping to return home soon with his mother and sister, but nobody can tell them if it is safe to do so.

Our boat finally appears mid afternoon and we say goodbye to our little gang, shaking hands and passing around packets of biscuits. I ask the Burundi lad if there are any toilets around and he smiles and shakes his head. 'No,' he says, 'not for white people. Only for black people.' As I suspect our transportation will be light on bathroom facilities, I wander off and do my business amongst a few leafless trees unshielded from any passer by who cares to glance my way. I have performed this once private activity in public so many times now I have ceased, almost, to be embarrassed.

When the captain gives the word, we balance our packs on our heads and wade out towards the boat, climbing up the ladder and hauling ourselves aboard. A narrow bench seat runs around the entire rim and we edge our way along to the bow, dropping our packs onto the piles of jerry cans and timber and children that fill the open hold beneath—it takes over an hour to load up, every inch crammed with people and cargo.

As we leave Kibelezi the wind picks up, providing a modicum of relief from the scorching midday sun. We chug gently down Lake

Tanganyika with the faint outline of Congo to the west and red colobus monkeys swinging through the Tanzanian jungle to the east. Parrots squawk from the lower branches and fish eagles swoop down from the tree-tops to the crystal water below. Every now and again, someone takes an empty Coke bottle, lowers it on a piece of string and drinks from the lake. Once again, we are the only tourists around and, given there is no other way to reach Gombe, I wonder if we might have the park to ourselves.

A sandy beach appears at the foot of the rainforest—wooden huts used to dry the catch dotted along its length—and our boat slows and angles towards it, picking up a fisherman and a family heading down stream. Sarah and I 'chat' with the women and I find myself jiggling a baby on my knee, while anyone with two words of English is practising on us. I explain we have no children, nor indeed husbands, and they frown. 'You are very old,' they say. 'What is wrong with you?' Within fifteen minutes of leaving Kibelezi we're laughing and sharing stories with half the boat.

Since we've been travelling with Rick and Navid, I've realised there are actually advantages to women travelling together; I had only ever thought about the problems, the safety issues, the vulnerability. People are far more likely to approach us, to chat or offer assistance, or to dangle babies for our inspection, than they are to the boys. Two men are more of a threat; Sarah and I don't worry anyone.

The Park entry is unassuming—a wooden sign on a shallow beach with dense forest rising on either side—you wouldn't guess it costs a hundred dollars a day just to be here. We drop over the side of the boat, our packs held aloft, and are greeted by our guide, Jim. He escorts us to our accommodation, a long baboon-proof bunkhouse with wire mesh covering the door and windows. As I hoped, there is no one else here. He shows us to our rooms—basic single beds, bare light bulb and a small wooden table—but it looks clean enough. We dump our gear and follow him along the baboon-lined path to the shop where my hopes of discovering something edible—a vegetable perhaps, some kind of bread product—are dashed. The only consumable item, for a complete change, is Coke.

Jim shows us the 'kitchen'—a dark hut with a wooden bench along one wall, and firewood scattered about the dirt floor. If we want to prepare food, he explains, we must do it here and carry it back to the bunkhouse. First, we must make sure we shoo away the baboons on the track—if they see or smell food, they will attack.

As lunch was some time ago, and not terribly substantial, I grab our limited supplies, shove them under my shirt and sprint from the bunkhouse to the kitchen, bolting the door behind me. When I am sure the hut is secure, and there are no baboons close, I set up the stove and cook the rice. It takes longer than usual and I sit on the floor listening to the variety of grunting and barking sounds that emanate from the trees just outside. Sarah appears after an hour to check on me and it's still not quite done. 'Almost there,' I say, removing the rice from the stove and boiling the corn.

When it's all cooked I fix a lid on the rice and slide a bowl over the plate of corn, balance one on top of the other and hold them close against my stomach. 'OK. I'm ready.'

'We'll have to be quick.'

'Yeah, I know. It's OK.'

'If you drop it, that's the end of dinner. There's nothing else.'

'Yeah, thanks Doll. I know.'

Sarah eases open the door, scouring the track on both sides for signs of baboon activity. 'I'll go in front. You stick close behind.' She raises her arms in the air and begins to sway, like a child pretending to be an aeroplane, and with a loud accompanying wail, dashes from the hut, spinning her arms wildly and weaving in and out of the trees.

I fall in as close as I can behind her, hugging dinner precariously, and trying to keep up as she swoops through the bush. I dodge between the trees, jumping over protruding roots and kicking up piles of leaves. From the corner of my eye I spot something large and primate-ish in the bushes, its head raised, its nose sniffing the air.

I pick up speed, my arms encircling dinner as the lid of the rice disappears into the bush. 'Hang on,' shouts Sarah. 'We're almost there.' With the corn pressed tightly against my shirt and the rice sliding down into my shorts, I make a final dash for the bunkhouse. Rick swings open the door and we barge through slamming it quickly behind us. 'Well done girls!' he says. 'Well done.'

I drop the food on the bench, dusting a few pieces of fluff from the corn and picking some stray leaves from the rice. We pull up chairs and grab plates. Some butter would be good, or salt and pepper, anything really, but there is nothing with which to relieve its blandness. The rice is still crunchy, despite cooking it three times longer than usual, and the sweetcorn isn't actually sweet, but tastes rather like I imagine cardboard might. 'Maybe it's a different sort of rice than we're used to,' Sarah suggests.

'Yeah and maybe a different sort of corn.'

It is almost inedible, but there is nothing else, so we sprinkle it with Coke and eat it anyway.

The notice board in the bunkhouse is lined with articles about Jane Goodall from the *New Scientist*, BBC *Wildlife* magazine and numerous international newspapers. Goodall was invited to Kenya for a holiday by a school friend in 1960—she was twenty-three at the time and had just finished secretarial college. While she was there she met the paleontologist, Dr Louis Leakey who employed her to assist on the digs at Olduvai Gorge. Leakey was keen to set up a study of the Gombe chimpanzees, believing that close scrutiny of one of our nearest genealogical relatives might provide insights into our own origins. He wanted a woman for the job—someone patient and observant—and asked Goodall. The British controlled authorities were reluctant to allow a single woman to live alone in such a remote place and she was only granted permission after her mother agreed to accompany her. 'Can you imagine,' I ask Sarah, 'what it must have been like then? No one would have even heard of Tanzania. I can't imagine her mother would have been too chuffed.'

'Darling have you thought what you'll do with your shorthand typing now you have your certificate?'

'Oh yes Mum. I'm thinking about going to Tanzania—it's in Africa— and living in the jungle and tracking chimpanzees. Fancy coming?'

Now, Goodall heads an internationally renowned institute and travels widely, raising money for campaigns and lecturing on animal rights and environmental issues. The Institute buys chimps who have been kept in captivity—in South American shopping malls or Third World zoos—and transfers them to sanctuaries. It also promotes the humane treatment of primates used in research, encouraging laboratories to keep them in pairs and provide stimulating activities and environments. Currently she is campaigning for a kind of 'Bill of Rights' for the great apes, which would acknowledge their special status as our closest animal relative.

We clean up the plates from dinner and head down to the lake for a swim. The shore is not strictly part of the National Park, which means the local people can wander freely and still have access to the villages on either side. The local fishermen set up small camps, building makeshift huts where they stay for three weeks each month—they don't fish when the moon is bright. A light attached to their boat attracts the tiny silver daaga and, when the fish have gathered in sufficient numbers, the men beat the side of their boats sending the fish into a panic and making them crowd together. Then they just scoop them up in a giant net.

There are no fishermen on the shore tonight, but we can see a sprinkling of lights in the distance and every now and again hear the rapid drumming as the daaga are lured. We slip into the cool water and float in the dark, Rick swimming out towards the centre of the lake. There are no villagers about and the baboons seem to have disappeared into the trees. For a few moments at least, we have Lake Tanganyika, the mountains of Congo and the vast jungles of Tanzania to ourselves.

Back at the bunkhouse I settle down with my book on Gombe Stream. We share ninety-five per cent of our DNA with chimpanzees and, as Goodall discovered, have many things in common. Chimps live in complex, hierarchical societies, can adapt to different environments and use tools to help them acquire food and clean themselves. They are capable of problem solving and demonstrate a range of emotions, including sadness and joy. They will sometimes care for other family members when they are sick or injured—one young female at Gombe fetched food from the tree-tops for her mother who was unable to climb. They have sophisticated linguistic abilities and, in captivity, have learnt and used sign language to communicate with their carers. And, something Goodall also discovered, they like bananas.

The Gombe chimps live in large communities, but tend to move about in smaller groups. Family ties are close—a baby will stay with its mother until it is weaned at about three years old, and juveniles will stick close until they are eight or nine. Even when they reach adulthood, at about ten or eleven, they spend a lot of time with their families. They feed for up to six hours a day, primarily on palm nuts and fruit, but will also eat seeds, insects and small mammals. The Gombe troops have developed 'mental maps' of the region and know where different food supplies are at different times of the year. They have even been known to search out particular plants for medicinal purposes; the 'aspillia' for example which is used by the local people as an antibiotic and to treat worms.

They are, of course, wild animals capable of aggressive and some-times ferocious behaviour. They can be cannibalistic and will kill and eat their own young—a fact much disputed when first identified by

Goodall. The chimps at Gombe are 'habituated' which means that, though they are still wild, they have become used to people. They have been observed for almost forty years now—the longest study of its kind—and everything about them has been recorded: what and when they eat, where they travel, how they interact, what they fight over, how they sleep, and all the different types of social behaviour they exhibit. The researchers can recognise individual chimps by their faces and body shape, and even their voice—and each chimp has been given a name.

Sarah appears, hovering at the bottom of my bunk. 'Anything interesting?'

'They're very like us you know.'

'Oh yeah. And they don't mind if we just rock up and invade their space? They don't get…edgy?'

'Well according to *What to do in the presence of chimpanzees* we'll be fine as long as we don't make any sudden movements or loud noises, and crouch rather than stand when we see them. We should talk quietly, wear dull-coloured clothes and never get closer than five metres.'

'And if they get a bit agitated do we run in zig-zags, climb a tree or play dead?'

'Actually, none of the above. It says: *If a chimp charges towards you, do not scream or run away. Stand up, move to the nearest tree and hug it very tightly.*'

'You're kidding?'

'Nuh. Straight up. Wrap your arms around the closest trunk and hope they think you're so crazy they run away.'

'Hmm. But they don't actually…ever really come close…do they…Babe?'

We are interrupted by Jim, who drops by to tell us we should be ready by seven and that we may be in the forest all day. He will check on the whereabouts of the chimps with the researchers before we leave—they may be close, or they may be far off in the hills—we may not see them at all.

He reiterates the warnings in my book, but is anxious to reassure us. 'There is only one chimp, who we call Frodo, who is really any danger,' he says. 'He sometimes gets aggressive and has been known to grab tourists by the arms and shake them vigorously. If you wrap yourself tightly round a tree he won't be able to grab you. Just hang on and he'll eventually give up.'

Thanks Jim…for the reassurance.

In the morning I stir to a whisper from across the mosquito net. 'Am I allowed to wake you up yet?' The springs of my bed begin to squeak and gentle kisses float across my neck and shoulders. 'I've been awake for ages—can we get up now?'

In my half sleep I recall an article I read recently about how serotonin levels affect moods: lower levels are thought to contribute to 'Seasonal Adjustment Disorder' and now to something called 'General Morning Grumpiness'. I wonder if an excess can lead to something called 'General Morning Chirpiness,' and if so, whether Sarah has it. 'I'm sorry,' she says. 'I know it's early, but…it's a bit like Christmas morning. Let's go find the chimps eh?'

After a quick banana breakfast the four of us follow Jim up a steep track into the forest which almost immediately closes in on us, the thick canopy cutting out the light. It is intensely humid and before long we are breathing hard and slowing our pace. Giant ferns spill onto our path from both sides and we breaststroke through them, ducking to avoid branches that swoop down above our heads.

The ground is wet and slippery, thick mud quickly clogs the soles of our boots and slops over our laces. We scramble up a steep bank, our heads bowed beneath the undergrowth, and slide down the other side, mud oozing through our fingers as we grab at roots and branches. We drag ourselves up another incline and down again until we reach a small clearing. Jim places his hands either side of his mouth and mimics the sound of the chimps' call—often they respond and make tracking easy—but the only sound today is our heavy breathing and the occasional squawking of parrots. 'Higher,' he says. 'They like the palm nut trees on the ridge.'

We continue up a sharp incline, the branches and ferns forming a tight tunnel that blocks the sun completely. It is dark, but not cool, and my shirt clings to my back and my hair falls lank about my face. No one utters a word. We reach the top and descend again, scrambling down a short steep slope where the branches spread low across our path. We duck under them, crawling on our hands and knees through the mud and over the mass of protruding roots. Thick, twisted vines dangle above our heads and we grab them, hauling ourselves up and attempting to swing across the logs and fallen branches Tarzan style.

We pause for a drink while Jim looks for signs of the troop. It is a good hour since we left the bunkhouse and we are filthy and exhausted already—I'm not sure any of us are prepared for a day of this. Jim chivvies us along and we drag ourselves up another wet slope and down the other side, emerging finally onto a patch of dirt that might be a track.

Without warning there is sudden burst of sound, a series of 'uh uh uh' calls loud and close. As we round a corner we see a young chimp sitting in a tree, barely four metres from us. 'Gimbo,' Jim whispers, 'a male juvenile.' We stop suddenly, standing in single file, each of us peering around the person in front.

Gimbo grabs a branch, pulling off palm nuts and popping them in his mouth one after the other, his thick pink lips moving rapidly up and down. He drops onto a lower branch, stripping the fruit as he swings, and jumps onto the track. I can see the wrinkles of his knuckles, the dirt around his fingernails and the pale whiskers on his chin. His hair, parted in the middle lies flat against his head like a bad seventies cut.

He sits, arms folded, resting his elbows on his knees and looks at Sarah, at Rick, at me, his eye contact direct, focused, *human*. 'Move around him slowly,' Jim whispers. We step into the bushes and tiptoe through the undergrowth emerging a little further along the track. I glance back, watching his head shift furtively, the backs of his sticking-out ears pink against his thick mat-black coat.

There is a rustle in the bushes ahead and a huge adult chimp swaggers out and lies on the track in front of us. He crosses his legs and pops one arm under his head in a classic pose of relaxation. 'That's Galahad,' says Jim, 'an older male.' Galahad scratches his belly, picking out a tick and flicking it into the bushes with his thumb and finger. He raises his head slightly, glancing at us, then flops back down, tugging his beard. His face—having lost of all the pink of its youth—is completely black, like his eyes.

Suddenly, the forest fills with a great cacophony of chimpanzee calls: loud screeching hoots that raise the hairs on the back of my neck, and deep, haunting 'ooh ooh oohs' that literally make me shiver. I freeze, searching frantically in the trees, my head jerking back and forth. I can hear them rustling, feel their shouts echoing above me, but I can't *see* any of them.

A loud heavy panting emanates from the trees close by and I watch as the branches slowly rise and fall. Behind me, I hear a shuffling and grunting and a then loud, steady drumming as they beat their arrival on the tree trunks. I spin around, check the tree-tops—I hear can them *breathe*—but still can't see them. Seconds later, a high-pitched screech rises from the undergrowth next to me, and somewhere, a dozen chimps join in, and we are completely encircled by a long, piercing, terrifying wail.

I look for Sarah and catch sight of Jim who is standing perfectly still, his hand raised in a 'stay exactly where you are' gesture. Deep barking grunts fill the forest and the screeching builds to a crescendo like a primeval scream. My heart beats faster. My legs shake. A cold sweat drips down my back. I have never felt so close, so *intimate*, to a wild animal as I do now.

Jim beckons us away and we step gingerly down the track, the grunting and screaming still echoing around the trees. As we walk, the noise slowly abates as the troop begins to settle. Rick and Navid have disappeared around a corner and we quicken our pace to catch them. Sarah is about three metres in front of me walking briskly with her head down. Suddenly, a huge full-grown male chimpanzee breaks through the bushes and strides towards her. He swings his arms, leaning on his front knuckles, his bottom swaying from side to side. Sarah stops. Freezes. She squeezes her eyes tight shut, like a panicked five-year-old—if she can't see him, maybe he can't see her.

Oh God! I say silently. Please don't let it be Frodo.

He moves closer to Sarah, pausing for a moment to look behind, then shuffles across the track, barely a metre from where she stands, petrified. He sniffs the air, takes another look around and ambles into the trees on the other side.

I run down and grab her. 'Sarah, you OK?' Her face is ashen. 'Sarah. Look at me,' I say. She opens her eyes—wide and staring. 'I didn't scream,' she says, 'or run. You know it said in the book not to scream or run.'

'I know Doll. It's OK. He's gone now.'

'Do you think it was…Frodo?'

'No. I'm sure it wasn't. You're safe now. It's…'

Before I can finish my sentence, another adult chimp comes bounding out of the bushes and lurches towards us. He stops, rocks gently on his knuckles, and looks us up and down. I wrap my arms tightly around Sarah. The chimp—Frodo maybe, who knows?—nods in our direction and starts to grunt. I try to persuade myself it's a friendly greeting, a sort of chimpanzee welcome, and hope he doesn't follow up with a pat on the back, or a friendly hug.

We stand. Frozen. Waiting. I can see the lines around his eyes, his wide nostrils, scars and scratches on his face and chest. After what seems like half an hour, but is probably half a minute, he shakes his head, steps over the path and disappears into the bushes. 'Jesus, Doll. There can't be any more. Can there?'

I fix my eyes on the spot where they are emerging and almost immediately another comes shuffling out, this time a juvenile. He glances vaguely in our direction and wanders across the track hardly a metre from us. Another adult follows close behind, then another, and another, and another. We stand silent, transfixed, barely breathing.

When the rustling in the bushes finally stops and the last chimp has past, I relax my grip on Sarah. 'You OK Doll?'

'Yeah…I think so. Are they done?'

'Yup. I hope so.'

We pause a moment longer just to be sure. 'That was like…I don't know. Nothing I've ever experienced.'

'I don't know either, Doll, but let's get out of here.'

We head quickly down the track catching up with the boys who are standing in front of a tree, snapping frame after frame, paparazzi style. A young mother, Fifi, has emerged from the trees and dangles by one arm, her sleek glossy coat sparkling in the rays of sunlight that sneak through the canopy. It's as if she knows she has an audience and is putting on a show, swinging from branch to branch, looking at each of us in turn and popping palm nuts delicately into her mouth.

'You alright girls?' Rick asks. 'Look a bit pale.'

'Fine thanks. Close encounter. Fill you in later.'

We leave Fifi and Frodo and all the others and head up to 'Jane Goodall Point', a clearing high above the rainforest that looks over the lake. It is a slow, gentle climb, a chance for our adrenaline to ebb and our heart rates to return to normal. It *was* scary, but it was more than that. It was *awesome* in the true sense of the word. 'They were so close we could have touched them,' says Sarah.

'I know. So much for keeping five metres away.'

'And so much for hugging trees.'

We emerge into a clearing and sit on a rock looking down across the rainforest to the mountains of Congo. The air is cooler up here and a quiet breeze drifts between us. We are too far away to see the chimps, but far below, beneath the canopy, we can still hear them calling. Such a combination of fear and excitement, of thrill and panic, I can't recall, but I know, nothing I have ever experienced has made me feel quite so alive.

CHAPTER 12

TOUCHING
THE WAZUNGU

THE MV *LIEMBA* LEAVES Kigoma once a week and chugs down Lake
Tanganyika to Mpulungu on the border of Zambia. It has been doing
this since 1924 and you can tell. The greying hull is chipped and dented,
and the once white railings are now tinged with red where the rust has
slowly eaten them away. A line of bolts gently corrodes leaving long thin
ferruginous stains, like tea dripping down the side of a china cup.

We have booked a 'first class' cabin for the two-day journey to
Kasanga on the southernmost tip of Tanzania, and as we idle at the
dock waiting to embark, Navid shares third-world ferry stories. 'Do
you remember the one that sank in the Plili…'

'Yes. Thank you Navid, I do remember.'

'And wasn't there another that went down in…'

'Yup, I think there was…Shall we embark?'

A gangplank is thrown across the water and we shuffle aboard,
heading straight for the upper deck. We are greeted by a man in an
epauletted white shirt who escorts us to our cabin and hands out keys.
The cabin is a pleasant surprise—if I stand in the middle with my arms

outstretched, I can't touch any of the walls. It looks recently repainted in a tasteful cream and burgundy, and a window facing the deck provides light and air. There is a small wardrobe that accommodates both our packs, a table and chair, and a sink from which water runs...or at least dribbles. The two large bunks have thick foam mattresses and a reading light above each—that works.

We unpack our sleeping bags and a few toiletries—after confirming there is no way this section of the boat can detach itself from the rest. It is only a step from our door to the railing from which there is an excellent view of the lower deck, the bow and the gangplank where small boys sell chapattis and Cokes from ice-filled eskies. Boarding is in full swing—a long queue of people stretching back along the dock. Travelling light in Africa, it seems, means an overstuffed bag under each arm and a basket on the head, but most people like to take a few extra bits and bobs: half a dozen full-size mattresses, a pile of buckets stacked precariously like the Leaning Tower of Pisa, two dozen pineapples tied up with raffia, a huge bundle of bright orange cloth.

There is no limit to the number of people who can board, nor any baggage restrictions, and after an hour I wonder if we haven't just taken on the entire population of the local refugee camp. A fog-horn sounds and boarding becomes frenetic. A cardboard box filled with saucepans is thrown onto the deck, sacks of flour are swung onto the bow, and the Coke boys race along the dock, catching shillings and flinging up bottles. Minutes pass and still more people appear—in fact, if anything, the line has stretched further. The fog-horn blows again and again—the pace quickening and slowing with each blast.

A young man, expensively dressed in a Nike shirt and shoes, appears behind us and, with accentuated politeness, asks if we can make some space at the railing. We move aside as he ushers a woman forward. She is veiled in black, her hands buried beneath folds of cloth, her head bowed. She stares down at four women peering over the edge of a high brick wall. They are similarly veiled and, but for slight differences in height, look identical. 'Her sisters,' explains the young man. Sarah notices the faded henna on the woman's wrists. 'Have you just married?' she asks her. The man nods and explains he is taking his new wife to Johannesburg, a journey of five or six days by lake and road—it will be a long time before she sees her family again.

The sisters stand, heads bowed, except for an occasional upward glance which is met with slow tears and a barely perceptible wave. The fog-horn blasts one final time and they raise their heads, a sharp look of despair in their eyes. The new bride pushes closer against the railing, waving silently as the boat pulls away from land. When they are no longer in sight, her husband steps forward, takes her hand, and gently leads her away to their cabin.

The notice outside the bar at the end of our deck says: 'First Class Restaurant Only' and I confess, Sarah and I are quite excited at the prospect of a smoke- and stare-free meal. Alas, within minutes of departing, the plastic tables and chairs are filled to capacity with men and cigarettes. We hover in the doorway, watched by the entire crowd. 'Hmm?...How about we eat in tonight?' I say, and we head back towards our cabin.

Next door to us is a group of women—three young mothers, a grandmother, two children, three babies and an assortment of potties, nappies and baby food—all in the one cabin. The two children, a boy and a girl no more than three or four, hover in the doorway watching Sarah and me. They are torn between the tremendous excitement at finding *wazungu* in such close proximity, and their fear of the unknown. They edge out of the cabin, clinging tightly to their mother's leg, and from behind a *kanga*, point and squeal. 'Mama *Wazungu! Wazungu!*' The women grab the children shushing them, and smile, slightly embarrassed, at us. Sarah crouches down and holds out her hand to the oldest. He is thinking this could be fun, you don't get to see *wazungu* very often...but ah...maybe not just now.

As the sun comes down we stand by the railing eating fresh pine-apple and watching Congo drift by. Most of the other passengers are in the restaurant, or settled on the lower decks, and we enjoy a rare stare-free interlude. The evening is still and warm and the lightest breeze whispers around our ears. The reflection of a three-quarter moon ripples across the water and we linger, hand-in-hand, breathing in the balmy air and searching out the stars. Though it feels a little like a scene from a bad American soap, we indulge in the romance of the moment nonetheless.

We are awoken in the early hours by sudden shouts and loud banging, and what sounds like more than a dozen men in heated argument. 'Ticket check?' I suggest. The engines are suddenly quiet and we pull on some clothes and step out. Two huge spotlights illuminate the deck and the turquoise water below. Approaching the *Liemba* from the shore are six or seven small wooden boats propelled by young boys paddling frenetically. As they near, they shout and wave and bang into each other, pushing off with the blade of their paddles. They split into two groups, one heading for the stern, the other for the bow, and manoeu-vre their boats as close as possible to the *Liemba*, shoving the others aside in their battle for the best position. The shouting becomes more agitated and is accompanied by a kind of manic gesturing at the people waiting on the deck.

At the bow, a group of men have gathered, surrounded by bags and boxes which they prepare to drop some twelve to fifteen feet into the boats below. The young boys throw down their paddles and balance precariously, raising their arms like cricketers preparing for a catch. Blankets, crates, buckets and bananas are dropped into the boys' arms and stacked in the tiny wobbling vessels. Once they have thrown over all their luggage, the men begin to clamber over the railing and climb down the hull of the Liemba, jumping into the boats beneath. There is no let-up of the jostling while all this is going on—the boys continue to shout and shove each other aside in order to maximize the number of passengers they take on board.

A young woman, with a baby wrapped in a *kanga* on her back, is lowered bodily over the rail by two men grasping her wrists. She is dangled above the water while another man in the boat below attempts to grab her legs and reel her in. Two more women follow, and a handful of children, thrown down like bags of maize. I glance at Sarah, catching the look of horror on her face as we both realise what's happening. There are no docks or jetties anywhere along this route and there is only one way to leave the *Liemba*. This is disembarking.

The fog-horn blasts and there is a final scramble—mattresses float down, crates and sacks are rearranged, and a man who slipped between two boats is dragged out of the water. As the boys again take up their paddles, the boats tip wildly from side to side, boxes and bags spilling onto the passengers while the children sit terrified, grabbing at the edges. A final blast sounds and the boats move quickly away as the *Liemba's* engine revs. The spotlight is switched off and we are again in darkness, the noise abating as the procession of boats heads back to the shore.

Back in our cabin I lean over my bunk to check on Sarah who hasn't said a word for ten minutes. 'OK, Hon?'

'Fine,' she says. 'Absolutely fine. And just so you know, I am not, under any circumstances, leaving this boat in that manner.'

We share a fried egg breakfast with Rick and Navid, watched by the entire restaurant clientele—we are the only *wazungu* on board and the general level of interest is persistently high. We leave our audience and grab a couple of chairs, settling outside our cabin to watch the day go by. Boys wander up and down selling single cigarettes and sticks of gum, and a few old men lounge on sacks of maize, smoking and spitting sugar cane onto the deck. Next door, the babies are fed, changed, bathed and dangled, and the two older children edge a little further from their mother's skirts and wonder whether it might now be safe to touch the *wazungu*.

Unfortunately for us, the rest of the passengers have decided to spend their day people watching too, and while we can choose from a couple of thousand passengers, they are interested in only two.

We head over to the restaurant and attempt to secrete ourselves in a corner. A bad seventies movie about a ferry hijacked by terrorists is showing on a single TV screen padlocked to the wall. I last about five minutes before my attention wanders and, as I glance around the room, I discover most of the patrons have given up on the movie too, and are watching us instead. Out of sheer frustration I stand and face them, raise my arms, place my thumbs in my ears, wiggle my fingers and spin around on the spot making loud 'wah wah' noises. Sarah chokes on her drink and spews Coke all over the table—the rest of my audience, unfortunately, remains unembarrassed. They smile, nudge each other and retain their fixed stares, waiting for Act Two.

We move to the other end of the restaurant where there are fewer people and Sarah orders a fresh Coke. The barman speaks excellent English and he asks how we are enjoying our trip on the *Liemba*. Sarah suggests that the method of disembarkation is a little unconventional and does not inspire confidence in *wazungu* used to slightly higher standards of health and safety. The barman agrees—it is very dangerous. 'Only last year,' he says, 'a lady died—she slipped between two boats and was trapped underneath.'

Sarah gives me an 'I-told-you-so' look and I attempt to usher her away from the barman and his doom and gloom stories. 'There was another time,' he says 'very bad—fourteen people were killed when their boat was sucked down by the *Liemba*. They didn't get away quick enough and were caught in the propeller.'

'Oh really,' I say, grabbing Sarah's arm and dragging her out onto the deck. We pause by the railing and she looks at me squarely. 'You are not, let me make this absolutely clear, dropping me and my pack from two storeys up into a wobbling little dugout floating on the deepest bloody lake in Africa. Is that *quite* clear?'

I put my hands on her shoulders and attempt to conjure an earnest, reassuring tone. 'It won't be that bad Doll, honestly. We'll avoid the stern and the propeller…it'll be safer at the bow and…'

She throws off my arms. 'I repeat. Under no circumstances am I leaving this boat in that manner. If we have to, we'll go to Zambia and disembark there.'

I linger by the rail as she stomps off to the cabin. I can't say I'm thrilled about this plan myself—I think *we* could make it over safely, but I keep seeing my beautiful pack and hundreds of dollars worth of gear disappearing into a watery expanse of turquoise.

The fog-horn announces our arrival at another village and we position ourselves on the deck so we have a clear view of the port side and bow. We can see the boats racing towards us in the distance and already hear the hysterical shouts of the boys. Like last time, the jostling begins long before they reach the *Liemba*, the boats barging into each other, water splashing over the edges as they clash.

The first one to reach us manoeuvres its way alongside the *Liemba* directly beneath the bow where the departing passengers have gathered. The moment it stops, another boat sweeps in behind, the boy at its helm adroitly forcing the first boat out of the way and taking command of the best spot. Three or four more follow up the rear, swinging close to the *Liemba's* hull and ramming those in front in an attempt to dislodge them.

On the deck, the men drop four large oil drums, the Leaning Tower of Pisa and half a dozen ten-metre timber poles. Then, they clamber down the side, or just jump into the water and swim. The women perch nervously at the rail.

A middle-aged man emerges from one of the first class cabins carrying a brand-new racing bike in one hand and a goat in the other. He is followed by a long line of boys carrying his luggage, who shuffle past us and weave their way through the crowd on the lower deck. The man lowers the bicycle and the goat over the side and supervises as the boys approach the rail and drop his other cargo: six huge frying pans, four reels of pink nylon rope, two old-fashioned metal laundry tubs, three large sausage-shaped sports bags, a roll of corrugated iron, a dozen sticks of sugar cane, a backpack, three bags of bananas, a crate of car parts, a briefcase and a large multi-coloured golf umbrella.

Our attention is diverted from him to the very front of the bow, where there is a small rusting crane tentatively affixed to the deck by four bolts. While the first class guy is dropping the contents of a small house over our side, a heavy chain is being attached to the top of the crane and dropped over the other. A line of twenty or more men lean over the rail pointing and shouting orders at whoever is below. On the deck, people and cargo are shifted from one end of the bow to the other—and back again.

As the crane begins to take up the slack, the creak of splitting wood echoes around the bow. The four bolts strain like champagne corks about to pop as a huge fishing boat rises from the water and is hoisted high into the air. It dangles precariously above a few hundred third class passengers, swinging wildly back and forth. The women grab their children and scatter to the rails, hands thrown protectively over their heads. The men hover beneath the boat, screaming instructions at the crane operator and attempting to guide it safely onto the deck. The boat jerks down, as if the chain is repeatedly caught and suddenly released, and lands with a crash, tipping over to one side and sending the men scurrying backwards.

'Perhaps I could arrange to have you lifted off by crane,' I suggest to Sarah.

At dinner we pick at our beef and rice and plan the next few days with Rick and Navid. From Kasanga, if we manage to disembark, we have to get to Sumbawanga, the nearest town about eighty kilometres east, and from there somehow reach Mbeya just over the Malawi border. On the map, it looks about four hundred kilometres, but there is no public transport, and at this stage, we're not even sure there are roads.

Sarah is quiet. I haven't worked out any other method of getting us off and have only a vague, and not particularly reassuring plan, for protecting our packs involving Rick and a small piece of nylon rope. We have watched every disembarkation for two days and have assessed the best place and tried to establish the safest method. There is a small ledge—maybe ten or fifteen centimetres, but enough for a toe-hold—halfway down the hull. If we edge over the railing backwards we should be able to drop down onto it then grab the bottom of the railing and shuffle down into a waiting boat. Rick and Navid will lower our packs which will remain attached to the *Liemba* until safely in our hands. Sarah, poor love, is unconvinced by my plan.

On the way back to our cabin we pass the boy and girl from next door. They are a little bolder, standing in front of their mother and breaking into a smile as we approach. We linger by the rail, about two metres away watching them watching us. The boy shuffles forward and Sarah hunkers down so she is squatting at his level. He turns to look at his mother who nods and smiles that it's OK, and he steps a little closer. A few inches away he pauses—Sarah remaining absolutely still—and, with another quick look at his mother, he steps forward and places his hand tentatively on Sarah's leg. He is fascinated by her skin and her tiny blonde hairs. He pinches a few between his thumb and finger and pulls, squealing with delight as Sarah winces. He moves his hand slowly up her leg, focussed totally on her skin, until his arm begins to disappear up her dress. Sarah breaks into a laugh and grabs his hand as his mother steps forward and gently pulls him away.

His younger sister has been watching, her arm wrapped around her mother's leg, afraid she might be missing out. I crouch beside her, holding out my hand as she fixes me in her gaze. Slowly, she unravels herself from her mother's *kanga* and takes a step towards me, then another, until she is barely a metre away. She stretches out her hand and I shuffle forward on the balls of my feet, our fingertips just a few centimetres apart. She raises her eyes to her mother, looks again at me, and at her hand so close to mine. She stretches her fingers almost imperceptibly until suddenly, her head shoots up and I meet her wide brown eyes filled with panic and excitement and fear and delight. She is not quite sure how, but somehow, she is touching the *wazungu*, and it is all a little overwhelming. In a split second she squeals, snatches her hand back and darts into the cabin.

We pull into Kasanga at 2.00 a.m. The border to Zambia is closed until 6.00 a.m. and, as it is only an hour from here, the *Liemba* must wait until 5.30 a.m. before continuing—we are allowed to remain on board until then.

I wake every half an hour, check the time and listen to Sarah lying awake beneath me. At four it begins to rain, gently at first then heavier, until it sounds like a troupe of Cossack dancers performing on our roof. A great clap of thunder sends a shudder through me and the cabin is lit with a flash of white light. I lean over the bunk and grab Sarah's hand. 'Oh God,' I say. 'I'm sorry, Doll.'

We lie awake, watching the sound and light show, and listening for the tell-tale shouts of the boatmen. We really can't go on to Zambia and disembark there—it would send us days out of our way—but how the hell I am going to get Sarah and our packs safely off this goddamn boat I really do not know.

At five, I crawl out of my sleeping bag and perch on the edge of Sarah's bunk. She props herself up and looks me in the eye. 'OK,' she says. 'Let's do this thing.'

The spotlights have been turned on and, as I open the cabin door, great curtains of pelting rain sweep across the lake and the sky fractures with myriad bolts of lightning. Huge drops of rain dance on the deck and claps of thunder shake the cabin walls. Rick and Navid emerge, buried in Gore-tex and nod silent hellos. There is still no sign of our boatmen and the four of us hover on the deck waiting for some miracle that will transport us safely to land.

After another quarter of an hour and still no boatmen, Sarah wanders off to see if she can find anyone while Rick and I fiddle with our gear. We knot together all the pieces of string and spare bootlaces we have and tie them around the handle of my pack. It's not going to be easy, especially with the rain pelting down and the deck slippery as hell. I peer through the darkness looking for boats—perhaps they just don't come out when the weather is this bad.

Suddenly, Sarah comes bounding down the deck, the rain bouncing off her jacket. 'Thank God!' she says, '*Oh thank God!*'

'What?'

'We're OK.'

'*What?…How?*'

'They've built a dock. It isn't in our guidebook because it's new.'

'You're kidding?'

'Nuh. That's why there are no boats. There's a gangplank over the other side. I've seen it. We're OK.'

'We don't have to go over the edge?'

'No. We don't have to go over the edge.'

'Why didn't someone tell us that?'

'Who cares? Grab those packs boys and girls. We're out of here!'

CHAPTER 13

BY AMBULANCE TO SUMBAWANGA

THE SPOTLIGHTS ARE suddenly switched off and the *Liemba* chugs away from the shore and disappears down the lake to Zambia. The four of us stand in complete darkness on a patch of scrub at the end of the small wooden dock, the still pelting rain collecting in puddles at our feet. We glance around in a full circle and see nothing—absolutely nothing. There are no shadowy houses or huts, no structures of any nature, no roads or tracks, no crops or enclosures, just a flat black expanse of wet nothing. 'What do you reckon guys?' I ask.

'Well…let's er…walk…forward, I suppose. Maybe… we'll bump into something.'

We shuffle into the blackness and trudge towards nowhere in single file, the rain swirling in our faces and pouring down our jackets. As our eyes adjust to the darkness, we identify a cluster of large rectangular silhouettes a few hundred metres away. Gradually, the outline of a truck becomes clear, then another behind it, and three or four more. A faint 'jambo'—a Swahili 'hello'—drifts towards us through the rain and I dig out my torch and shine it in the direction of the voice. I can't see anyone, nor any movement, nor, in fact, any sign of life.

The voice 'jambos' at me again and I flash the light towards it. Between the ground and the undercarriage of the nearest truck there are six men huddled together, wedged between the giant wheels, sheltering from the storm.

We crouch alongside them, smiling in the darkness and attempting to communicate in slow English and the odd word of Swahili—if we can work out where they are heading, we may be able to hitch a lift. They smile back and attempt to communicate in slow Swahili and the odd word of English. Neither approach is very successful and, after failing to establish either where they are going, or when they might go—or anything else—we give up.

We stand in a circle staring at each other and watching the rain drip off our noses. It's not like we have so many options. Rick drops his pack, shoves it under a truck and squats beside it, and we follow, wedging ourselves behind him, to wait for daybreak.

An hour later, as the sun rises, we crawl out damp and stiff and check our surroundings—even in daylight all we can see is low empty scrub which rises to a faint bump a few kilometres away. A teenage boy emerges from underneath another truck and we attempt to communicate our desire for a lift. He nods encouragingly and tries to find out if any of the drivers are heading to Sumbawanga—or at least we hope that's what he's doing. After five minutes of discussion he returns, shaking his head and throwing his arms in the air—either the drivers are not heading our way, or they don't want to take us, or the boy hasn't a clue what we're talking about—which I suspect is really what's happening.

He gestures towards a track and mutters something that might be English. '*Village?*…is that…*bus station?* or maybe it's just Swahili for "I don't know about you guys, but I'm knackered and I'm going home".'

I am a little sceptical about finding *anything* in this tsetse-fly infested swampland, but, as our options are once again limited, we fall in line behind him.

We trek away from the lake, our young guide assuring us every few minutes that...something...I'm not really sure what...is 'just round corner'. The rain has soaked through my pack and I shift its dead weight from one shoulder to another and trudge, head down along the track.

The path is lined with deep potholes which periodically give way, my feet sliding through the sludge, the water flooding over the top of my boots. Gradually, the holes become bigger and the spaces between them smaller, and the path turns into a gentle brown river, the water nudging at our knees. Along the banks, between fields of drowned maize, there are a handful of white-washed huts, but there is no sign of any villagers—or anyone or anything else—and I am completely confident there will be no sign of a bus station either.

We schlep up a long winding hill that takes us out of the flood and away from the village. Navid is struggling under the weight of his pack, which, we discover, contains a hundred and fifty rolls of film, six pairs of shoes—in case he's invited to something a bit more formal— and *six* Lonely Planet guides. Rick is trying to keep the pace up—he has to be in Nairobi in four days to catch his flight back to Canada.

We reach a fork in the road where three women sit on bags of corn, chatting and scraping the mud from their thonged feet. 'Bus station,' announces the boy.

Oh I don't think so. This is a fork in the road; a 'bus station' requires the addition of certain other items, even in Africa, not least of all, buses.

'The bus has gone,' he says with some confidence, though unless he has radioed the depot and checked out today's timetable when we weren't looking, I'm not quite sure how he knows this. 'Tomorrow, another will come.'

We drop our soaked packs onto the sopping wet dirt and sit amidst the puddles. Apart from the few village huts, we have seen nothing that might offer food, or shelter or a bed for the night. The view is the same whichever way we look: plots of half-grown, half-drowned maize with shrivelled husks of corn littered across the dirt. Banks of earth slip away forming piles of soft squishy orange mud and, for as far as we can see, every hole or dip or trench is waterlogged.

Rick wanders down the hill to see what he can find while I put my mind to how we might enliven our next three meals of not quite ripe, not quite sweet, sweetcorn. Kasanga, it is safe to say, is not strictly on the backpacker circuit, or even on the 'off the beaten track' circuit, and I suspect our dinner options may be limited to a delicately boiled *ugali*, served on a bed of fresh *ugali* with a fragrant *ugali coulis*.

From the bottom of the hill I hear the rough straining of an engine, and a small beaten-up old van the shape of an American school bus lurches up the road. Rick is hanging out the doorway, a 'look-what-I-found' grin on his face. 'He'll take us to Sumbawanga,' he shouts, 'it's only eighty Ks.'

'*Good work!*' we shout in unison and grab our packs out of the mud.

The bus has deep crimson flock wallpaper around the windows and red carpet on the ceiling. If I had seen it anywhere else I might have thought it was owned by a circus troupe. Four rows of bright red seats are squashed in—the vinyl held together by black tape, grey pock-marked stuffing poking out the edges. The floor is laid with brown lino through which we can see the ground in the spots where it has thinned. There are no other people on board and, as it's only eighty kilometres, I estimate, even by Africa time, we should reach Sumbawanga by mid-afternoon.

We pull away from the 'bus-station' and head into now familiar country—wet low scrub with occasional patches of bedraggled maize and the odd hut. There is no improvement in the track and, with the complete absence of suspension, each bump sends us six inches in the air and we have to bow our heads to avoid hitting the ceiling. We cling to the seat in front and bounce along, like a group of children on a fairground ride. The metal frame of my seat pokes through the vinyl and repeatedly bangs against my thighs and bottom. I roll up my fleece and shove it underneath where the stuffing used to be.

We stop amidst a sad cluster of huts to pick up some passengers—there are no stalls selling bananas, no Coke stands, no kids running along shouting, 'Give me pen'. A couple of scrawny chickens peck in the dirt, and a handful of children stare in silence—naked, barefoot with crusty eyes and noses and huge distended bellies. Behind them, stand a row of teenage girls in faded *kangas*—all bearing babies on their backs. They glance towards the bus, too anxious, too indifferent maybe, to approach.

They look weary, not tired after a hard day, not exhausted by work or responsibility, but worn down by the daily routine of hunger and hardship. It's not the first time we've seen poor villages, underfed babies and skinny kids, but this is quite different. There's no *movement* here, no sound or activity, no sense of *life*—not even the hope that a bus load of tourists might bring the transitory comfort of a loaf of bread, or a western trinket.

A young father, supporting a twelve- or thirteen-year-old boy in his arms, manoeuvres onto the bus and squeezes into a double seat at the back. He adjusts his arm and cradles his son's head like a baby, shooing flies from his face. The boy looks pale and sickly, barely conscious, and Navid is itching to examine him, but with no way of communicating, no drugs nor even the most basic facilities, there's little point.

It is very slow going, the pot-holes turning into long trenches where the road has fallen away completely. Every now and again we ease out of a ditch and weave through what were once fields of corn. We lurch from side to side, leaning so far over I am squashed against the window with Sarah weighted on top of me. A few inches more, a pack suddenly shifting, and we would topple over completely.

I revise my estimated time of arrival.

We stop for a late lunch at a dank concrete hut serving rice and stew, and as I haven't seen anything resembling a cow for days, I stick with rice. The boys are rather more adventurous and chew their way through a pair of gristly knee joints while Sarah and I fill up on Coke.

After lunch we weave through four, five, six meagre villages, picking up boys with sacks of flour hoicked on their shoulder, or up-side down chickens slung at their sides. At the back of the bus the sick lad is still stretched out across the seat, his father periodically placing a cup of water to his lips and gently encouraging him to sip. There is a clinic of sorts at Sumbawanga, but Navid is sceptical they will be able to help.

We stop at a village where a crowd has gathered, clearly awaiting our arrival. A young woman, maybe nineteen or twenty, is carried aboard by three men. The steps to the bus are steep and she is hauled bodily, her arms dangling loosely at her sides, her full breasts falling out of her bright yellow dress. We shift our packs and clear away crates to make room for her. The villagers lay her on her back on one of the double seats, folding her arms across her chest. The seat accommodates only two-thirds of her body—her legs bend at the knees so that her bare feet are flat on the ground.

A woman of similar age, her sister maybe, steps up carrying a very young baby. She edges around the sick woman's knees and sits silently at the back. A much older woman and a young man, we assume the mother and husband, step up next. They deposit a small bag behind one of the seats and hover over the young woman, not quite sure what to do next.

The husband wedges himself awkwardly between his wife and the seat in front and covers her with a blanket, tucking it carefully around her hips and waist, and pulling it up beneath her chin. Navid is watching from the front of the bus, this time unable to hold back. He stands, head bowed under the low ceiling and approaches the husband, smiling and gesturing towards the woman. He checks her pulse and lifts her eyelids to examine her pupils. 'She's catatonic,' he says. 'How long?' he asks. 'How long has she been like this?' His question is met with blank faces and we grab the driver who knows a few words of English. 'Three days,' he says. 'She gave birth three days ago and has been like this since.'

The remaining villagers alight, offering the mother a spare *kanga* and a small bottle of water which she stows carefully at her feet. The driver jumps back into his cab and we pull away slowly, heading up the dilapidated dirt track, the quickest route to Sumbawanga.

The road is a nightmare, and the bus bounces violently even at slow speeds, throwing us out of our seats and sending boxes crashing into each other. We shift our packs in an attempt to immobilise them, and give the woman and her family a little more room. The husband remains standing, checking his wife repeatedly, carefully smoothing and re-tucking the blanket each time it's disturbed. The mother brushes away flies from her daughter's face and spoons some kind of tonic that looks like blackcurrant cordial into her mouth. She has a stoop and the wrinkled skin of a seventy-year-old, though she is probably closer to forty. Her hands shake ever so slightly and grief is writ large in her eyes.

Navid is perched on the edge of his seat, leaning forward with his hands clasped between his knees. He looks across to the young woman and mutters to himself, shaking his head. *He is an American doctor. He should be able to fix this.*

The bus continues to dip and lurch as it is hauled in and out of great gaping scars in the road. Periodically it swerves violently, fishtailing across thick mud and throwing us up against the windows and back across the seats. I lose track of how long we've been travelling, and there's no way of knowing how far we've come. The sun is dropping and the shadows of the acacias are lengthening. No one is very chatty, and it occurs to me that in all this time, and with all this jostling, we haven't heard a sound from the baby.

The bus plunges suddenly and we slide off our seats, tripping over bags and struggling to stay upright. The engine revs and strains trying to pull us out of the dip, but the tyres spin, sending great circles of mud high into the air like Catherine wheels. After five minutes and no movement we pile off the bus, leaving the young woman and the father and son on board. The driver grabs a spade from the roof and starts to dig while we hover awkwardly by the roadside.

It takes at least half an hour to dig us out, and when we re-board, Navid leans over the young woman placing his fingers on her wrist and checking his watch. He shakes his head, looking around the bus as if there might be something that could help. There is a long bench seat where we were sitting which could accommodate the woman more comfortably and make it easier for her mother and husband to attend her. Sarah and I shift packs and boxes while Rick and Navid and the husband position themselves around the woman. They struggle with her dead weight, lifting her over the back of the seats, her arms falling lifelessly to her sides. They shuffle the few steps to the front of the bus and lay her down, Rick unravelling an emergency blanket that crackles open to a huge piece of tin foil, and gently tucking it around her feet. He steps back to make way for the mother who crouches by her daughter's head, stroking her cheek with the back of her fingers.

Navid checks her pulse and pupils. Her extremities are cold and her breathing rapid and shallow. 'Maybe she didn't deliver the placenta,' he says. 'Could be septicaemia.'

The road, at long last, flattens out and, though there are still potholes, we lurch and strain a little less—we might even be travelling at more than twenty kilometres an hour. Before long, however, we start to slow again and with a groan and splutter come to a dead stop.

We have run out of petrol.

The driver jumps down from the cab, grabs a jerry can from the roof and heads up the road—where on earth he will find petrol amidst this desolate swampland I do not know. Rick, Sarah and I step down from the bus, leaving everyone else on board. We wander up and down the track, kicking the dirt and following each other in silent circles. A few flat top acacias interrupt the otherwise featureless savannah, and the air is heavy and still. A thick black band of safari ants weaves in and out of the wheels of the bus and a dung beetle struggles with a ball of mud twice its size, heaving it up a rut in the road and chasing it down the other side.

After a few minutes, the mother steps from the bus and falls to her knees by the side of the road. She gathers her *kanga* tightly around her and begins to weep, her whole body gently shaking beneath the purple and orange cloth. We shuffle away from her—looking and not looking—staring out across the trees. Slowly, she begins to rock, her head and shoulders lurching back and forth, her arms tight across her breast. Her quiet sobbing rises to a howl and the air is cut with a long piercing wail.

Navid slumps down from the bus, and a moment later the husband emerges, head bowed, hands hung limply by his side. He makes no motion towards the mother, but turns towards the bonnet of the van, standing still and silent. The young woman's sister steps down, crying quiet tears into the baby's swaddling. At the side of the road, the old woman slumps forward, her face almost in the dirt, her body racked with loud choking sobs. Around her, the trees darken to silhouettes, and pink and purple clouds spill across the horizon in an exquisite African sunset.

I squat down next to my dung beetle, helping him up the bank with a twig and making a rut in the dirt so he can reach the safety of the scrub more easily. The sun sets so quickly here, in a few minutes I won't be able to see him. I look up, trying to make sense of the bizarre tableau in front of me: six people—three black, three white—from different worlds and a newborn baby, lingering by a broken down bus on the edge of the savannah. There is no interaction between them, no words spoken, no glances exchanged. Everyone is absolutely still, save an old woman, who rocks in grief at the side of the road. In the bus is the corpse of a woman. A young woman, barely half my age, whom I have just watched die—and die from childbirth, something that surely belongs to history. Her newborn son, cradled in the arms of its aunt, is silent, and I wonder whether he will die also. Just now, I can barely take it all in, and I linger by the track, head bowed in a silence I hope passes for respect.

It is another half an hour before petrol arrives and we climb, somewhat reluctantly, back onto the bus. I edge my way up the stairs and shuffle onto my seat. This isn't a question of not looking, of averting one's eyes; the woman is spread out before me covered from head to toe in bright shiny tin foil. I flatten my back against the seat as much as I can and angle my legs holding my knees in tightly, but there are still only inches between her and me.

Sarah and Rick and Navid wedge themselves onto the other seats, and the mother and husband crouch at either end of the body, the sister and baby tucked into a corner behind them. At the back, the boy lies pale and inert in his father's arms, his hold on life gently slipping away. Our driver cranks the engine and we head off again towards Sumbawanga.

The road is flatter, but still rutted, and as the bus lurches in and out of the pot-holes, the body of the dead woman rolls towards the edge of the narrow seat and brushes against my knees. The mother and husband grab the shoulders and feet beneath the tin foil to stop it falling off. Each time we hit a ditch or bump the body bounces awkwardly, the head jerking, an arm flopping down, dangling by my leg. Each time, the mother carefully takes her daughter's hand and pushes it back underneath the foil.

I can think of nothing else, see nothing else, feel nothing other than the overwhelming presence of a dead woman lying at my knees. I can see the dirt under her fingernails, the pock-marks on her forearm, feel the coldness of her hand as it brushes my calves.

A sudden deep trench sends the body high off the seat into the air and inches from my lap. I panic, turn and shoot to the back of the bus. 'Guys, how about swapping places?' I say. Dead bodies are more their line of work than mine, after all.

It is dark by the time we hit the sealed road into Sumbawanga and we pull up by a non-descript concrete building. I squint through the window trying to work out where we are. 'Is it the clinic?' asks Sarah.

'God knows. Doesn't look like a clinic. Not even an African one.'

Rick peels the tin foil blanket from the woman and folds it carefully. He and Navid grab her under the arms while the husband gathers up her legs. They lower the body awkwardly down the steps, her hands dragging along the filthy floor, her still full breasts once again exposed.

On the street, a crowd quickly gathers and two rows of men form a line to receive the body. They carry her shoulder high—like a much mourned religious leader—the mother, sister and husband trailing behind. We watch silently as the body disappears into the darkness, and within seconds, the crowd disperses and everyone returns to their usual business.

Back on the bus, the father and his son are still sitting awkwardly, having barely moved since they boarded some eight hours ago. We head towards the main street, to a 'Mama na watoto' clinic where the driver shouts through the window to a young nurse. After a brief exchange he revs the engine and pulls away. 'Too old,' he says to us. 'The boy is too old. We must go somewhere else.'

We turn off the main street and head down a narrow, pitch black road, pulling up at an open concrete room lit by a naked bulb. The driver bangs on the back of his cab and the man gathers up his still unconscious son and clambers down the steps. He shuffles towards the building looking for a doctor or nurse, anyone who might offer help, but the clinic, if it is one, is deserted. He sits on a concrete bench, laying the boy across his lap, and brushing the flies gently from his face. We leave him there, waiting for help that doubtlessly won't come and, even if it does, won't save his son.

We are dropped a few minutes later at a guesthouse in the centre of town. In the eleven hours it has taken to travel the eighty kilometres from Kasanga we have watched a boy and baby struggle to hold onto life, and we have watched a woman die. Today, Africa is somehow different. Or maybe we are.

Our journey is still far from over—from Sumbawanga we have another three hundred or so kilometres to Mbeya, the one major city in the south from where we should be able to access transport to Malawi. The bus that does the trip is currently undergoing massive repairs and won't be ready for days. Our book says the journey should take six hours, but the road is completely down in places—huge banks collapsed under the weight of water—and we are being quoted any- thing from twelve to thirty hours. Rick has to be back in Nairobi for his flight in three days and is worried.

While we rest, he spends the day trying to find a lift and eventually manages to track down a half-decent vehicle and driver. After much negotiating—and payments up front in American dollars—we secure four seats in a Land Cruiser. 'It may take some time,' says the driver, 'but I will get you through.'

At 6.00 a.m. the following morning I haul myself wearily into the awaiting four-by-four—there are no seats as such, just two facing nar- row wooden benches. Sarah grabs the front with the driver, and I squash in with the other seven people and all our gear. The road out of Sumbawanga is tarmacked for the first twenty minutes, then returns to dirt. It is reasonably intact, but the driver puts his foot down and we bounce awkwardly between the low ceiling and the hard seat.

An hour out of town we pass a broken down car with a family hovering by the side of the road. After an exchange with our driver they extricate a couple of suitcases, some sacks of food and a chicken and climb on board. The mama, with a broken arm in a cast and the scrawny *kuku* squeeze in beside Sarah, and the four men and their gear push their way into the back. I am shoved up the bench, wedged between the driver's seat and a skinny, mud splattered old man.

I shift my fleece under me and kick the box at my feet. I'm tired. I'm fed up. I'm hungry. I've been hungry for days. I haven't showered in a week and my hair is crawling. My back's killing me and my arms and legs are covered in bruises. Yesterday I spent the day watching someone die and today...well today I'm just not sure I love Africa quite as much as I did.

We rattle down the road in a tedious parody of our ride from Kasanga, our four-by-four straining through deep ditches, and skirting the almost vertical banks where the road has collapsed. We pass three, four, five bogged vehicles, our driver periodically zipping off-road and into the cornfields to avoid getting stuck.

After three hours we meet a bogged convoy: a Pepsi truck, a mini oil tanker, a 'business class' coach, and an assortment of missionaries in jeeps and Land Cruisers. Our driver contemplates his best option and revs the engine in preparation for a fast manoeuvre around the edge. Great chunks of road have fallen away and the larger vehicles lean at a forty-five degree angle, their wheels and undercarriage half exposed, half buried in the mud. Our driver mounts a bank, hauls us up onto a small ridge, passes the Pepsi truck, weaves around the missionaries, and comes to a slow, gentle stop alongside the business class coach.

We pile out onto the mud and tiptoe through sludge to the side of the road. There are dozens of people milling about, passengers from the vehicles, and local villagers who have emerged from nowhere. Groups of men, barefoot or in gum boots, shovel huge piles of sloppy earth in an attempt to extricate the trapped vehicles. A long line of women and children watch from the side.

Digging and pushing is definitely not a girl thing and we leave Rick and Navid grabbing spades from our driver and join the women on the sidelines. We stand chewing sugar cane, watching the guys and attempting some basic non-verbal communication with the women. A couple of kids appear, followed by a few more, until there are twenty or so gathered around us in a circle. I feel like a busker, my audience captive and waiting. 'A dance perhaps?' I suggest to Sarah.

'Sure.'

We try a cross-ball-change routine—or rather Sarah does and I fake it—which goes down very well, and elicits general smiles all around. We repeat the performance, adding a couple of spins and finishing off with an elaborate bow. The women turn to each other and laugh and the kids smile and slap their thighs.

Our vehicle is still buried axle-deep in the mud and looks like it will be there for some time. 'Hmm…what next?' I say.

'Er…how about a clapping game?' suggests Sarah, 'Emma and I used to play them.'

'Sure.'

Sarah and I stand opposite each other and raise our palms so they are a few inches apart. We begin to sing and clap in time: *C C my playmate, come out and play with me, and bring your dollies three*. It must be twenty-five years since I've recited this, but it returns instantly. The kids love it and start jiggling about in time and doing high fives, though they are still careful to maintain their distance.

Sarah faces a small girl at the front of the crowd, maybe five metres away, and crouches to her level. She recites the song again, doing the hand actions to the air. The girl raises her palms and, from a distance, starts to imitate Sarah's moves, unsure at first, but, after a few attempts, imitating perfectly.

Sarah shuffles forward and they repeat the game, this time only a couple of metres apart. She edges closer—the girl concentrating intently—until they are face-to-face and their hands come to together in a sudden clap. The girl smiles, a big surprised delighted grin, and the rest of the kids gather close. Soon they are all facing each other in pairs, clapping and singing, *CC my playmate* echoing though the maize plants.

Some of the older kids speak a little English, and after establishing names and ages, we try to teach them 'Head and shoulders, knees and toes,' accompanying each word with an action. When they have it down pat—which does not take long—they attempt to teach us the Swahili version, though of course there's no way of knowing whether we're really playing 'Hair and shirt, leg and boot.' We struggle with the unfamiliar combinations of letters and they laugh as we repeatedly mispronounce each word.

As we play, one of the young girls reaches up towards Sarah and fiddles with her ponytail. Sarah pulls out her scrunchy and bends over, shaking out her hair. Within seconds, twenty tiny fists are grabbing at her head, tugging in different directions. Sarah suppresses her screams and, after some time, manages to resurface, the kids now grabbing her hands and hanging off her arms.

With the whole pack firmly in tow, we amble back towards the boys to check on their progress. Rick and Navid are coated in thick mud up to their knees and have brown sludge splattered across their arms and faces. We watch as the driver revs the engine and the spinning wheels send sheets of mud high into the air. I'm sure they all know what they're doing, but it's rather difficult to tell whether any progress has *actually* been made.

It takes the boys a good two hours to dig us out—Rick looks terribly pleased with himself and Navid looks completely shattered. We scrape off the excess mud and squeeze back onto the bus. God knows how far it is to Tunduma, the one town *en route* to Mbeya, but breakfast—weak tepid coffee and a slice of bread—was a long time ago, and it would appear that today's schedule does not include a stop for lunch.

We drive throughout the afternoon and evening, weaving our way through flooded cornfields, passed decrepit trucks that look like they've been stuck for days. The road is unrelenting, and every hour or so we grind to a halt and pile out. The guys shovel the mud away from the axle, and we chock the wheels, throwing our shoulders against the back and pushing. It is a long, *long* day—the rain falling, the sun setting, and still no sign of food.

About an hour outside Tunduma we pause at the bottom of a steep hill. Through a tiny semi-circle of windscreen we can see the rain pouring down on a deeply furrowed incline. 'I'm sorry,' says our driver. 'Too much weight. I will go ahead, and you must follow on foot. I'll wait at the top.'

I lean over and bury my head in hands. '*I can't bear it*,' I say. I am desperately hungry, filthy and exhausted, and so sick of this bus and everyone in it. I just want to *be there*. To have a halfway decent meal and go to bed.

'Come on Babe,' says Sarah. 'Let's just do it.'

We climb out for the hundredth time today and watch the van tip and lurch up the hill. As it disappears over a crest some fifty metres away, we are suddenly left standing in absolute darkness—no stars, no moon, no artificial light of any kind, our torches buried beneath piles of luggage in the back of the van. It is completely, utterly black.

I lean my head against Sarah's shoulder. 'How the fuck are we going to get up there? I can't even see my feet.'

'We'll be OK, Babe. We'll hold hands and just take it really slowly.'

I pull my jacket tight against the sheeting rain, put one foot in front of the other, and begin the trudge up the slope. The ground is rutted all the way—thirty centimetres between the top and bottom of each bank—and with each step I have no way of knowing where my foot will land. Sometimes—bingo—I hit the top of the rut and shuffle a few metres forward, then my foot slides into a ditch—water flooding over my boot—and I tumble headlong, grabbing fistfuls of mud as I go.

The other passengers are out of sight in seconds and unless Sarah stays within a few feet I lose her too. We throw ourselves at the darkness, hoping we'll stay vaguely upright and reach the top with ankles intact. I stumble every few metres, never quite sure how soon I'm going to hit the ground, not knowing whether my hand will sink or jar. We are the last up, but at least everyone else looks as filthy and fed-up as we do.

The lights of the town slowly start to twinkle and I think longingly of my promised plate of beef and rice, and dry, flat bunk bed. The driver pulls over to the side of the road, turns off his lights and gestures to two of the young men in the back. They open the door and walk around to his window, and, after a muffled exchange, pocket a wad of shillings and drag a couple of jerry cans from the roof. Oh God! Not again.

'We have a problem,' says the driver. We should not really be on the road—no traffic is allowed after 10.00 p.m.—and it is still one hundred kilometres to Mbeya. The petrol station will be closed, but the boys will be able to fill the cans and we will sneak past the police road block.'

Yes of course. An excellent plan, and far more sensible than finding somewhere to eat and sleep in Tunduma and continuing in the morning. I stretch out my legs—kicking mud all over someone's suitcase—and pull my hood over my face in an attempt to forget where I am.

After half an hour our boys have not returned, and the driver is getting agitated. A pair of headlights appear in the distance and we wonder if perhaps they have been able to hitch a ride. As the vehicle approaches and stops, our driver groans. Two policemen emerge and after a brief chat—during which our guy nods and smiles a lot—we are packed off to town and the nearest hotel.

Tunduma's one guesthouse comprises half a dozen small concrete rooms with one shared low-style, and a water pump in the courtyard out back. There aren't enough rooms to accommodate us all and Rick and Navid volunteer to crash on our floor. We wolf down a barely edible, been-around-all-day portion of beef and rice and, as we are leaving at 4.00 a.m., and it's now almost midnight, head straight for our room.

A damp threadbare blanket covers an ancient mattress on a rickety wooden frame—you can almost see the bed bugs bouncing. I lie—minus boots and jacket, but otherwise fully clothed—on top of the blanket and shove my fleece under my head. Rick and Navid kick off their boots and unroll their thermarests onto the concrete floor. Between the creaking of the beds, the shuffling and snoring from the boys, the biting bugs, and the collective sock and body odour, it is not a restful night. Rather, it is not a restful four hours, as we are awoken and imprisoned back in the van by four-fifteen. Why it is OK to drive in the dark after midnight, but not before, I don't ask. When we will next eat I don't inquire either.

I fall into a bumpy sleep, dreaming of toast and cornflakes and tea and a clean firm bed with fresh white linen. I become vaguely aware of someone calling me and shaking my shoulder. 'Jac. *Jac!* Wake up Babe.'

'*What!* For Christ's sake! Can't I even dream in peace?'

'We have to get out, Hon. Dodgy bridge.'

'Fuck the bridge. I don't care. Just drive over it.'

'Come on. Get up.'

The bridge can take the weight of our Land Cruiser, and its collective fifteen passengers, but not, apparently, at the same time. When the vehicle is safely over the other side we schlep across and—I dare not hope, for the last time—climb aboard.

We are dropped, finally—soon after daybreak—at Mbeya bus station where we pile out for the last time, hauling our packs from beneath the mountain of luggage. We stand and stretch and rub the sleep from our eyes and I scan our immediate surroundings for breakfast opportunities. Navid wanders off and we arrange to catch up later in the day and travel together to Mzuzu—the first town in Malawi.

A coach heading for Dar es Salaam blows its horn and screeches past us. Rick grabs his bag and rushes towards it, banging on the door. 'We're full,' the driver shouts.

'This is Africa,' I yell to Rick. 'There's no such thing as a full bus.'

He jumps back up, grabbing the handle of the door and falling onto the steps as it disappears out of the station.

'Bye Rick. Nice travelling with you.'

Sarah and I drag our mud-coated packs onto our backs and head for a small wooden café. We devour half a dozen fried eggs and two loaves of bread. It's not very nice, and it's not enough, but it's a start.

CHAPTER 14

LUXURY ON LAKE MALAWI

'Madam! Madam! Excuse me Madam. May I prepare breakfast for you on the beach? I can make pancakes with banana, sugar and lemon.'

'You can make *pancakes?!*'

'Yes Madam. And if you like, I can make tea.'

'And *tea?!*'

'Yes Madam.'

I grab my pack from the four-wheel drive and glance at Sarah. 'Doll, there's a young lad here wants to cook breakfast for us on the beach. What do you reckon?'

'Do they really *have* food here, or is it just a tease?'

'No, I think they do. Honestly.'

I smile at the charming boy offering unthinkable delights. 'Thank you,' I say. 'We'd love breakfast on the beach.'

'You're welcome. My name is Iwa. I will meet you tomorrow on the beach.'

We have been dropped at the top of a sandy track that leads to the tiny fishing village of Cape Maclear on the shore of Lake Malawi. There is a handful of low brick buildings and an unattended craft stall displaying tall 'chief's chairs' and elaborately carved circular tables. A couple of teenage boys lounge under a gently flapping tarpaulin selling hand-made bracelets, and some of Iwa's buddies lie on the sand flicking rounded pebbles like marbles. A solitary backpacker scribbles postcards, sipping a long glass of what I strongly suspect is fresh fruit juice. I note, with some excitement, small piles of avocados and tomatoes spread out on hessian sacks. 'Doll, there are vegetables! There might even be fish, too.'

We head down the main track which runs alongside the beach, stepping around a line of dug-out canoes, and past a bamboo hut advertising scuba diving and kayaking. The water's edge is sprinkled with large thatched umbrellas where groups of backpackers lounge, passing around fat drooping joints—they look like they've been there some time.

The track leads to an unobtrusive whitewashed block, one of a handful of small hostels in the village. Four small tents are pitched on a sandy patch of bush beneath a couple of scrawny trees that provide dappled shade. A young woman—arm flopped loosely by her side, her face to the sun—swings in a hammock, a dog-eared paperback open across her stomach. On the beach, a pair of saronged Scandinavians sunbathe topless, rubbing cream onto each other's backs.

After the bus of death, and the long haul from Sumbawanga, we are keen to stop for a few days and do something that suggests we are actually on 'holiday'—I don't know...*eat* now and again...sleep a bit maybe—and besides, Sarah has made it abundantly clear that she is not getting on another bus for at least a decade, and unless an alternative to beef and rice is immediately forthcoming, she will have to dump me and fly to Cape Town.

A bamboo café-cum-bar runs down to the water's edge where a group of happily stoned residents play cards and swig beer. The barman appears, black wraparound sunglasses and a tight white vest, long loose dreadlocks falling across his shoulders. He fiddles with the CD player and turns to us, smiling broadly, a cigarette drooping from the corner of his mouth. 'Yo! Girls,' he says, 'Patrick. Room?'

'Ah?…maybe.'

'Cool.'

The CD begins to play and Patrick clicks his fingers in time to the beat and gently sashays around the bar. 'Tell me, Sarah, that's not…*Blowin' in the Wind*.'

'I think it just might be.'

One of the card players approaches wearing a lazy, stoned smile and cradling a guitar across his stomach. He is short and wiry with a pock-marked face and faded tattoos from wrist to shoulder. 'Hi. I'm Brian,' he says, in a thick Scottish accent. 'Can ye sing?'

'Er…no. I can't. Sarah can a bit.'

'Greet. Ya stoppin' then?'

'Er…Yeah. I think we are.'

We book a room for a week—a tiny hot box in the whitewashed block with a tin roof and an iron grille for a window. It is slightly smaller, and not quite as luxurious, as an average prison cell—no fan or light, just two single beds and a wobbly wooden table at one end. But it's cheap and clean, and a step up from the tent and, unlike the minimum secu-rity prison in Mombasa, this place does actually have some *atmosphere*.

As we squeeze our packs into the room, I notice the guy in the box next door sprawled across his bed. He is sweating profusely, his face an alarming shade of scarlet. 'Hi,' I say. 'New neighbours.'

'Wotcha,' he replies, struggling to lift his head. 'I'm James—got malaria.'

'Oh you poor thing. How long have you had it?'

'This is day three, another couple to go I reckon.'

'Where did you pick it up?'

'Dunno. Kenya maybe or Tanzania. I was takin' that chloroquine\Paludrine combination. Load of bollocks, though. Kept forgettin' to take 'em. Feels like me insides are on fire, and someone's playin' football wiv me 'ed.'

'Oh Sarah did you hear? James has malaria. Yes he was taking the chloroquine\Paludrine combination, BUT HE KEPT FORGET-TING AND NOW HIS INSIDES ARE ON FIRE AND SOMEONE'S PLAYING FOOTBALL WITH HIS HEAD!'

'Oh…Better start taking mine then.'

'Can we get you anything James, water or something?'

'Nah. There ain't none. I'm fine. Cheers.'

The blackboard above the bar promises cornflakes, Weetabix, orange juice, Milo, sausages and bacon, and though we are hopeful that Malawi might bring the longed for change in diet, we are now all too familiar with the yah-boo-sucks style of menu. A young boy slouches across the kitchen bench watching our eyes run down the list. 'Do you actually have any of this?' I ask.

'No.' he says.

'What do you have?'

'I can do scrambled eggs on toast with tomatoes, avocado and baked beans and tea.'

'We'll have that twice please.'

We settle at a wooden table underneath the bamboo awning and contemplate the thought of eating more food in one sitting than we have had in the whole of the last three weeks. It's a relief not to be digging buses out of foot deep sludge, trekking across ankle breaking terrain in the dead of night, or witnessing someone's lingering death from childbirth. I suppose the real Africa—the bits you don't see on safari—just caught up with us; floods, famine, everyday grinding poverty. The infant mortality rate in Malawi is around twenty per cent and, while what we saw may have been shocking to us, it is really quite unexceptional. Even so, we are feeling pretty exhausted. Cape Maclear looks like the very place to hang out for a week and do nothing.

I look out onto the calm clear waters of Lake Malawi, a couple of tree-covered islands in the distance, an occasional fishing boat idling by. 'How about a swim after lunch?' I suggest.

'Sorry Babe. Bilharzia.'

'Bil-*what?*'

'You know, bilharzia—minute worms that live in the snails that feed on the reeds. They multiply until there's a few million of them, leave the snails, then bore through your skin and attach themselves to your intestines by way of the veins in your bladder. They munch away at your bowel for a while and you start to get severe abdominal pain and pee blood. It's excruciating apparently.'

'Don't hold back, Babe. Tell it like it is.'

'It gets worse. They swim around the rest of your body and start attacking your other organs, laying eggs and multiplying inside you. If you don't get to a doctor pretty quickly, you die. The lake's full of them.'

'I'll take that as a "No" then, shall I?'

Our food is an hour coming, though there are no other orders and the young boy in the kitchen appears to be busy the whole time. When it finally arrives, we are overwhelmed: a huge mound of light fluffy scrambled egg on one side of the plate, baked beans cascading down two slices of thick white toast on the other, wedges of fried tomato and thick slices of avocado arranged around the edge. The tea is hot, doesn't taste of charcoal, and might even be made with fresh milk. Sarah grabs her knife and fork. 'OK. Maybe I won't dump you.'

A door slams on one of the hot boxes and a young woman emerges, a grim look on her face. She plonks herself at an adjacent table and a moment later is joined by a young man with an equally thunderous expression. I smile and venture a gentle 'Hi' and they both immediately perk up, clearly happy to have someone else to talk to. They are Fi and Tyrone, a New Zealand couple spending a year in London earning 'obscene amounts of money' in banking. They live in a three bedroom flat with only four other people which is something of a record. Most people they know—Aussies and Kiwis doing their 'OS year'—live three or four to a room, with a couple of extras on the landing or in the hallway. It's the only way they can afford the rent.

'Do you know they still have meters,' says Fi, 'for the electricity. You have to stockpile fifty p's and scramble in the dark every time the lights go out. And they don't have showers. If you're lucky they might have a rotten rubber hose that doesn't quite fit on the taps and squirts water up the walls. And even when there is a shower, the water pressure is so crap it's like standing underneath a dripping tap. And it's really filthy, you know, the city—if you blow your nose after you've been on the tube it comes out black. Bloody great place, though. Love it don't we darling?'

'We do, my dear. Bloody great place.'

We order more tea and I think about whether I could ever live in London again. I miss it, I really do—the diversity of the people, the theatre, the history, most of all, the friends I grew up with. But there's something about Melbourne that's so *easy*, so *comfortable*, and something about London that's so not.

'Have you met Bri and James?' asks Fi. 'We're all having dinner on the beach tonight if you'd like to join us.'

'Sure.'

'We're next door. We'll call for you.'

We grab our tea and find a shady spot under the trees. A man appears with a shopping basket full of old paperbacks and we buy Bill Bryson's *Neither Here Nor There* and a Ruth Rendell mystery. 'Let's not go anywhere for a while eh?' I say. 'No dramas, no adventures, just a bit of peace and quiet. What do you think?'

I look over to Sarah's hammock, but she hasn't heard me. She is miles away already—wandering around Kingsmarkham with Inspector Wexford.

As the sun comes down, I finish my chapter and head over to the ablutions block. I take a long, slow shower, enjoying the extravagance of fresh water and, as I head back to our room, I fantasise about dinner— we are promised fish prepared on an open fire with rice and a tomato and onion sauce.

Through the walls of our box I can hear Fi and Tyrone in mid argument. 'For God's sake, Tyrone, will you grow up—you're behaving like a spoilt child.'

'Oh well that's choice coming from little Miss-I-always-get-my-way Fiona.'

'Let's just drop it, shall we, and try to enjoy the evening.'

'*Fine.*'

'*Fine.*'

We hover outside their door and knock tentatively. 'Hi. How's it going?'

'Hi. Good. Yeah. Me and Fi were just sorting something out, but we're cool now aren't we darling?'

'Yeah. We're fine. Really. Aren't we honey?'

We amble down to the beach, Fi and Tyrone making a remarkable recovery, chatting and holding hands by the time we reach our group.

David, our cook, hovers over a small pit in the sand, guarding two saucepans and a whole *chambo* balanced precariously on three pieces of driftwood. 'Good evening,' he says, 'welcome to the beach.' The food smells fantastic and looks close to done. 'Evening,' I say. 'Smells great.' He gestures for us to sit, and we squat down by the fire and twist open four cold beers.

James is lying on the sand, looking ragged and gaunt, but a little more cheerful than this afternoon. ''Ow's your 'ed?' I ask.

'Still thumpin', but it's gettin' betta.'

'So you heading home?'

'Back to London soon as I'm fit. Gotta get ready for the surfin' season.' James is short and pale—not in the least bit muscley, or blond, or tanned—and has a rough crew cut more reminiscent of a skinhead than a surfie.

'Popular is it these days, surfing in England? Long season?'

He smiles. 'You takin' the piss? You've been in Oz too long. As a matta of fact it's very popular. All them Aussie soaps, you see.'

Brian arrives, guitar in hand, and settles down between us. He's been here a month, funding his trip through a little dope-dealing at home. It works out cheaper to live here for a year, he reckons, than to stay in Glasgow. 'It's a good place Glasga', but it's 'ard and ya gotta be 'ard to survive. I know fellas who are banged up and they think it's greet, 'cos it proves how 'ard they are. Fuckin' stupid if y'ask me. I'd rather be 'ere. You dinna wanna always be 'ard di ya?' And, as if to prove his point, he picks out the tune to 'Stairway to Heaven' and makes us all sing.

We are joined by an American couple who are not staying in the hot boxes—they are thirty years older than everybody else and three thousand times richer. Terry is a consultant engineer, and Alexandra a financial adviser who works with senior executives in Washington. They collect art, antiques and countries—they are aiming to become members of the 'Century Club', an organisation for people who have travelled to over a hundred countries.

They've been all over the world. They have *even* visited Australia, they explain, *and* they walked down Oxford Street, *by themselves!* 'We were warned, of course,' says Alexandra, 'but thought we'd risk it anyway.'

I think about lively, innocuous Oxford Street—shops, traffic—not especially renowned for its gangs or muggers. They are from DC after all.

'Warned about *what?*' I ask

'You know...*the gays*...that we might be approached.'

I splutter into my beer and try to avoid Sarah's gaze. Oh in your dreams, darlin'.

'Really...that's very...interesting,' I say, 'and how long have you been in Malawi?'

As the sky darkens, I lie back on the sand watching the stars emerge, and listening to the easy hum of conversation. It is warm and soporific—the waves of the lake breaking gently on the shore—and I persuade myself that the water here is reed-free, and flowing fast enough to risk a nighttime swim.

As I contemplate a dip, David announces that dinner is ready, and I abandon the idea until later. He slices into the *chambo*, cutting a thick wedge of the delicate white flesh, sliding it onto a plate and passing it around the circle. We pile on the rice and cover it in sauce—it is hot, fragrant and tastes divine.

We send Tyrone off to the bar for more beer and everyone shuffles around the circle, Terry and Alexandra making a bee-line for Sarah and I. We chat about travel, art, the States and we try, in the nicest possible way, to come out, but despite frequent references to 'partners' and 'girlfriends,' repeated use of endearments, and random acts of physical affection, they fail to twig.

They head off pretty soon after dinner, shaking hands with everyone and giving David a huge tip. 'We really enjoyed talking with you,' says Alexandra. 'It's swell you girls are travelling together—you seem like such *great friends*.'

'Er...yup. Really...great friends.'

She slips me her business card and holds my hand in her hers. 'We would sure love you girls to come visit and spend a weekend on our yacht.'

Ah...a whole weekend...yes...on a yacht... 'That would be lovely. Thank you.'

'You're welcome *anytime* girls.'

We shuffle closer to the fire and Brian quietly picks out 'House of the Rising Sun', while Fi continues her favourite topic. 'They actually sit on the beach *in the rain*, I'm not kidding. And sometimes, if it really starts to pour, they get out an umbrella and sit underneath it. I say "beach" but there's not a grain of sand in sight. It's all just stones, you know, and when the sun does come out—maybe for five minutes if you're lucky—everyone gets excited, pops the umbrella away and spreads their towels on the rocks, adjusting the pebbles to make them a bit more comfy. Truly.'

I smile to myself and think back to childhood trips with my Mum to the south coast. Did we really do that? *And* think it was completely normal?

In the morning, Iwa is on the beach as promised with a billy full of batter, an orange, and a little bundle of sugar wrapped in paper. He leans over two skinny smouldering sticks fanning the flames with a piece of cardboard. 'Good morning,' he says.

'Good morning, Iwa.'

We sit on the sand beside him as he pours the mixture into a frying pan and shakes it over the fire. He is eleven, he tells us, and will soon finish primary school. He would like to go to secondary school, but it is very expensive, about 6000 kwacha (US$400) a year, and his family makes only a little money from fishing. He is charging us 75 kwacha (US$5) for our pancakes, and I suspect he must pay at least a dollar for the ingredients. 'It will take you a long time to save,' I say.

'Yes,' he replies. 'You must tell your friends to have pancakes also.'

He slides the pancake onto a plate, sprinkling it with sugar and orange juice and wrapping it around a banana. 'You make great pancakes Iwa,' I say. 'We will tell all our friends.'

We retire to the hammocks with our tea, swapping books and settling in for the day. Around noon, Sarah sends me off to the bar to find a little something for lunch and I return with ice cold orange juice and sausage sandwiches.

'I asked Patrick for a drink of water Doll, but he said there isn't any. Hasn't been any for days.'

'Oh…where do they get the water for our tea?'

'I don't know Doll. *Where do you think?*'

'Oh…And what about showers? Have we been…washing in it as well?'

'Washing in it. Drinking it. Eating off plates washed in it. Cleaning our teeth with it.'

'But…what about the bilharzia?'

'I don't know, Doll. Perhaps they get knocked out by the teabags, or maybe they choke on the toothpaste. Whatever. Either it's safe or we're already fucked, so it doesn't matter. I'm going for a swim. Coming?'

We have booked a cheap, three day 'island hopping' kayak trip— gentle, low key, no chance of vehicle breakdown or close encounters with death. Though neither of us has much kayaking experience, the waters of Lake Malawi are still and calm and the islands do not look terribly far off. The distances are small and the weather reliably good.

Sarah, of course, takes national pride in being able to handle any small watercraft—it is, after all, what Canadians *do*.

Really, what can go wrong?

Our guide, Samuel, runs through the basics on dry land: how to hold the paddle, when to use the rudder and what to do if we capsize. He demonstrates how to effect a safe entry—without putting our feet through the fibreglass, or tipping ourselves into the lake. He grabs the edges of the kayak and in a swift easy movement slides one leg in, then the other, and plonks himself neatly on the seat.

Sarah and I attempt to emulate Samuel's effortless action, and though our entries are not quite as smooth—both involve just a *little* hopping—he nods, and we are allowed to drag our kayak onto the lake.

We wade out until the water is up to our knees and spin the kayak so it's pointing at the island. Sarah leans over it, placing a hand on either side of the rim as instructed, and lifts her leg. Unlike the dry run however, on a flat unmoving surface the kayak wobbles, making the entry rather tricky. And, as it tips, little waterfalls cascade onto the seat and form a river in the bottom of the boat.

She straightens up, pauses a moment and approaches the kayak again, gripping the edges and attempting to steady it before resuming her entry. She balances on her right leg, shuffling a bit to adjust her position, then lifts her left leg and pops her foot over the rim. As she stands—one leg in, one leg out—hugging the kayak, it slowly starts to slip away, and she hops, once…twice…three times, chasing it down the lake.

'You OK Doll?' I shout after her.

'*Fine! Thank you.*'

She bounces along the shoreline, attempting to edge her thigh further over the rim, and get at least one buttock onto the seat. Each time she manages to catch up and pull the boat close—and is about to launch herself—it slides away, drifting down the lake towards Mozambique, Sarah hopping frantically after it. I watch from a distance, not totally confident that any offer of assistance from me at this stage will be well received.

With her left leg still dangling over the seat, she seizes the boat with both hands and drags it to her chest. Slowly, it begins to spin, turning towards the islands, then the shore and around again. She hops backwards, bobbing up and down in a tight little circle, desperately struggling to stay upright.

With the kayak still on the move, she makes a decisive lunge, launching herself into the air in the hope that some part of her will end up in the right place. She performs a desperate kind of Frosby flop, landing heavily on the seat and balancing for one hopeful second until the boat tips to a forty-five degree angle, and she slides head-first into the lake.

'Don't. Even. Think. About. It.' She says, emerging from beneath the boat and squeezing the water from her ponytail.

'Not a word, Doll.'

She splashes after the kayak and drags it back, and I fix what I hope is a supportive expression on my face as she prepares for a second assault.

'Sweetheart…can I…? Perhaps I…'

'…Why don't you just look the other way and admire the pretty view.'

'Sure. Yup.'

I turn away, trying to occupy myself with something else, though it's a little difficult when I'm standing in the middle of a lake completely surrounded by water and can hear everything that's going on behind me. There's a muttering, a little more splashing, some swearing, and finally a heavy thump, as Sarah's bottom hits the seat.

'Well done Doll,' I say. 'You did…'

'…Stop there. Just get in.'

I grab my paddle and drop easily into the front seat. 'OK. Let's go.'

We point ourselves towards Mumbo Island some ten kilometres away. Samuel, in a two-person kayak loaded with all our gear, gives the thumbs up and we head off.

Paddling is also somewhat more tricky than on dry land—every time I lift my oar the water flows down its handle, along my arm and onto my T-shirt. When I lower it, the water splashes across my lap and down my legs. Within minutes I am soaked and an inch of water is sploshing around my feet. Sarah is squelching and grunting behind me—I suspect, experiencing similar difficulties.

We attempt to minimise the flow of water into the kayak and propel ourselves forward in a vaguely straight line, though we tack the first kilometre out of the bay. As the mainland disappears and we head into open water, the waves become choppy, and our little boat is tossed from side to side, more water splashing over the bow and into our laps.

The still, calm Lake Malawi has somehow metamorphosed into a wintry Atlantic, and the island—that only looked a hop and a skip away from the shore—is now a distant speck on the horizon.

Sarah is having a few problems with the rudder and we alternate direction with each stroke. 'Doll. You're sending us all over the place.'

'*Babe!* Just paddle and let me worry about where we're going.'

'Well there's not a lot of point my paddling if we're heading for the middle of nowhere, *is there?*'

'Jac! If you paddled consistently we wouldn't be heading for the middle of nowhere.'

Samuel is way ahead, pausing every now and again to check we are OK. Though we have only been paddling a few k's my back is aching and my arms are beginning to tire. I can see the island ahead clearly enough, but it isn't getting any bigger, and we are still zig-zagging wildy.

'For God's sake Sarah. Are we going to meander the whole way there? I feel like we're on the bloody Mississippi.'

'The reason we're meandering all over the place is that you can't string together half a dozen decent strokes.'

'Oh for *Christ's sake* Sarah. You're being ridiculous.'

'*Fine.* Paddle your fucking self to the island.'

Sarah hauls her oar out of the water and drops it across her lap. I stop, leaving my paddle dragging through the lake, as our kayak spins around the open water like a compass needle.

'Sarah, what are you doing?'

'I'm being ridiculous.'

'Doll. Please. We need to…cooperate here…otherwise we're going to drown.'

'Well. I will resume paddling as long as you make no further comment on my steering, and as long as you cease paddling intermittently.'

'OK. Agreed.'

It's a long, silent paddle to the island where we arrive soaked and exhausted. The mainland, at least, looks a gratifyingly long way off, though I remind myself we have to 'hop' back there in two days, after our other 'hop' tomorrow.

We are greeted by Francis—keeper of the camp—who hauls our kayaks onto the beach and grabs our packs. We follow him along the shore, across a shallow inlet where the warm water laps our ankles. He leads us up a rough track buried by trees, and we emerge into a clearing on a high promontory, the lake splashing the rocks below on all three sides.

The camp is a glossy-travel-magazine-definitely-not-for-riffraff-budget-travellers type camp, and we pause behind Francis wondering if someone has made a terrible mistake. A large bamboo structure houses two long wooden tables, with alternating cream and green director's chairs arranged neatly around them. Wicker arm chairs with deep cushions circle a bamboo coffee table, and patterned rush mats in complimentary colours cover the baked earth floor. A bookcase—with a couple of shelves of recent paperbacks—sits arm's length from a bamboo *chaise-longue*.

Behind the dining area there is a long low bar, an urn at one end with mugs and jars of tea and coffee, and a terracotta water cooler at the other. A low wicker table is covered with up-market nature magazines, and African field guides. The whole camp is beautifully light and airy, a gentle breeze rustling through the trees, a series of bamboo blinds providing protection from the sun.

Francis gestures for us to sit, pours two long glasses of fresh fruit juice and potters about the kitchen. He is separated from us by a low bamboo wall hung with carved cooking utensils, frying pans and pots. Clay jars are arranged neatly on shelves and the foodstuff packed in two large wooden chests. He carefully balances a pot of water over some hot coals, and lays the table with napkins and polished glasses and cutlery. We look onto the grove of trees that edge the camp—hammocks strung at intervals—and sip our juice. 'Nice place,' I say.

When we have finished our drinks, Francis escorts us around the camp along a series of neat gravel paths, dozens of tiny rainbow lizards darting across our feet. A bamboo bathroom is hidden amongst the trees—a clean toilet with a wooden wash basin, and a towel rack, paper holder and soap dish, all in bamboo. A large metal bucket with a tap and shower head attached is suspended overhead, and a window cut into the wall at eye level provides a perfect view of the lake while you shower. 'When you are ready,' says Francis, 'just let me know and I will prepare hot water for you.'

Our tent is in its own private clearing away from the main camp, a small awning out front providing shade to a beautifully carved chief's chair. Inside, there are two single futons with fresh sheets and pillowcases and a lightweight duvet. There is mesh on either side and the canvas is rolled back to allow the breeze to drift through. 'If there's anything you need,' says Francis, 'just let me know. When you've unpacked, lunch will be ready.'

We shove our bags in the end of the tent and lie back on the futons.

'Wow!' I say.

'Wow!' says Sarah.

Francis places a pot of tea, cups and saucers, fresh milk and sugar on the table in front of us, and a large bowl of salad comprising ingredients not seen since our Turtle Bay extravaganza a couple of months before: lettuce, cucumber, capsicum, as well as tomato and avocado, all tossed in a light vinaigrette. The main course is a fresh, tasty homemade macaroni cheese, sprinkled with freshly ground black pepper. There is enough to feed four people, but Francis and Samuel eat separately and, as there appears to be no one else on our island, we eat the lot. 'Is anyone arriving later?' I ask.

'You are here alone tonight.'

God. Can't wait for dinner then.

After a rummage through the bookcase and a swing in the hammocks,

Francis asks whether we might enjoy a guided paddle around the island. Sarah and I exchange looks. Neither of us is keen to disturb this very pleasant peace, but we do have to paddle together again and maybe this would be a good opportunity to practise. 'How about we change places in the kayak and try to be more patient?' I suggest.

'OK.'

'That'd be great Francis. Thanks.'

We walk down to the water's edge, slip into the kayak with relative ease, and head west along the shoreline. The wind has settled and, away from the open water, paddling is less strenuous, though we still can't quite master the straight line thing. 'Jac, Sweetheart. We're sort of…meandering a little bit…you need to use the rudder…'

'Thanks Honey. I think I've got it. If you just paddle, my love.'

I jiggle the rudder with my feet, trying to keep us away from the shore and a long line of overhanging branches, but the kayak is unco-operative, and we head straight for a shallow bank and come to a slow, gentle stop. 'Bugger,' I say.

'Bit trickier than it looks that steering thing isn't it, Babe?'

I attempt to push us off using my paddle like a gondolier's pole, but as I poke the blade into the sand, the front of the kayak swings around and wedges itself further up the bank. Sarah tries to dislodge us from the front, but her paddle sinks into the mud and we remain perched on the bank at a forty-five degree angle, unable to move forward or back.

'Hmm…what now?'

I throw myself repeatedly against the side of the kayak, trying to use my weight to dislodge it, but succeed only in cracking my hip against the fibreglass.

'Perhaps if we push together, Doll. After three…'

We lean against our paddles in unison and gently slide away from the bank into the deeper water. As we spin around, the nose of the kayak disappears into a patch of snail covered reeds, and a few billion bilharzia are treated to lunch.

I attempt to back out and in so doing am almost decapitated by an overhanging branch that catches underneath my chin. As I duck and shove it aside it whips across my arm leaving a bright red weal. 'Ouch! For Christ's sake. This shouldn't be so difficult!'

'Patience, remember, Sweet one,' says Sarah. 'Patience.'

We extricate ourselves from the reeds and I manage to put some distance between us and the shore. We follow Francis around to the end of the island, gradually developing some rudder control and paddling synchronicity. We manage, eventually, to proceed in a vaguely straight line.

Huge high crags alive with seagulls and lizards rise from the water, and giant monitors cling spread-eagled to the rock. There are literally thousands of cormorants, all sitting upright and facing the wind, their gullets wobbling like full sails in a breeze.

Francis drops a fishing line over his kayak and hooks three fish in as many minutes. 'Look,' he says, pointing skyward. 'The eagle, you see him?' A huge, white crested fish eagle perches on top of the trees, his head jerking rapidly from side to side. 'Watch.'

He grabs a fish and throws it into the water a couple of metres from our kayak. The eagle launches from the tree, spreading his huge wings and swooping down in a smooth controlled dive. He glides in a huge wide arc, gradually veering towards us, his wings fixed and perfectly still. As he approaches I feel a rush of air on my face, can see the pattern of his feathers and his dark, beady pupils. Not three metres from us, he grabs the fish in his talons like a magnet, swerves around and shoots back up to the crag.

The whole performance lasts only a few seconds and we are awe-struck, Francis clearly delighting in our enjoyment. As he grabs another fish, I scramble for the camera anticipating photographs of *National Geographic* proportions. I ask Francis to hold off a minute while I focus on the eagle and prepare to pan the shot—I've seen how they do it on the telly. 'OK. I'm ready,' I say. 'Let's get him.'

He throws another fish and instantly the eagle launches off his branch, spreads his wings and swoops down towards us. I hold him in the frame for…a second…two, but as soon as he swerves toward the water, he drops out of my picture and I'm focussing on a lichen-covered crag.

'Did you get him?' shouts Sarah.

'Er…almost, but not quite…Next time.'

Francis prepares another and this time I am ready. As the eagle leaves his perch I follow the arc of his dive, anticipating his direction and holding him in the frame for a good…two milli-seconds. As soon as he disappears, I glance over the top of the camera, check where he is and re-focus, but the whole show is over before I can hit the shutter button. The eagle is safely home with his catch and I have three shots of the lichened crag.

While Francis paddles off to catch more, Sarah and I discuss the finer points of wildlife photography. How can you pan the damn thing when it goes so bloody fast and swerves all over the place? Should we focus on the fish rather than the eagle and just snap when it comes into frame? How can you zoom in, focus and compose all at the same time? And how the hell do you do all this from a very wobbly kayak?

'How about continual shutter release?' suggests Sarah. 'Isn't that what proper photographers do?'

'Yes! Excellent idea.' I reset the camera enabling me to snap a whole series of shots in quick succession, and when Francis returns, lock on the eagle once again.

He tosses in another fish and the eagle drops from his perch and swoops down. As soon as he leaves the tree and I hit the button, there is a repeated clicking and whirring as the camera eats up film. I cannot say for sure, of course, until I see them, but I think I have six shots of sky, three of the water and maybe one of a talon in the top left-hand corner of the frame.

Francis grabs his last fish and we decide to try a different approach. I will stay clear of the eagle altogether and focus on the fish, while Sarah provides a running commentary. She will tell me as soon as the eagle is about to come into frame, and I will immediately press the shutter button. This way we should we should capture eagle, fish, talons and all.

I brace my elbow against my knee, frame the fish and re-check the focus. 'OK. I'm ready. Let's go.' Francis throws the fish and Sarah watches the eagle. 'OK...he's leaving the branch now...picking up speed...swerving...looks like he's coming in from your right...getting closer...CLOSER...CLOSER. NOW! NOW! NOW!'

I hit the button in a flurry of panic, the camera whirring through four, eight, ten shots.

'DID YOU GET IT, DOLL? DID YOU GET IT?'

'Er...yeah...bloody brilliant...talons and everything...Or...I don't know...maybe...maybe not the talons...and maybe...not the eagle either...but definitely the fish. Yup...the fish...the dead fish...bobbing about in the water.'

We spend the rest of the day dozing in the hammocks, sipping ice-cold beer and watching the sun set over the lake. Samuel lights half a dozen kerosene lanterns and hangs them along a path from the dining area to our tent.

As darkness falls we are summoned to the table, to a row of warm terracotta pots lit by candlelight. Wafts of fragrant steam circulate as Francis removes the lids and invites us to begin. The food is overwhelming: light fluffy rice, a spicy, delicately flavoured catfish stew, steamed carrots and green beans coated in butter, tiny individual roast potatoes and a green salad—all in vast quantities. It would be an excellent meal anywhere, but prepared completely over charcoal, in a bamboo kitchen, it is quite incredible. 'Francis, this is just superb,' I say. 'Thank you.'

After dinner Samuel and Francis clean up and then disappear to their shelter on the beach. Sarah and I finish our coffees, swing in the hammocks, flick though the magazines, and finally, stroll down the path of lanterns to our tent. We have the whole camp to ourselves and I feel like we're in the best cubby house in the world and our parents have left us unsupervised for the night.

For the first time in weeks I feel physically comfortable: clean, satiated, my skin relieved of its worst mosquito bites, and for once, I can lie in a tent without feeling hot or itchy or irritated. A strong breeze drifts through the flyscreen and I stretch out on the futon, my body glowing from the sun and exercise of the day. Through one side of the mesh I can see the half moon, and through the other, the lanterns around the bar which, without my glasses, look like the Southern Cross. Sarah is asleep in minutes, but I lie awake listening to the water and the wind in the trees. A storm is picking up a few kilometres away and lightning flashes across the canvas. I pull the duvet up around my shoulders and drift into a gentle easy sleep.

I awake sparkly and refreshed and crawl under Sarah's duvet to say good morning. 'Oh my God!' she says. 'What *do* you look like?'

'Not quite the response I was looking for, my love.'

'No, sorry. I mean your eye. It's all swollen.'

'Oh…Feels OK.'

'Hmm…maybe it got whacked yesterday when you were caught in the trees.'

'Don't think so.'

'Well. I'll keep an eye on it today.'

Francis and Samuel have prepared another remarkable meal: tropical fruit salad, a huge jug of just squeezed juice, poached eggs and fried tomatoes, and a loaf of freshly baked bread with butter. We eat to the sound of thunder and rain which, although comforting last night, has a rather different effect this morning. We are neither of us terribly keen on dragging our small and insubstantial bit of fibreglass onto open water and into the eye of a storm.

We linger a while, packing up slowly and hoping it will pass. 'Shouldn't we wait?' I venture to Samuel hopefully.

'No problem. I will stay close. You will be fine.'

We trek down the path to the kayaks, the rain drifting across the lake in sheets. The boats fill as quickly as we can bail them out, and we abandon our sponges and plonk ourselves on the soaked seats. Samuel pushes us out from the shore, the shallow waters immediately around the island, at least, only mildly churned up.

As we enter open water, the waves become high and choppy and, despite our newly developed synchronised paddling, we are tossed all over, the boat tipping and spinning wildly. Great anvil thunder clouds billow on the horizon, and a sea of white-caps dance around us. Samuel hovers close, and we paddle frenetically, struggling to stay upright.

As the sky blackens, the rain pelts down filling the kayak with water, and we alternate bailing and paddling. 'You OK, Doll?' I shout, though all I can hear is rain, and all I can see through my glasses is blur. My neck and shoulders are aching, my arms twitchy and weak, and my eye is beginning to feel very peculiar. We paddle together, somehow finding a rhythm, and haul ourselves through the storm.

Gradually, the rain shift towards the mainland, the wind drops and the waves subside. The last twenty minutes are exhausting, but the sky begins to brighten, and we can bail out without instantly filling up. We arrive at the island soaked and shaky, crawl out of the kayak and follow Samuel up the beach.

The camp is smaller and a little less plush than Mumbo, but beautifully secluded and, once again, we are here by ourselves. Jacob, our new cook, serves a light pasta lunch and we settle around the dining table where we remain for the rest of the day.

By evening my eye is huge, an angry rash covering the skin between my eyebrow and eye lid. I dab at the red raw flesh with some cotton wool and warm water, and Sarah administers some antiseptic cream. Samuel and Jacob take a good look, but it's not like anything they've seen before—and it's certainly not a whack from a branch.

I have a restless night, waking repeatedly to wipe the gunk seeping down my cheek, and in the morning my eye is sealed shut. However hard I try, I can no longer open it. The rash has turned yellow, a crusty scab covering a thick layer of creamy pus, and the left side of my face is red and swollen. It doesn't feel particularly *painful*, but is horribly uncomfortable, and just a little worrying.

We pack up as quickly as we can and paddle back to Cape Maclear, the sun shining, the water calmer, and the paddling easier than it's been for days. We are greeted by a welcoming party of James, Brian, Fi and Tyrone, who stare gobsmacked at my eye. 'Oh my God,' says Fi. 'What on earth happened to you?'

'I'm not quite sure,' I say, 'but I think I should probably find a doctor.'

There are no doctors in Cape Maclear, or anywhere in the surrounding area, and we have no choice but to stay the night and head to Blantyre, the nearest major city, in the morning.

We spend our final night barbecuing on the beach. James is fully recovered from malaria and is heading home to search for the perfect wave off Land's End. Brian has made a deal with the hostel owner and is running the bar and kitchen in return for free meals. Tyrone has done a scuba course while Fi wrote letters home, and they are friends again.

In the morning, we hitch a ride to the main road and take the 'M1'— straight and sealed—to Blantyre, where a brisk German doctor examines my eye. 'Spider bite,' she says. 'Probably when you were asleep in the tent.' She prescribes cream and antihistamines and promises it will clear up in a few days.

We are fourteen weeks into our trip and it looks like things might get a little easier as we enter southern Africa. The break in Cape Maclear has been good, a chance to recuperate, renew our energy. Malawi, it seems, is a dividing line between some of the poorest parts of the east, and the relatively more affluent south. Quite frankly I'm done with being rugged, and am looking forward to the civilised delights of Harare. I can live without collapsible roads, starvation diets, death in close proximity, worms in my water and spiders that bite in the night.

CHAPTER 15

FOREVER ENGLAND

ARRIVING IN HARARE is like hitting downtown London or New York—thousands of people march up and down the pavement and bumper to bumper cars spew exhaust, their drivers tooting repeatedly. Glass fronted department stores display fancy clothes on mannequins, and fast food outlets advertise burgers and fries. Fresh fruit and vegetables are spread out on the street—oranges and plums, tomatoes and apples—and stalls piled high with fresh bread rolls. Rows of shops sell everything you can imagine: cassette players, stationery, blankets, pots and pans, school uniforms, jewellery and baseball caps.

We walk back and forth over a pedestrian crossing, just because we can, and pause outside a cinema showing a recently released mainstream movie. I check out a western-style hairdresser where a bouffant woman asks me whether I normally have 'number one' or 'number two?' Do I prefer wax or fudge? We drop into Cleopatra's Hydrobath Beauty Salon and Nail Bar where Sarah buys moisturiser, and gets her legs waxed. Afterwards, we take tea and scones at the beautiful Meikles Hotel and, for the first time in Africa, feel underdressed.

We check e-mail and post-restante and phone Maria and Jacki in Melbourne. They are manically preparing for their departure and working ridiculous hours to free themselves for their trip. They have some final purchases to make to complete their safari wardrobe, and we remind them, again, that we'll leave them at the airport if there is even a hint of khaki four-pocket shirts, long socks or pith helmets.

It's a week until they arrive and we've hired a car and planned a trip to the Eastern Highlands on Zimbabwe's beautiful sealed roads. But, we have a slight problem.

Sarah is the driver in this relationship. I managed very well in London as a non-driver, as many people do, and only learnt when I came to Australia. Without dredging up the sordid details, it's fair to say I experienced some difficulty acquiring my licence. Not because I couldn't drive, you understand, but because every time I sat the test, my left leg would shake so badly, my foot bounced like a jack hammer, which made controlling the clutch rather tricky. I even saw a doctor who prescribed beta-blockers to suppress the adrenaline, but they didn't work. My instructor, of twenty years' experience, said he'd seen people pretty shaky before, but never anything quite like this.

After a number of attempts I transferred to an automatic and passed with flying colours. Now, though, whenever I get close to a manual, it's as if my leg *remembers*, and out of some perverse instinct, returns to its former uncontrollable state. Sarah, although a competent and experienced driver, has never driven a manual.

The nice young man at the car rental company demonstrates the features of our Mazda 232 and I settle in and wait for him to leave. I shift my seat back and forth, adjust the rear-view mirror, and fiddle with the buttons on the dash. He stands at the door of the office, arms folded across his chest, watching—maybe it's part of the service to see us safely out of the car park.

I start the engine, press my foot on the clutch, and shift into reverse. The rental guy leans back against the wall, one foot casually crossing the other. He smiles, waves and…waits. Sarah stares straight ahead, pretending she's not sitting right here beside me.

I push gently down on the accelerator and start to lift my left foot from the clutch. The tell-tale twitching begins; a definite wobble in my foot which spreads up through my ankle to my calf and out to my thigh, like a ripple of water spreading across a pond.

I pause, take a deep breath, and gently stroke my leg, willing it to be still.

Slowly, I ease out the clutch, twisting in my seat, my head turned towards the back window. The car remains absolutely still, but my heel starts to bob up and down, gently at first, then more quickly, until my foot is bouncing on and off the pedal and the whole left side of my body is jiggling violently.

There is a faint snicker from my left.

'Don't even think about it,' I say.

I shove the clutch in roughly, leaning back in my seat and straightening my leg. When my foot's against the floor I'm OK, but the minute I lift it, I'm done for.

I massage my thigh and calf and tell myself it's all in my head—it's complete mind over matter. This is *not* a difficult thing.

Sarah shuffles in her seat and gives me a weak, encouraging smile.

'It's *not* funny, Sarah, so please don't grin at me in that childish fashion. *I'm* trying to get us out of here!'

I gently release the clutch again, my foot springing into the air—sometimes landing on the pedal as it descends, sometimes not—my knee repeatedly knocking the steering wheel. I am utterly unable to control it, but unless I can engage the gears, we are stuck in Harare for a week. I lift my leg, hit the accelerator and hope for the best. We bounce, once…twice…three times out of the parking lot and lurch onto the main road.

Once I am driving and can take my foot off the clutch, the shaking abates and I am able to shift though the gears with more confidence. It is a five-minute drive to our hotel and we make it back with only two sudden stops, three blasts on the horn from our fellow commuters, and one threatening gesture from a man in a BMW.

I step out of the car, stretching my legs, and wander around to the passenger side. Sarah slips into the driver's seat and places a tentative hand on the gear stick. 'OK,' I say. 'It's all about balancing the clutch and the accelerator—too many revs and we'll shoot forward, not enough and you'll stall.' Sarah looks at me with raised eyebrows.

'I'm fine on the theory.'

Sarah depresses the clutch—her leg perfectly controlled—whacks down the accelerator and we bunny hop away from the hotel, bouncing along the quiet back street. We practise turning, reversing, parking, and all the tricky slow stuff. Sarah, like me, is great once we're out of first gear, but those early manoeuvres are still not terribly smooth. We agree that I will attempt to drive out of Harare and onto the highway, and Sarah will take over from there.

We check out of the hotel, booking a room for our return, and one for Maria and Jacki. Sarah sits with the map across her lap trying to work out a route, while I start the engine and deal with the leg thing.

'OK,' she says. 'Up to the end of the road, right, then left, then straight over the roundabout.'

'You sure Doll?'

'Jac!'

'I'm only asking.'

It takes a little while to find the A14 to Rusape and the Highlands and, *en route*, we enjoy a tour of the local prison, take a short drive up a one way street—courtesy of Sarah's left/right problem—and check out a number of Harare's outer suburbs.

'OK,' says Sarah. 'So it's not my best thing.'

Away from the city, the scenery is very familiar: tall gum trees line both sides of the road—you can even smell the eucalyptus—and thin bushy scrub sprouts through the dry red dirt. Pine plantations form sharp lines across the hillsides, and sawmills dot the slopes. We even pass a semi-circular sign, divided into sections with a movable arrow, indicating the day's fire risk.

We are heading for Nyanga National Park, the former home of Cecil Rhodes who, upon deciding it was the most beautiful place in Africa, bought it—or at least, a hundred acres of it. Rhodes was sent here from England in 1870 by his father, hoping the climate might improve his son's poor health. In less than twenty years, Rhodes had founded De Beer's Diamonds and established the British South Africa Company with support from Queen Victoria. A royal charter granted him enormous power to pass laws, make treaties, engage in trade, and even maintain a police force.

Rhodes was the quintessential colonialist—not content with merely amassing a huge personal fortune, he wanted to extend British 'civilisation' throughout the continent, envisaging a sphere of influence, and a railway from Cape Town to Cairo. The area north of the Limpopo River, where he aimed to expand, was Matebeleland, controlled by the powerful Ndebele chief, Lobengula. In 1888, Rhodes tricked Lobengula into signing the Rudd Concession, a deliberately mistranslated document that gave the British mining rights to tribal land in return for rifles and money. Despite the Concession there were continued skirmishes between Ndebele warriors and Rhodes' private armies. The Ndebele were eventually defeated, and Lobengula died of smallpox, a disease introduced by the British.

The next ten years saw a consolidation of white control throughout the region, the blacks forced to settle on marginal, tsetse-fly infested land discarded by the British, or become indentured workers on white-owned farms. Europeans flocked to the country, spurred by stories of instant wealth from gold, diamonds and land.

By 1922 'Rhodesia' had become a self-governing colony, the white population maintaining almost exclusive control of farms and factories. *The Land Apportionment Act* in 1930 enshrined this control in law, excluding blacks from owning any of the country's farmable land. Other laws followed in 1934 that kept them out of the professions and skilled trades, and strictly controlled where they could live. Rhodesia's *Apartheid* was firmly in place.

Most of the good farmland is still in control of the whites and there is a strong push for some of it, at least, to be returned. The government has issued a list of farms targeted for redistribution, but many people, both black and white, are worried. Lands previously taken by the long-standing President Mugabe have ended up in the hands of his friends and family, or abandoned—valuable crops left to rot. If the farms are taken, there is no guarantee the land will end up in the control of the people who actually need it.

Most of the white-owned farms are hi-tech commercial concerns producing export crops that are the mainstay of an increasingly ailing economy—breaking them up will bring its own problems. But, the land was stolen, and black workers are paid subsistence wages while the white owners reap huge profits. Something clearly needs to change—a redistribution that recognises both the value of the farms to the economy, and the needs of poor blacks who originally owned the land. Given the endemic corruption, this may be hard to achieve.

As we drive further from the city, the trees disappear and the landscape turns from red to grey—from gum trees to barren rocky outcrops. In the sunshine it reminds me of the Grampians—the Australian ones—and when the cloud rolls in, I think of Scotland. As it begins to rain, the thought of camping is all of a sudden less attractive and we find a self-contained lodge which, after the accommodation in Malawi and Tanzania, is luxurious. A clean and functioning toilet and bathroom, a kitchen—with gravy boat and toast rack—beds with fresh sheets, and a lounge with a settee and coffee table. For the first time in weeks we are able to cook, and we eat in front of the open fire.

We are awoken in the morning by the sound of washing up. Our 'attendant' has arrived to clean up after us. He scrapes away the remains of last night's dinner, washes, dries and puts away the crockery, sweeps the floors, lays the fire, removes the rubbish, cleans the toilet, and straightens the lounge. Most of the guests who stay at these lodges are white Zimbabweans or ex-pats here for a spot of golf or trout fishing, and who, I presume, take such services for granted. I, on the other hand, am not used to having a middle-aged black man clean up after me and I stay in bed until he leaves.

Sarah has decided it makes sense to take advantage of our current situation to consolidate her manual driving skills: we have a hire car whose gears we can crunch with impunity, there are only a handful of vehicles on the road, and we're unlikely to bump into the local traffic police. I am more than happy to avoid any recurrence of the leg-bouncing scenario and happily cede the driver's seat. We pull out of the lodge and bounce along the track to the main road, taking a few fast corners into the National Park. The ranger at the entrance smiles as the gear box whirs and clunks and we lurch through the gate.

We head over to the ruins of a 15th century fort, a row of crumbling lookouts still discernible though the aloe plants and msasa trees. There are a number of ancient 'pit structures'—low grassy enclosures surrounded by thatched huts that were used for holding cattle. Though more than four hundred years old, they don't look very different from the villages near by.

We see only two other people all morning: a terribly well-spoken, retired English couple picnicking by Rhodes' Dam. We entertain them with stories of trekking through jungle in search of chimpanzees, of hot nights in Zanzibar, of young women dying on buses. My accent, I note, slips into BBC broadcaster mode, as it occasionally does, my Ts and Hs returning, my glottal stops disappearing. They are charmed, like the American couple in Cape Maclear, and after a quick rummage through her handbag, the wife hands me a card. 'You must come for tea when you're home,' she says. 'We'd love to see you.'

'Well...if we're ever passing through...'

I glance at the address and smile: The Reverend and Mrs. G. H. Walveridge, Brook House, Dorset.

Excellent. Lesbians take tea with the vicar.

Nyanga, just outside the park, could be in Oxfordshire or Kent. A narrow road, bordered by high privet hedges and rhododendrons, leads to a neat village green. Thatched cottages, with names like 'Bonny Doon' and 'Leprechaun', nestle amongst tidy rows of daffodils and bluebells behind iron-lattice gates. By the roadside, a sign points to 'The Village Inn' and a shop, 'Santa's Grotto', where a couple of blue-rinsed old ladies discuss their lace doily purchases. 'Do you think young people still use them?'

'Oh, I think so, for special occasions.'

At the edge of the green there's an ivy clad church, St. Catherine in the Downs, with a Norman arch—copied from an original in Northampton—and a bell, donated by a woman who retrieved it from her husband's boat on its return from Dunkirk. A fallen tree in the churchyard has been hewn into a rough table where the vicar serves tea after the Sunday service. A notice board announces the forth-coming events of the Rotary and Lions Clubs, the Boy Scouts, the Philatelic Society, the Wine Circle and the Women's Institute Choral Club.

Clearly, Rhodes was not the only British person to settle here.

The drive through the Honde Valley that borders Mozambique takes us out of England and back into Africa—banana palms, rows of maize and rich red soil. It is mid-afternoon and uniformed schoolchildren line the road with their thumbs out. We pull over and open the door, with half a dozen kids sprinting towards the car and squeezing onto the backseat. I turn around to six eager, smiling faces. 'Hi, I'm Jacqui. This is my friend Sarah.'

''ello, 'ello,' they chorus.

'Do you speak English?' I ask.

'A little. We learn at school.'

Sarah attempts to pull out, and we lurch and jolt onto the road, the kids laughing and bouncing up and down with the movement of the car. They clamber over each other, poking their heads out of the windows and waving at their friends still walking. There is no public transport in this area and very few vehicles—a ride in a car is clearly a big event.

'Where shall we drop you?' I ask.

They smile and shrug their shoulders, clearly not keen to stop yet.

We drive for a few more minutes, three heads hanging out of each window, a dozen hands waving at anybody on the path. We pass a village, and then another, and I check with the kids.

'Here?' I say. 'This village? Shall we stop here?'

They fall silent and look at me blankly, and I realise this is not a lift at all, it's a *ride*, a fairground attraction. We are actually taking them away from home. Sarah pulls over and they pile out. 'Thank you, ladies,' they say. 'Thank you very much. Have a nice day.'

'You're welcome,' I say. 'You have a nice day too.'

We drive down the northern flank of the valley, the Mtarazi Falls—the highest in Zimbabwe—tumbling over the cliff tops above us, Shona villages littering the floor below. Everything is lush and green, fertile and abundant.

Slowly, we emerge from the valley into an oil painting of gently undulating hills washed in a late afternoon haze. The emerald green bushes of the vast Aberfoyle Tea Estates spread east and west across the horizon, the smooth lines and neat rows of tea as ordered as the English who drink it. A number of roads lead into the plantation and we choose one at random. Sarah has mastered gears two to five, and as long as we don't have to slow down or stop too often, we manage very well.

Our road quickly becomes narrow—bush on one side, and rocks on the other—and then disappears completely. We stop at the end of the track and consider our options. I am mildly concerned about the level of clutch control involved in a tight, three point turn, but I'm not sure reversing up a winding path with jagged rocks and branches at window height on either side is a great idea either. 'Don't worry,' says Sarah. 'I've really got the hang of it now. Honestly.'

She slips into gear and bounces through the first of the three points—a tell-tale tinkling emanating from the front headlight area. 'Oop la!' she says, reversing into the second point, and wedging both back wheels snugly into the ditch by the side of the road.

She revs the engine, trying to drag us out, but the wheels spin and the mud flies and we remain securely fixed. After a number of stalls and re-starts, the engine splutters and dies. 'Bugger,' she says. 'It's stopped.'

'I think you've flooded it, Doll.'

'Oh…Can you do that?'

We half open the doors and squeeze out to check the damage—the front light is smashed, and at the back, there are two dents just above the bumper. 'What now?' I say.

'Maybe we could…like…bounce it out. You know…like they do on the telly?'

'Yeah. Why not? It's worth a try.'

We position ourselves either side of the boot, one foot firmly behind the other and, on the count of three, push down together, leaning as heavily as we can.

There is a barely perceptible shift, a faint compression of the suspension, as if it whispers, 'Dream on girls. You'll have to do better than that.'

We stand up and edge around the back of the car, earnestly examining the wheels, kicking the tyres and nodding to each other with knotted brows.

'Hmm…we could maybe try…jumping on it…like…we both turn around and after three…sort of…you know…throw ourselves onto the boot and kind of…move up and down. It might create a bit more force.'

'Er…OK…Sure. Let's give it a go.'

We lean our backs against the end of the car, our palms flat on the boot, and begin the count. 'One…two…three…jump!'

We land in perfect unison, the boot letting out a loud crack and buckling beneath our weight.

'That's not what happens on the telly.'

'No. I think we need to be men, and there needs to be six of us.'

We haven't passed a village, or seen anyone for at least an hour, and I'm not sure this particular part of the plantation sees much action. Sarah tries the engine again.

Nothing.

We wander around to the back of the car again, lean into the boot and try pushing. We are just not strong enough to shift it.

I try the engine again.

The sun is on its way down and there is not much of the day left. 'We might just have to walk,' suggests Sarah.

'Where to?' I ask.

I sit in the driver's seat and fiddle with the keys. After another five minutes I turn them, and again after ten…after fifteen…and twenty.

Suddenly, after four more tries, the engine kicks over and we haul ourselves out of the ditch and back onto the main track. We head into the plantation and, just as the sun goes down, reach the Aberfoyle Country Club, a narrow, single storey brick building with a tidy garden out front, and a neat parking area painted in white lines.

The décor of the reception is a cheap safari lodge, English bed-and-breakfast mix. Half a dozen lounge chairs, in a bright zebra motif, are arranged around a bongo drum table, with a carved tribal mask lampshade. Jars of local honey are displayed on a blue gingham table-cloth, and yellowing plants spill out of bronze pots onto the parquet flooring. Behind the desk, a glass fronted case of mounted butterflies hangs next to a pastoral watercolour.

There is no one about, and we wander into the dining room with its arresting smell of last night's steak and kidney pie mingled with this morning's stewed prunes and burnt toast. A long trestle table is covered with jars of Heinz Tomato Ketchup, Coleman's Mustard and Lee and Perrin's Worcestershire Sauce. Fifties retro tables are dotted about the room, the tablecloths a mixed motif of traditional Ndebele art work and traditional English ship and anchor.

In a corner, half a dozen brown vinyl chairs are arranged in a semi-circle around a record player and a wire rack of LPs: the Royal Scottish Dragoon Guards Military Band, The Bachelors, Vera Lynn's War-Time Favourites. Above the record player there is an amateurish mural—a guitar, a trombone, and two flamenco dancers—and on the adjacent wall, a flock of painted parrots perched on bamboo branches. In the opposite corner is an upright piano, dog-eared sheet music falling off the stand. 'Maybe we should pop back later,' I say to Sarah. 'I reckon it'll be hopping.'

The manager eventually appears, explaining there are no camping facilities at the County Club, but he will let us erect our tent on the golf course. We follow him across a fairway and around a green to a patch of rough under some trees. 'Here,' he says. 'You may pitch your tent.' Though it's almost dark the ground looks as if it's…shifting. I step closer and squint. There is no wind at all, but the grass is definitely moving…a kind of gentle rippling.

'Urgh!' I scream, stepping back suddenly. The ground is completely covered—*blanketed*—with bright orange termites. 'Termites!' I say.

'No problem,' he says. 'They will move as soon you put down your tent.'

'Well OK then. That's fine isn't it? No problem. I'll just keep my boots on if I need to pop out in the night eh?'

We throw the tent on the ground and start to unpack as the manager heads back to the club. In a few minutes it will be pitch black, and I don't imagine he'll return to check on us. I drag the tent onto the fairway—as far away from the termites as possible—and, though I suspect it's not strictly golfing etiquette, erect it near the twelfth hole.

We return to the club for dinner. We are the only patrons and have packet mushroom soup, steak and onion pie with tinned peas and carrots, apple pie and cream for pudding, followed by cheese and biscuits.

We could be in Bournemouth.

In the morning we arrange to visit the Aberfoyle factory to see how the bright green leaves, that don't look or smell anything like tea, end up small and brown and floating around a teapot. We are met by Walter, the factory manager, who greets us with long enthusiastic handshakes and broad smiles. He has worked at the factory for thirty-four years—starting as a builder, becoming a foreman and then manager. He clearly delights in having guests, and hovers by the factory door like an estate agent about to show off some prime real estate.

The factory is Dickensian: long mechanical conveyor belts operated by oily cogs and pulleys, and a line of heavy, clunky machines that fill the room with firing pistons and rhythmic clangs and gasps. Fires burn in huge glass fronted ovens and the air is thick with floating ash and fine particles of tea that settle over everything like coal dust. The high ceiling lets in little light and the bare concrete floor is stained with oil and grime as old as Walter. There is nothing hi-tech about production here—just the old traditions of a century past.

'This is where the process begins,' says Walter, as a tractor pulls up ladened with huge sacks of freshly picked leaves. The bundles are hoisted on to a large industrial weighing machine, then hooked to an overhead gantry. 'The tea,' he explains, 'has just come in from the fields and must be weighed so the pickers' salaries can be calculated.' They are paid thirty cents a kilo; a good worker can pick up to two hundred kilos a day which we calculate would earn them around twenty US dollars a week. 'Some pickers are lazy,' he says, 'and drop stones in their baskets to try to fool the weighers, and some pick leaves from too far down the stem.' The finest quality tea comes from the two newest leaves at the top of the plant; leaves picked from below will produce a lower quality tea. The factory employs two hundred pickers who, between them, harvest the new crop every eleven days.

'Who owns the factory?' I ask

'It is owned by an Irish company, but leased to a Kenyan.'

'To get around the land redistribution list?'

He smiles. 'I am just the manager,' he says.

Sarah and I duck repeatedly as the bright green bundles swing around the gantry just above our heads like something out of *Charlie and the Chocolate Factory*. The workers, in dark blue overalls and thongs, grab the bundles as they pass and empty the leaves onto long metal tables. 'The first part of the process is withering,' says Walter.

'To dry it?' I ask.

'No! No! Not *drying*, absolutely not. *Withering*,' he replies, waving his finger at me. 'Drying comes *much* later.'

'Oh…Sorry.'

'Withering takes between six to twelve hours, depending on outside air temperatures.' He grabs a stem from the table and holds it in front of us. 'When you can twist the stalk around the leaves without breaking it off, the tea is withered. You see?'

'Yes I see. Absolutely.'

He ushers us into the next room where the withered tea is passed by conveyor belt through three separate machines: a sifter, a cutter, and a roller. Another group of men in bare feet and boiler suits pile the tea from one machine to another with huge flat wooden shovels. 'Here the tea is *sifted* to remove any grit or stones the pickers may have dropped in, then *cut* to remove the stalk, and *rolled* to crush it. It may be rolled a number of times to make it as fine as possible. There is also a magnet which removes any tiny pieces of metal that may have got mixed up with the tea. 'For our best quality, for London, the tea must be very pure.'

Walter grabs a handful as it emerges from the roller and scrutinises it in the palm of his hand. 'There is too much stalk here. Can you see? It will produce a lower grade. And here, there are specs of green. Not good. The leaves were too old.' I nod and smile enthusiastically, as if I can detect these minute differences.

We follow Walter into the fermenting room where he shouts above the noise of the machines. The tea is fermented for one to two hours—turning from green to a pale brown—then piled like great mountains of sawdust around the room. Close up, it is damp and lumpy, like the stuffing used in old fashioned furniture. '*Now* it is ready to be dried,' explains Walter. 'We use steam for this part—to dry it and to separate the tea that still has stalk and fibre. This machine has just been replaced—the old one was thirty years old and it made the tea too smoky. London did not like it.'

Dried, the tea turns from the sickly looking sawdust into a darker, richer brown, and finally resembles the stuff I buy in Twinings packets at Safeways. I grab a handful, holding it to my nose and letting it run through my finger tips. I love that in twenty-four hours the unrecognisable plant outside can be transformed into something so familiar. It's a bit like discovering turmeric in a field.

Now that it looks and smells like tea, the final grading process takes place. It is passed through a sorter which removes any remaining stalk and bits of fibre, and is then piled on a set of tiered grills, each with holes of increasingly smaller diameter. The grills are mechanically shaken, producing the effect of a giant sieve. The coarser leaves stay at the top while the finer, better quality leaves, are filtered through to the lower level.

Walter beckons us to a crate where he has assembled samples of the ten grades in small flat tins. Each looks like tea, but they are *actually* different: a darker or lighter shade of brown, bigger or smaller particles, more or less green and flecky. 'One teaspoon of this,' says Walter, pointing to the top grade, 'will make an excellent cup of tea, but two and half spoons of this—the lowest grade—will not make such a good cup of tea.' The top five grades are packed into brown paper bags lined with tin foil to keep in the flavour, while the others are stored in plastic sacks. Tea chests are no longer used, because they are too expensive. The lower grades are distributed to hospitals, schools and prisons, and the quality tea sold to a broker in London, who blends the various grades to produce the final product.

In the office, Walter shows us samples that have been removed during the day. He can tell if the tea is being processed correctly and, if there is anything wrong, at what stage the problem is arising. He can also identify each of the ten grades by taste. He measures exactly six milligrams into a ceramic dish and allows it to brew for exactly six minutes. 'The tea may still have green flecks or fibre, it may be too light or too dark, it may be very bitter, or not bitter enough, or it may be over-fired and smoky.'

He strains the brewed tea into another dish and takes a large soup spoon, scooping the tea and bringing it up to his mouth. He slurps, loudly, throwing his head back, washing the tea around his mouth, and spitting into an urn in classic wine taster's style. 'Hmm...Good,' he says. 'Not too smoky. A rich, deep flavour. Excellent. London will be pleased.'

CHAPTER 16

TEAR-GAS BEFORE BEDTIME

I AM STANDING in one of the bathrooms back at our guest house quietly doing my ablutions when I hear Sarah outside the door. 'Jac, is that you?'

'Yes. How did you know?'

'I can recognise the sound of you brushing your teeth.'

'Oh God. Do you think we need to spend some time apart?'

We are four months into our trip and, apart from some minor discord over kayaking, and a difference of mood in the mornings, we have managed to avoid any real conflict. That said, we are both looking forward to Maria and Jacki's arrival, to having new and different conversations, to spending time with someone who hasn't done exactly what we've done, every day for the past sixteen weeks.

We arrive at the airport early and grab a beer to take the edge off our nerves. It has the opposite effect, and by the time we reach the viewing platform, we are manic, bouncing up and down over people's heads to catch sight of the plane. It is almost dark, a giant spotlight shining on the portable staircases dotted about the tarmac, the lights of the airstrip narrowing to a distant 'V'. We hover in the crowd, checking and re-checking the time, and listening for the sound of the plane. As we wait, we discuss meeting protocols; some friends throw their arms around you and it's all big hugs and long embraces. These girls, we decide, will be a little more restrained. Jacki's an engineer and, well…she's from the country—that's what we put it down to anyway. Maria?…well, Maria doesn't really do intimacy—they're just not the huggy, kissy type.

As the Qantas 747 with its distinctive red kangaroo logo glides into view, I have a pang of nostalgia—lovely, safe, reliable, *Australian* Qantas. As it starts to empty, we jostle for a position closer to the railings. The steps down from the plane are obscured by an overhead canopy but, as the crowd spreads out across the tarmac, we catch the unmistakable silhouette of our friends: Maria, larger, rounder, a little taller; Jacki, short and skinny, both sporting distinctive, brand-new, matching Akubras.

Sarah shakes her head and smiles. 'Just be thankful they're not pith helmets,' I say.

We force our way through the rows of people and run to the end of the platform, waving and shouting at the emptying plane, though it's impossible for them to see us. We dash through the bar and hover at the arrivals gate. In minutes they are through, comfortable baggy pants and shirts, small sensible packs with ample room for African purchases.

'Thought you might like today's paper,' Maria says, whacking a rolled up copy of *The Age* against Sarah's stomach.

'Thanks. Good flight?'

'Yup.'

'Work finish up OK?'

'Pretty much.'

'Nice hats girls,' I say.

'Yeah. Cool aren't they? Matching.'

'Yeah. Very cool. Very matching.'

'They're "Squashies",' says Maria, grabbing it off her head and crumpling it between both hands. 'They go right back to their original shape, see…'

'…We bought them especially,' interrupts Jacki, nodding enthusiastically.

'Brilliant. Squashies,' I smile. 'Come on girls. Let's get you out of here.'

It's late by the time we return to the hotel, and we perch on the end of their bed and start getting used to each other again. Maria and Jacki potter around the room, unpacking their sensible zip-up toilet bags, their T-shirts times two, undies times five. They are experienced travellers—South-East Asia, the States, South America—though I suspect Africa will hold a few surprises. We've done lots of trips together—bushwalking weekends, cycle tours, soccer camps—but nothing on this scale. It's a bit weird, thinking of having them around all day, every day, for the next month or so, when it's just been Sarah and I for so long. There aren't many people I'd contemplate spending that much time with, but Maria and Jacki are kind of…*easy*—they won't freak out if a train is delayed, or if a hotel's a bit grotty, or if something doesn't go according to plan. You know, instinctively somehow, that certain people would be a nightmare to travel with. Maria and Jacki manage to be enthusiastic and laid-back at the same which makes them ideal. And if Maria sometimes gets a bit antsy—which, let's be honest here, is not unheard of—Jacki's always there to smooth things over.

I shift out of Jacki's way as she pops their toothbrushes by the sink and tidies their packs into the wardrobe. She flops onto the bed and hangs her arms loosely around Maria's shoulders. Like us, they have an enormous capacity for each other's company. '24/7' Jacki calls it—twenty-four hours a day, seven days a week—that's what a holiday means. They've been looking forward to it for months.

'Anything particular you want to do in Harare, girls?' I ask.

'Oh yes we have a list,' says Maria, grabbing her guidebook. 'We have been planning. A General Wander to begin with to orientate ourselves, a Walk Around African Unity Square to get a feel for the people and the city, a Visit To The National Gallery and Queen Victoria Museum to get a sense of the art and culture, and maybe a Tour Of The Craft Markets for a preliminary review of shopping opportunities.'

That's what I love about these girls—they're interested in just about everything there is to be interested in. They've done all the research, and they'll pack as much as is humanly possible into this trip.

'We're *very excited* about the shopping opportunities,' interrupts Jacki. 'Aren't we, Big Chica?'

'Oh yes. Very excited, Little Chica.'

'Well that all sounds doable,' I say.

'And perhaps a Cultural Activity, some music or dancing?' suggests Maria.

'Oh yes, definitely a Cultural Activity,' says Jacki. 'We *lurve* our new Thomas Mapfumo CD, don't we Big Chica?'

'Yes we *lurve* it, Mini Chica.'

I glance at Sarah who has a kind of have-they-always-been-like-this? expression on her face. I smile quietly. Of course they have, we've just missed it for a while.

'Well, girls,' I say, 'I think we can fit all that in. We can have breakfast here, and head out as early as you like.'

'Is there any…trouble?' asks Jacki tentatively.

'Few disgruntled war veterans and lots of talk about land distribution—but there's no strike or anything tomorrow so the streets should be pretty calm.'

'Good…that's good.' says Jacki, only vaguely reassured.

In the morning we walk into town, Sarah and I providing a guided tour through the packed city centre. A flame-throwing unicyclist juggles in the square, and kids and drunks, and young women in business suits hang out in the park. A hawker thrusts Harry the Hippo in Jacki's face, ''ello *kan-ga-roo* ladies,' he says. 'Free look for the *kan-ga-roos*.'

Maria glances at us somewhat perplexed. 'Why the kangaroos?'

'I don't know girls, maybe it's something to do with the headgear.'

The thing is, even without the matching Akubras—sorry, *squashies*—Maria and Jacki just look *Australian*. I don't know if it's the sun-kissed hair and skin, something about the laid-back manner maybe, but you could pick them out in a line-up any day. They are both fiercely proud of it too. They've seen a lot of other places in the world, but have no desire to live anywhere else. I've often wondered what that would feel like. To be so sure of your roots, and to know that however far you roam, you still call Australia home. Man! They could *be* a Qantas ad.

'Kangaroo ladies, please,' the hawker persists, 'perhaps a giraffe, or a pair of guineafowl.'

'Might we be interested in purchasing a giraffe, or a pair of guineafowl, Big Chica?'

'Perhaps not just yet, Mini Chica. It might be a little early for *actual* purchases.'

'Yes. I think you're right. A little early.'

Outside the Town Hall, a large agitated crowd gathers carrying placards, waving clenched fists, and chanting loudly. I smile at the guy standing next to me and ask what's going on. 'War veterans,' he says. 'They demand pensions from Mugabe. If they don't get them they will be *very angry*.'

'Perhaps we should move on,' suggests Jacki, 'just in case.' We walk quickly away from the centre of town to a side street of smart shops and cafés, and pop into the Zanzibar Collection, an up-market souvenir store where the girls can undertake their preliminary review of shopping opportunities.

The shop is full of painted ostrich eggs mounted on fake rhino horns, ivory chess-sets, embroidered table clothes of the 'big five', and umbrella stands in the shape of elephant's feet. Sarah spots a bookshop opposite and sneaks out, while Maria and Jacki check out the Ndebele cushion covers, and the genuine hand-carved-by-local-Shona-tribesmen—not—bows and arrows.

Suddenly, the security guard slams the door shut and I wonder if someone is trying to make off with the ostrich eggs. Outside, dozens of people dash past the shop, coughing and choking, tears streaming down their cheeks. A young man pulls a T-shirt over his nose and mouth, and a woman wraps a scarf around her face. They sprint past the shop in both directions, their heads bowed, hands protecting their eyes, bumping into each other as they desperately try to flee.

'Shit! Where's Sarah?' I say. 'She's out there somewhere.' I rush to the door and peer though the glass. She is standing in front of the bookshop opposite, her hand over her mouth, her eyes watering. She makes a dash across the path, the guard opening a crack in the door for her to squeeze through. 'You OK Doll?'

'Yeah, I'm fine, but it stings like hell. What's going on?'

'Tear gas,' says the guard. 'The police have fired on the war veterans because they protest.'

'About pensions?'

'Yes. Today, Mugabe has issued a list of the liberation fighters who will receive one, but Mugabe only rewards his friends.'

Maria and Jacki peer through the door at the mayhem, a slightly pained expression on their faces. Having been in Africa for four months now, a small tear-gas riot is just an interesting diversion from shopping for Sarah and me, but I suspect it's not quite what the girls had in mind for their first day in Africa. 'OK girls?' I check.

'Yeah…Yeah. Fine. Just not quite the cultural experience we had in mind—maybe we should move on to somewhere a little less…volatile?' Jacki suggests.

When the air is clear and the street seems calm again, we venture out, Jacki scouring the path on both sides for anyone who might vaguely pass for a riot police officer or protesting war veteran. We walk directly to the closest travel agent and duck in past the security guard. We are in the shop five minutes when the door slams and the street becomes chaotic again. Dozens of businessmen scatter in different directions, teenage boys sprint across the park, and women grab their children, covering their faces to shield them from the gas. We wait, protected inside the shop, watching a crowd bustle around a water fountain trying to rinse their eyes. The travel agency staff sit behind their desks and peer nonchalantly through the windows. 'This is just the beginning,' they say. 'It will get a lot worse.'

Maria and Jacki are looking slightly perturbed and I decide a trip to Meikles Hotel might be a good idea. It'll be secure and safe, and besides, both girls are rather partial to the odd gourmet snack. 'How about a nice chocolate milkshake, girls?' I ask, 'to settle the nerves, and a perhaps a lemon tart or two? We know a little place around the corner.'

'Ooh yes. Chocolate milkshakes. We like that plan, don't we Mini Chica?'

'Ooh yes. Big Chica, we do.'

'Chocolate milkshakes it is then.'

Maria has organised our first cultural activity, a performance of the Hohodza Hot Merimba Band and the Glamorous Dancing Queen Bees, just back from their sell-out European tour. There is only a handful of people in the audience when we arrive, but the band is already playing. Seven men in smart grey chinos and pressed white shirts fill a tiny stage in the dark downstairs bar. The drummer and his kit take up most of the space, and the brass players squash up either side, swinging their trumpets and trombones, and dancing in neat little circles. Maracas and tambourines and washboards and bells are passed across the stage and juggled between the other musicians, who shuffle and swing and spin in perfect time. We order beers and lean against the bar, four white chicks lined up like cartons of milk.

The room begins to fill—a youngish crowd in smart casual dress, couples and groups of friends. They are all local, all black, and though we become increasingly conspicuous, the stares and smiles are curious, but welcoming.

The band moves into their next number and the Dancing Queen Bees emerge from back stage and line up on the floor. Each one wears a narrow strip of bright yellow around her top, and a full skirt with black and yellow striped ruffles that rustle as she moves. They begin to dance, small steps at first, left then right, following each other in tiny circles. As the band quickens its pace, so do the Bees, jiggling their hips vigorously and gyrating around the floor. Conversation quietens and the whole room focusses on the dancers. At the bar, four white girls slowly start to shuffle.

The drummer beats faster, the trombone player spins and hops, and the other members of the band shuffle quickly from side to side swinging bells and maracas. The Queen Bees form themselves into a line and turn their backs to the audience. They begin to wiggle their bottoms, the ruffles of their skirts heightening the movement. As the tempo increases, the Bees wiggle faster until their bottoms are moving from side to side with alarming speed and ferocity. The effect is quite remarkable and we stare in awed disbelief. 'How…on earth…do they do that?' Maria asks.

'It's not actually…anatomically possibly, is it?'

'It's like…somehow…their bottoms have separated from the rest of them, and they're kind of moving independently.'

The temptation to try it is too much and we plonk our beers on the bar and start to swing our arms back and forth and wiggle our bums in vigorous imitation. We are still the only white people in the room and, Sarah excepted, not particularly well-endowed with dancing talent—Jacki never quite moving on from the Castlemaine Hop of her youth, and Maria only ever managing a reluctant shuffle at the occasional soccer function. We don't let this stop us though.

'Girls! Girls!' Sarah says suddenly. 'Steady. Please.'

We ignore her appeals for decorum and continue, heads down, elbows pumping, hips jiggling rapidly sideways.

'*Girls,*' says Sarah, '*Please!* Just look around.' The three of us pause a moment, straightening up and glancing around the room. The Queen Bees are no longer the focus of attention, the crowd having shifted its gaze to the peculiar display in front of the bar. Amused nudges and snickers circle the room and we smile awkwardly and grab our beers. 'Perhaps we should practise this at home?' says Jacki, resorting to a slightly more dignified thigh tapping.

We have eaten and rested, showered and slept, and it is time to leave lovely Harare, with its home-made scones and strawberry milkshakes, its beauty parlours and tear-gas riots and head off to real Africa again. Sarah has chosen one final cultural activity for us before we leave. She has never, *ever*, not even when she was on a kibbutz, not even when she was travelling around Andalusia—and watched it in Spanish—missed the Oscars.

'Doll, we're in Harare. In the middle of Africa. Do you see a lot of cable tellies?' I say.

'There has to be somewhere—maybe one of the posh hotels. We could like…sneak in and watch.'

'I think not.'

While Maria and Jacki do their Visit To The National Gallery, Sarah tries to track down an Oscar viewing opportunity. She calls the Harare Sheraton, the Holiday Inn, Meikles and a string of lesser hotels and lodges, but none, surprisingly, is throwing an Oscar party. 'Sorry Doll, you might have to miss it this time.' She leaves me flicking through the guidebook and wanders off to find the manager of our guest-house. Half an hour later she returns, bouncing into our room. 'Sports Bars,' she says. 'They have cable and there's one in Chitipunga. We can get a cab.'

It could be any sports bar in any city in the world—red vinyl booths and formica topped tables, signed soccer shirts and cricket bats decorating the walls. A huge screen with life-size wrestlers hangs above the bar, and a line of TV monitors flicker with cricket and swimming and basketball. There is no sign of Oscar, of red carpets, of skinny stars in ball gowns, or tuxedoed interviewers asking fatuous questions.

Sarah goes off to investigate while Maria, Jacki and I buy beers and settle into a booth. Each table has its own individual TV with a selection of channels, and I flick through hoping for Sarah's sake to find something. She is chatting with the tech guy—doing the smiley, ponytail thing—while he fiddles with buttons and levers and computer keyboards. It certainly looks like they should be able to find it.

After twenty minutes she returns to our table, head bowed and disconsolate. 'They have M-Net which means they should be able to receive it, but for some reason it's not working tonight.'

'I'm sorry, Doll. Come and have a drink and maybe we could watch something else…How about …skateboarding?…golf?…rugby?'

She slumps across the table and buries her head in her arms, and I flick through once more searching for something, *anything* that might salvage her evening.

'Ooh! Hon,' I say suddenly. 'Look what I've found—your favourite!'

She lifts her head a fraction and glances at the screen, then sits bolt upright. 'Ooh I *love* this episode. It's the one where Niles has a heart attack and the Nanny thinks he's going to die.'

We take the bus to Masvingo, the nearest town to the Great Zimbabwe Ruins. There are still five seats across where there should be only four, but for the first time it is not chock full of people and animals. The Great Zimbabwe Ruins are on the cover of every tourist brochure and guidebook, but are still relatively remote. There is no public transport from Masvingo, but we are told we should be able to find a cab.

We arrive early evening—the only tourists—and manage to organise a ride in a very small and dilapidated baby blue Citroën, circa 1965. The boot accommodates only one pack and we balance the other three on the roof, tying them on with two short pieces of parcel string. We wedge ourselves in, Maria at the front, Jacki, head bowed and perched on my and Sarah's knees in the back. Through the rusting hole at my feet I can see the ground just inches away.

Our driver speaks almost no English and Maria spends the thirty-minute journey trying to communicate that we would like to be picked up from the ruins in the morning of the day after next. He smiles a lot and nods, and points things out in Shona.

We pull up to a large site with shady trees, patches of green grass, and two small tents a hundred metres apart. There's an ablutions block, a stand-pipe and some concrete picnic tables. It is not unlike an Australian national park site, apart from the twenty or so monkeys hovering around the bins, and scampering up and down the trees. It is right next to the ruins, and the soft light of the fading sun filters through their meandering walls.

We pile out of the cab and rescue our packs while Maria tries to confirm with the driver that he will return to pick us up. He smiles and nods more, and points to the ruins, and I anticipate a long walk back the day after tomorrow.

We unpack our tent and Maria and Jacki carefully unravel the beautiful new Bergen, its first outing since the dry run in their lounge. Maria holds the pegs while Jacki clicks the poles into place and slides them through the pockets. 'It has a forest green exterior,' Jacki explains, 'designed to merge with the natural environment, but a bright safety-yellow interior that you can expose if you need to be rescued by helicopter.'

I'd forgotten Jacki's 'Safety First' philosophy—I think it's an engineering thing. Sarah's Dad is the same.

'Excellent Jacki.' I say. 'That's really very handy.'

As we settle into the evening, an overland truck arrives, pouring out its not insignificant contents onto a large patch of bush fifty metres from us. Twelve backpackers—six men, six women, all in their early twenties—scurry around the truck off-loading twelve canvas stools, six matching dome tents, a large portable table and a variety of industrial pots and pans. Half the group are on tent duty, the other half on dinner. We watch them prepare and eat enough spaghetti to feed western Tanzania and, afterwards, wash and dry the dishes, holding a plate in each hand and waving it vigorously in the air—tea towels, clearly, are an extravagance. A couple of casks appear and cheap warm Riesling is passed around in plastic cups as they settle in for a long night.

I would have loved a big group adventure when I was that age, but now I couldn't imagine anything worse. All that compulsory drinking and awkward sex. All those late-night D and Ms and midday hangovers. And all that awful twenties' angst. I look at Maria and Jacki—ten years into a relationship—holding hands and watching the sun set, and I look at Sarah, her stockinged feet laid casually across my lap, her eyes fixed on the backpackers, absorbed by a real life soap. I love where I am today and wouldn't be twenty again for anything.

We awake to a beautiful blue day, the air crisp and clear, and I feel like the sun is shining just for us. We zip everything away from the monkeys and walk the few hundred metres to the ruins, stepping along the remains of an ancient granite track, and squeezing through the narrow entrance to the Great Enclosure. Surrounding us is a massive outer wall, an eleven metre high dry-stone construction that encircles us for about two hundred and fifty metres. I open the guidebook; Maria, Jacki and Sarah standing in a line, looking eagerly at me like my old Year Seven home group.

'Great Zimbabwe is the biggest single ancient structure in sub-Saharan Africa,' I begin, 'believed to be the remains of a vast city inhabited between the 13th and 15th centuries. Its chief was the most powerful ruler in the south-eastern interior, extending political influence into present day Botswana, Mozambique and South Africa. At one time up to 20 000 people lived here—supporting themselves with cattle, sorghum and millet—and trading gold and ivory for porcelain and cloth.'

'What happened to them?' interrupts Maria.

'I don't know. I haven't got to that bit yet. We have to admire the wall first.'

The stone work is remarkable: neat, regular blocks fitted tightly together without mortar, creating smooth gentle lines interspersed with delicate zig zag patterns. Where the wall has encountered a boulder—a particularly resistant block of granite—it has been incorporated, the man-made structure blending with the natural shape of the rock. It looks like a fortification, but was actually built to celebrate the authority of the chief—the more important the person, the higher the wall surrounding his home.

'Reminds me of the Inca stonework in Peru,' says Maria. 'Do you remember Chica? How beautifully it was put together without anything to cement it. Hundreds of years later than this, though.'

The interesting thing about Great Zimbabwe is that, for many years, its history was disputed by white settlers and colonisers who denied its African origins, arguing that such a sophisticated settlement must have been built by outsiders—meaning 'whites'. They argued that its presence proved the necessity for external conquest and colonisation—that only through foreign influence could prosperity be achieved. As late as 1970 the Rhodesian Front issued instructions that no official publication could explicitly state that Great Zimbabwe was an African creation. Not until Liberation was it officially acknowledged that all the archaeological evidence conclusively proved it was African.

We step across a series of small raised platforms—the site of clay huts—with their own lower walls encircling them, and file past a line of granite pillars that look like they once held something up. Piles of rubble are heaped around the track and we edge around them, ducking through a narrow enclosure into a tight passage. Two high parallel walls loom above us, the air suddenly cooler and the light dim. I look behind to check everyone is keeping up. 'Hang on a minute, Julian,' says Sarah, 'I'm just waiting for Anne and Dick…'

'…The name comes from here, you know,' interrupts Maria.

'What name?'

'The name of the country, of course, *Zimbabwe*. It comes from the Shona word *madzimbahwe* meaning "the house of stone"—that's what we've been looking at for the last half an hour.'

'Ah…right. Yes.'

We squeeze through the tiny corridor in single file, shuffling along the walls and emerging into a small clearing where the great conical tower—the most photographed part of the ruins—looms in front of us. It is about ten metres high and five metres in diameter and beautifully intact. No-one is quite sure what it was used for; perhaps, like the wall, it was merely decorative.

We duck through another passage and come out at the southern end of the wall, where the midday sun illuminates the distinctive chevron patterning of the rim. I lead my little group up the adjacent Hill Complex where the huts and enclosures were built amidst a jumble of huge granite boulders. We clamber over a series of smooth rocky outcrops and perch atop a low cliff looking down the valley to the Great Enclosure. We have lost the handful of other visitors we began with and lie under the warm sun, watching the rainbow lizards devour our apple cores, and eagles swoop down from the cliff top.

'They look like the soapstone carvings,' says Maria, 'the Shona carvings we saw in the market.'

'What do?'

'The rocks. Look,' she says, pointing. 'The shapes of the boulders, the smooth lines and the curves—they're the same shapes you see in all the Shona stonework.'

The three of us look and nod in unison. 'She's right.'

We head back to the site, checking out the tiny souvenir shop, where Sarah and I covet some Ndebele wall hangings, and Maria and Jacki take advantage of an excellent shopping opportunity and purchase a matching pair of green ankle socks embroidered with the Great Zimbabwe Ruins motif.

The following morning we stand in a line staring down the dusty road and listening for the tell-tale signs of a dilapidated, pale blue Citroën. Miraculously, on the dot at 9.30, as arranged, our guy splutters up the road—sporting the same enormous smile and still muttering away in Shona—and drives us to Masvingo. We pick up a truly 'luxury' coach, spacious and comfortable, which delivers us to Bulawayo in three easy hours. After Kenya and Tanzania, travelling in southern Africa is a cinch.

Bulawayo is the centre of the Ndebele, long time rivals of the Shona who are concentrated further west, and who dominate politically, controlling most of the influential positions in Mugabe's government. Bulawayo has always been the second city. The wide, tree-lined main street, with its striped awnings and swept pavements, reminds me of photographs my parents took in Brisbane in the late fifties. Young men, black and white, saunter across the road in white short-sleeve cotton, and kids in neat shorts and pretty dresses peer through shop windows. Old Fords cruise slowly up and down, dropping people off in no particular hurry. It has that safe, gentle feel of a country town from a bygone time.

We make our way to the municipal campsite, a large area of flat green grass with a clean shower block, and a cooking area with stainless steel sinks and taps that gush with clean hot and cold water. There's a neat little office with photocopied flyers detailing prices and facilities. It's amazing how quickly Sarah and I have become accustomed to a higher level of order and organisation. Almost without noticing, we've slipped back into the ease and comfort of a place that functions normally—normally for us anyway. I wonder now how we got through those hideous nights on our first safari in Kenya.

We leave our gear protected by the team of security officers that guard the entrance to the site, and head into town to check out some local Ndebele culture. The art gallery has a charming café attached and, as dairy products and home-made cakes are still a novelty for Sarah and I—and as Maria and Jacki are a little down on their quota of gourmet snacks—we skip the art work and head for the tea and scones. We do manage to catch the souvenir shop before it shuts though, where the girls pick up a large hand-woven basket and some Ndebele cushion covers.

In the morning we are met by the jaunty and enthusiastic Stanley, our guide for the tour of Matopos National Park. Stanley is Ndebele—like most of the black population of Matebeleland, which covers Bulawayo and the south-east corner of the country. 'Matopos,' explains Stanley, 'is sacred to the Ndebele people.'

He stops the van just inside the park by a curiously out of place floral garden, with a white picket fence and bench seat. 'This is The Memorial of Turning Hearts,' he explains. 'A tribute to Rhodesian soldiers who died fighting my ancestors. But, long before there were Rhodesians, there were Ndebele, and this land has always had great spiritual significance for us. There are many sacred sites where my people come to pray—especially to the great spirit Mwali who controls the rain. When there is drought, even the politicians come.'

We park beneath a grove of amarulla trees and follow Stanley up a wide path of smooth lichen-covered granite. 'This is Malindidzimu Hill,' he says, 'the dwelling place of our benevolent spirits.' It is also the final resting place of another, somewhat less than benevolent spirit. Rhodes took rather a liking to the place, renamed it 'View of the World', and declared he would be buried here. His grave sits on a rocky outcrop marked by a simple stone: 'Here lies the remains of Cecil John Rhodes'. From the site you can see for miles across vast tracts of beautiful native African bush—the sacred lands of the Ndebele stolen by Rhodes and his armies.

Beneath the outcrop we pause on a rocky ledge by a long low cave covered with ochre paintings dating back ten thousand years—hunters chasing wildebeest, women grinding sorghum as they do today. 'Warriors used to hide in these caves,' explains Stanley, 'and the ground where you are standing used to be covered in thick reeds—a symbol of strength in battle for the Ndebele. When the Rhodesian army discovered this, they sent soldiers to destroy the reeds and cover the earth in concrete.'

We pile back into the van and head for the other side of the park. 'Perhaps, on our way, you would like to see some traditional dancing?' asks Stanley. 'I could take you to my village.' There is a moment's pause while Sarah and I recall a handful of T-shirted teenagers in traditional Nike hightops bobbing around a camp fire at five bucks a pop.

'Ooh. Yes. Traditional dancing. What do you think, Little Chica?'

'Ooh. Definitely. We're a bit low on cultural activities, Big Chica.'

We wait in the bus while Stanley goes off to check the traditional dancing opportunities in his village. This is clearly not part of the scheduled trip, but rather an entrepreneurial enterprise cooked up by Stan and his folks. He waves us over and we wander towards a patch of scrub where a dozen kids from six months to sixteen gather in a semi-circle. An old man, Stanley's Dad possibly, emerges from a hut and stands directly in front of us. He is wearing a white business shirt that has seen better days with a python skull necklace, and a skirt of jackals' tails. He smiles broadly at us, revealing a smattering of blackened teeth, and dons a huge feathered headdress. He has a whip-like wildebeest tail in his right hand which he raises above his head, and thrashes down to his side.

'Remember. This was your idea, girls,' says Sarah.

The kids start to clap and chant and Mr S shuffles from side to side and hops in little circles, the tails of his skirt springing in the air. The kids are actually quite tuneful—and clearly enjoying themselves—and Mr S, despite his advanced years, is remarkably good. Stanley joins us, explaining the meaning of the dance, and soon we are surrounded by the kids, and everyone is cheerfully clapping along in time.

Mr S nods to Stan and makes a beckoning movement with his wildebeest free hand, and I have a sudden, terrifying realisation that we are about to have an audience participation moment. Sarah clearly twigs at the same time. 'Oh God. No. *Please!*'

'I'm not.' I say. 'I'm sorry, but I'm just *not.*'

Maria makes a sudden dash to the back of our group and attempts unsuccessfully to hide behind a skinny three-year-old boy.

'You must dance,' says Stanley, smiling.

Well…I'd love to…really…it's just that…I've suddenly broken both my ankles…

'He is the Chief. You must dance.'

Right. Yes. The Chief. *Soo*…I suspect it all would be terribly culturally insensitive if I didn't.

Stanley grabs the wildebeest tail and holds it out to me. I hover, looking pleadingly at Sarah, who is pointedly staring at her boots. Maria is nowhere to be seen.

'He is the Chief,' repeats Stanley.

'Right. OK. If the Chief says…then…let's do it.'

As I stretch out my hand for the wildebeest tail, Jacki—friend, teammate, fellow wanderer and shining light of my day—grabs it. She bounds up to the Chief, whips the tail though the air, and dances the Castlemaine Hop like there's no tomorrow.

It's our last day in Bulawayo and Maria has decided we should see a soccer match—a good, grass roots, cultural activity. 'It's the Champion of Champions quarter final second leg between the Harare Dynamos and the Bulawayo Highlanders,' she announces. 'There'll be no tourists; it'll be different and fun. And they're the two biggest clubs in the country, so it should be a competitive match.'

Excellent idea, Maria. Let's go in search of an overcrowded and poorly maintained stadium miles away from town, and watch the Shona and Ndebele thrash out a few hundreds of years of enmity on the soccer pitch. 'Fine by me,' I say.

There are thousands of people milling around Barbourfields Stadium where our somewhat perturbed cab driver drops us. We join a long line of men—and a handful of women—in one of a dozen queues. The atmosphere is lively but good-tempered, though I note with mild concern the number of people swigging brown paper bags.

We squeeze through painfully narrow turnstiles, the weight of the crowd bearing down behind us, and I can't help wondering how my ribs would fare in the event of a minor skirmish. 'Let's hope we don't have to leave in a hurry,' says Jacki. 'Can't imagine the emergency evacuation procedures are up to much.'

We stick close, weaving through the tunnels until we eventually emerge onto the terraces. They are chock-full, packs of men lounging on concrete tiers, swigging beer and taking long slugs of gin. We are not, of course, inconspicuous, and rows of eyes pass from Jacki to Sarah, from Maria to me and back again.

'Any of these gentlemen you would particularly like to sit next to girls?' I ask.

There appears to be a lot more space on the opposite side of the stadium—on the more expensive concrete slabs—and we decide to take a chance, heading back towards the entrance. In order to reach the other terrace however, we have to leave the stadium and enter from a different side. A security guard stands by the exit—a bolted gate in a high chain-link fence. Hundreds of supporters are still outside, squashed up against the fence, and he is reluctant to unlock it for fear of a stampede. Quite frankly, I'm with him on this one.

Another dozen supporters latch on to us, and we are soon surrounded by twenty or thirty people bumping and jostling. I grab Sarah's arm and make eye contact with Maria and Jacki as we surge towards the gate. The security guard steps forward, arms raised and pushes us back. 'There is another way,' he says, 'but it is not General Admission and you must pay more.' We follow him along the inside of the fence, elbowing our way through the pack until we reach the other terrace, where another security officer controls the slow flow of people through a small makeshift entrance. We push through the crowd, trying to keep track of each other, as the guard takes our money and, one and at time, shoves us through the door.

We smile politely at the already drunk spectators, and attempt to find a spot of concrete not doused in beer. The atmosphere is not unfriendly, and mostly we receive amused glances that suggest they're not really sure why we've come, but they're happy enough for us to be here. It feels *reasonably* safe, but there's definitely an edge of something—a hint that it wouldn't take much for it all to go horribly wrong.

The stadium is packed—I guess twenty-five, maybe thirty thousand people—three...no...wait a minute...*four* other white people. The terraces are buzzing, and when the whistle blows for kick-off a mighty roar encircles us. The Bulawayo Highlanders have a slow start and after ten minutes a scuffle breaks out amongst disgruntled home supporters behind the goal. The police appear in seconds and fight through the crowd, separating the brawlers and dragging them off the terrace.

After twenty minutes, the home team miss a penalty and the crowd becomes agitated. A fight breaks out across a flight of steps a few metres from us, and we shuffle along the terrace as the two drunken combatants swing air punches and roll down the stairs. I glance around our section of the stadium and wonder just how we'd get out if things really started to hot up.

Just before half time, the locals score—much to the delight of the crowd—and to our immense relief. Five minutes into the second half though, the away team equalises and the euphoria is replaced by despondency. By now, most of the crowd have worked their way through half a dozen beers a piece, or a bottle of the local home brew and, at the very least, are swaggering precariously on the concrete steps, wielding glass bottles above their heads. A can of beer is thrown at the linesman who, clearly used to this, picks it up and drinks. More bottles rain down on the away team net, and a series of scuffles breaks out in the stand. 'Looks a bit tense over there,' I say.

Suddenly, a dozen police appear cradling huge automatic guns, rows of tear-gas canisters hitched to their belts. They line up along the edge of the pitch facing the crowd who, clearly less perturbed at this development than us, continue to lob bottles and cans. 'Oh God,' says Jacki. 'I do wish they'd stop throwing things.'

A substitution focusses attention back on the game and a new player—a white boy, the only one so far—emerges from the bench. Given the demography of Zimbabwe, the ratio of black to white on the park is probably about right. The four of us cheer loudly at his entrance, and the crowd around us exchange amused glances.

When the whistle blows for full-time it's a one-all draw and the players line up for a penalty shoot-out. The crowd are on their feet, cans kicked down the terrace, empty bottles rolling along the concrete. The penalties are even until the Dynamo keeper saves the fourth kick and the Harare crowd roar. The Highlander supporters—most of the stadium—bury their heads in their hands and kick whatever's close. 'Time to get out of here, girls,' announces Jacki.

We step over cans and broken glass, and edge carefully through the drunk, despondent and, noticeably edgy, crowd. Outside the stadium we hover anxiously looking for a cab, but clearly, most people don't take a taxi home from the football, and we join twenty thousand others walking up to the main road.

As we shuffle through the pack, I see a young man barge into Maria and make a grab for her watch. 'Oh God!' I think. 'I wish he hadn't done that.'

She turns suddenly, her eyes fierce, and yanks her arm from him. As she disentangles herself she gives him a hard shove and he stumbles back. A broken bottle drops from his hand and smashes to the road. Maria holds her ground and he suddenly turns and runs.

Man! Don't they know? *No one* messes with Big Chica.

CHAPTER 17

FOUR HAVE AN ADVENTURE

THE ROAD FROM Francistown to Maun—across the north-east corner of Botswana—is wide, tarred and flat, and the landscape through which it runs is unrelenting. Four hundred kilometres of pale yellow grass are interspersed with the occasional skinny bush clinging desperately to the dry dusty soil. The further west we travel, the more scraggy the vegetation becomes and the more the sand encroaches. We are driving along the edge of the vast Kalahari Desert which over-whelms three quarters of Botswana.

Most of the population live along this eastern border in the half dozen towns linked by the road. The 'Kalahari Bushmen' whom we learnt about in primary school—now more accurately known as the 'San'—have been virtually wiped out. Thousands were killed by the Boers in the nineteenth century, and the few who survived lost their hunting grounds to mining, cattle ranching or tourism. There are now only about 55 000 San, and only a couple of thousand who maintain the traditional nomadic, hunter/gatherer lifestyle. Their culture all but destroyed, most now live on isolated reserves supported by an indifferent government, their lives an on-going struggle with alcohol, disease and poverty. A somehow familiar story.

The San apart, Bostwana is one of southern Africa's success stories: a stable multi-party democracy that holds regular, peaceful elections, enjoys freedom of speech, and a free press. A year after independence, diamonds were discovered which provided Botswana with much needed foreign currency. The economy grew rapidly and the pula is now Africa's strongest currency. In just over thirty years, life expectancy has risen from forty-nine to sixty-nine. That is, of course, if you're not one of the thirty per cent of the population who are dying of AIDS. Superficially at least, Botswana looks and feels like a some-what more affluent African country.

Maun is the jumping-off point for the Okavango Delta, 'Botswana's Number One Tourist Destination.' The Okavango is a huge inland delta that sits between two fault lines, a narrow pan-handle pointing north-west towards Angola. Geological movements over a few million years have caused the waters of the Okavango River to slow and spread into a classic alluvial fan. In any given year, an estimated eighteen million cubic metres of water flows into the delta and, though I have absolutely no idea what eighteen million cubic metres of water looks like, it sounds rather a lot.

Thousands of people flock to the region every year to explore this spectacular watery labyrinth, to enjoy its magnificent lily covered and papyrus lined channels. Bird life abounds and animals gather in the thousands to graze the rich pasture. It is one of the rarest, most beautiful ecosystems in the world. Unfortunately for us, however, none of the eighteen million cubic metres is flowing at the moment. The delta is dry—bone dry—its picturesque meandering waterways a series of slightly soggy footpaths, its spectacular bird life all but disappeared. The dug-out canoes—the *mekoro*—in which we might have been poled effortlessly through this natural wonderland, are piled high and dry.

Of course we didn't actually know this until we were half way here—or at least we didn't really believe it—but it seems a shame not to see it now, having travelled this far.

There are no roads into the delta and the only way to see it properly is to fly into the middle—a short, twenty-minute hop in a six-seater Cessna. We gather our much-reduced luggage and walk onto the single airstrip just outside Maun. Sarah hovers around Shane, our Australian pilot, and after much pointing and whispering, climbs into the cockpit. The rest of us squeeze into the main cab—Maria at the back, and Jacki and I in front. There's less space than your average hatchback and we are cowed by the roof, our knees tucked under our chins.

Shane hands Sarah a headset—earmuffs and a mouthpiece—which she positions carefully on her head. She sits bolt upright, folding her hands neatly in her lap and, smiling at Shane, promises not to touch anything.

We bump down the airstrip—the wind blowing through the cracks in the window frame where the seals aren't quite tight—and Shane glances left and right, as if driving through a country intersection on a Sunday afternoon. We jerk and splutter into the air—my stomach struggling to keep up—and in minutes are high above the delta, the harsh grating roar of the engine filling the tiny cab.

Below us, clumps of trees sprout from the yellowing scrub and round thatched roofs form circles along the dry ox-bow lakes. Where the river and its tributaries are supposed to be, there are dark green meanders where new plants have found a foothold in the moist soil. Beyond these channels, though, everything is dry and dusty, and there are no signs of the much lauded bird life, or the elephants and hippos who normally graze here.

Sarah is deep in conversation with Shane and Jacki is snapping photos. I dig out the camera and try framing a shot, but my head is a little spinny, and my stomach still hasn't quite caught up with the rest of me.

I realise, for something completely different, I am going to be sick and grab a bag from the pocket of the seat in front. As I vomit quietly to myself I reflect that it really would be nice if, just for once, I could negotiate a new form of transport without throwing up.

Sarah is pointing at the instrument panel and nodding earnestly, and the others are too caught up with the pretty view below to notice anything else. I lean my head against the window, taking advantage of the free flow of air through the seals, but with the next lurch of the plane I am hunched back over my bag, trying to angle my vomit into its narrow opening. I poke Sarah in the shoulder, summoning my best 'Look-at-me-Doll,' 'Don't-you-feel-sorry-for-me,' expression.

'Yeah. Yeah, Babe,' she says. 'Just talking to Shane. Be with you in a minute.'

I rest my head in my hands as we begin the descent, vaguely aware of Jacki shuffling beside me. As I look across, I notice she is bent double, her deathly white face a few inches from mine. I grab a fresh bag, thrusting it in front of her and we practise synchronised vomiting until the plane finally comes to a bumpy stop.

We fall out of the cab, clutching our folded bags like little packed lunches, and hover on the dusty airstrip taking long deep breaths. Sarah bounces down from the cockpit, oblivious. 'That was *brilliant*,' she says. 'Shane was *so* interesting. Can I take flying lessons?'

We are met by our guide, Xhata—'X' for short—who escorts us through the bush to 'Oddball's Camp', the only affordable accommodation in the inner delta. The Botswanan government has adopted a policy of 'high cost, low impact' tourism to maximise their returns while protecting the environment. Most of the visitors to the delta come via international safari companies and stay at one of the exclusive lodges.

Oddballs is built entirely of local wood and thatch—not unlike the camp at Jumbo Island—though much bigger. The main social and dining area is on stilts and surrounded by an open deck from where you can look out across the water...when there is any. Long communal tables fill the main room and lounge chairs face out onto the balcony. The bar itself is an upside down *mokoro* supported by a line of poles. Hanging above is a huge buffalo skull and horns sitting comfortably next to a framed portrait of Nelson Mandela.

'We have a bit of a problem with elephants,' explains X. 'The camp used to be surrounded by an electric fence to keep them out, but they were too smart. They would stand just outside the wire and bend branches onto it with their trunk. Then, with the fence earthed, they would simply push it down.'

We are greeted by a young Kiwi woman who scribbles down our details and allocates a couple of tents in an adjacent clearing. Jacki picks up a ring-binder with a series of dog-eared photocopied sheets and flicks through. 'The...er...River Lodge?' she asks. 'What's that exactly?'

'It's a hundred dollars a night Jack, is what it is.'

'Is it...nice?'

'Yes. It is rather,' says the Kiwi. 'I think you'd like it.'

'Hmm...is there another?' asks Sarah, hovering at my shoulder.

I grab the folder and sling it back on the desk. 'Settle, girls,' I say. 'We're camping.'

Five minutes and a hundred dollars later we linger at the bottom of a huge Jackalberry tree by a ladder leading up to a giant tree-house four metres above us—River Lodge is a childhood fantasy writ large. We climb slowly up the broad flat steps emerging into a huge room dominated by a king-size four poster bed. It is carved from a heavy dark wood, about waist height, and buried in pillows and a six-inch duvet. I grab Sarah's hand and we launch ourselves onto the deep spring mattress, bouncing up and down like over-excited children at bedtime. 'Look Doll, pillows! Dozens of them.' We flop down and lie spread-eagled, staring into the bamboo rafters that are delicately interlaced with the branches of the tree. The morning sun is already filtering through the cracks, and a breeze tapping at the half open bamboo blinds that drop on either side of the room.

Behind the bed is the bathroom: a proper 'high-style' toilet, a miniature carved *mokoro* for a sink and the promise of warm water. The shower floor is made of round branches placed a few centimetres apart and when I step onto them I can see the dense undergrowth metres below where the water runs through.

We climb back onto the bed, prop ourselves against the huge headboard and look out onto the open savannah. A herd of red lechwe graze amongst the reeds and half a dozen bull elephants amble across the horizon. How many places are there in the world as beautiful as this, I wonder. 'OK. You win,' I say. 'I'm glad we're not camping.'

We jump down and head for the bar where X and Maria and Jacki are waiting, having just checked out their matching tree house.

'Nice accommodation girls?' I ask

'Oh yes. We like it very much. Don't we Mini Chica?'

'Oh yes. We like it *very much* Big Chica.'

Oddballs is on the edge of the Moremi Game Reserve, a large region of the inner delta protected since the early 1960s. It comprises permanently and seasonally swamped areas, though neither is wet at the moment, and a tongue of dry land through the centre known as Chief's Island. As we hike out of the camp we pass a dozen *mekoro* piled onto a shallow bank. 'I have never seen the delta so dry,' says X, 'and I have lived here all my life.'

We follow him though thorny scrub and dense reeds until we reach a huge anthill—big enough for the five of us to sit on—and X runs through the safety talk. 'There are no hippos or crocodiles because of the drought so we need only worry about buffalo, elephant and lion. Buffaloes are by far the most aggressive land animal and if we are charged…'

'Yeah. Yeah. Been there. Done that. Run in zig zags and climb the nearest tree.'

Maria and Jacki look askance. I forget this is all new to them. 'Climb *what* tree?…Maybe it's just me, but I can't see any trees,' says Maria. 'Can you see any trees Jacki?'

'No trees, Chica. I can see no trees.'

I peer around the flat, featureless plain. 'Well…the nearest ant hill then.'

'You will be fine,' interrupts X. 'Just remember, if there are lions you must not run. But sightings here are infrequent, perhaps only once a month.'

'And…dare I ask…you last saw one when?' asks Jacki.

'About a month ago,' he replies, deadpan.

I am less anxious about the wildlife than when we first ventured onto the Masai Mara a few months ago, though having said that, this is the first time we have wandered into the bush without an armed guide—X is carrying nothing that might assist us if we were to upset the buffalo.

We follow him deeper into the reserve, a few mokolani palms looming at the edge of the old flood plain. Even without the water the delta is beautiful, vast banks of reeds waving in the breeze and lechwe skittering between. Groups of wildebeest with too much time on their hands chase each other in circles and kick up the dry dust.

X pauses, squatting down by a sandy track and points to a perfectly formed set of lion prints. 'Fresh,' he says.

'How fresh…exactly?' asks Jacki.

'Hmm…Difficult to say, but he's been here recently.'

'Excellent.'

'Don't worry,' says X to Jacki. 'It's OK. Once—when I was accompanying a group of German tourists—a lioness emerged from the reeds and started to walk towards us. She came very close and I told everyone to be absolutely still. She didn't look like she was hunting, but you can never be sure. She walked straight up to me, sniffed my trouser leg and flopped down on to my feet. My heart was beating so fast and my whole body shaking, but I tried not to show it. After a minute, she stood up and wandered back into the bush, and we continued our walk unharmed. You see, even if a lion does approach, there is really nothing to worry about.'

There's a long pause while we absorb X's reassuring story. 'Thanks. I'll bear that in mind,' says Jacki.

It is good to be on foot after spending most of our safaris in the back of a bus. Though the animals are less abundant here, there is something quite special about meeting them at ground level, knowing the only thing between you and them is a small stretch of savannah. It feels somehow…fairer, like we're entering their territory, but this time there are no guns, no vehicles, just us—it kind of levels the playing field, I suppose. Not that I have the remotest inclination to encounter lions or buffalo close up, but on foot you actually *feel* closer, even if you're not.

We pass through a grove of palm trees, the trunks partially uprooted, branches strewn everywhere, the grass bent in all directions. The ground is pitted with giant holes—reaching up to Sarah's knees—and a nearby termite mound has been completely flattened. 'The elephants have had a party,' X explains. 'They eat the amarulla fruit which makes them drunk and then sleep it off using the termite mound as a pillow. You can see the shape of the elephant's head and shoulders where the grass has been flattened.' A sudden trumpeting sounds from beyond the trees where a group of adults nurse their hangovers and recount the events of the night before. They are probably…fifty metres away—which is really quite close when you're talking elephants—and though they don't look terribly interested in us, X ushers us in the opposite direction, nonetheless.

We amble across the scrub, past the occasional acacia thorn and lead-wood willow, and through patches of reeds that bite sharply at our calves. We rest awhile on another termite mound overlooking the one remaining waterhole. Scattered pairs of zebra lean their heads on each other's rumps and giraffe make the long journey down to drink. Baboons splash around the water's edge, periodically nudged out by visiting reed and water buck, and the ubiquitous red lechwe hover in huge packs looking nervous—heads up, noses in the air—as if perpetually anticipating attack.

We climb down from our viewing platform and head back through the dried marsh where solitary egrets and the occasional white heron peck the dirt. Beyond the marsh, perhaps two hundred metres away, a large herd of buffalo jostles and stomps. Maria and Jacki spot them immediately, spinning around in search of tree climbing opportunities. X continues to walk slowly, and we follow tight behind. 'They have seen us,' he says, 'and they are agitated.'

A great cloud of dust rises up around them as they pound the dirt with their hooves, the vibrations echoing under our feet. There is really nowhere for us to hide and nowhere to run, though we step up our pace regardless. 'It's OK,' says X. 'Just ignore them and walk away.'

We adopt a kind of power walking posture—bums out, arms pumping by our sides—and stride towards camp. Maria is at the head of the column with the rest of us marching in single file behind. After we've put some distance between us and them, X slows us down. 'It is safe now,' he says, 'and we are close to home.' We relax a little and amble back along the track to camp. With the River Lodge in sight, X hunkers down again and examines the dirt. 'Look,' he says, 'two front and back paws equal distance from each other, and a low thin smudge in between. He sat down here.'

As we lean over X's shoulder, a distinctive growl rises from the reeds, and the four of us freeze, wide eyes focussed on the offending bush. 'He is close,' says X casually, as if referring to the imminent arrival of the postman. We do not wait to ascertain his whereabouts further, but make a rapid dash towards the lodge stepping as quickly as we can. We are not *technically* running, so we are not *technically* behaving like prey, but I'm not sure our growly friend in the bushes would draw such fine distinctions.

Back in the beautiful River Lodge I prepare to shower. There is something perverse about standing under gallons of steaming hot water in a place suffering its sixth year of drought, but for one hundred dollars a night I am prepared to overcome my scruples. The scarcity of the water, in fact, makes the experience even more indulgent. As I step into the shower the steam mixes with the cool night air and I bury my face in the fresh clear flow of water. I watch it run down over my toes and disappear through the branches into the undergrowth below. I wash away the dirt and dust of the day, staring into the darkening twilight through the small bamboo window. As I look, I see two tiny beads of green light staring back at me from the bush. Hmm?…I wonder. What might his plans be for this evening?

Maria and Jacki arrive with four cold beers and we sit on the wicker chairs of our balcony and watch the sun drop over the elephants ambling across the horizon. I've known Maria and Jacki as long as I've known anyone in Australia. When I first came, I joined the Melbourne University Soccer Club as a way of meeting people; Maria was the long time player/manager and all round organiser. At the time, I was unemployed, penniless and a bit desperate and, on the basis of a very new acquaintance, Maria lent me money, and was a friend when friends were a bit thin on the ground.

When Sarah arrived at training one night two years later Maria invited her—'the loud Canadian'—to dinner, and the rest, as they say, is history. The four of us have been knocking around together ever since. The funny thing is, people get Maria and Jacki wrong in the same way they get Sarah and me wrong. Everyone thinks Maria and Sarah are a bit full on, kind of loud and pushy, and they worry that poor Jacki and I get bossed about. We know, of course, it's actually the other way around; Jacki and I have the real power, we just exercise it a little more quietly. It works though, the difference in temperament; I couldn't imagine going out with someone like me, and Sarah says she'd go crazy in a relationship with someone like her. I think it's the same for these girls too.

When the sky has turned black, we follow the path of kerosene lanterns that lead to the dining area and settle around our table with a very nice bottle of South African red. Dinner is an excellent beef stroganoff with rice and freshly baked bread, and a fruit tart for dessert. 'Do lions climb trees?' asks Jacki, out of the blue.

'They can—we've seen them at Lake Manyara—but they don't always for some reason.'

'Do they…in the Okavango Delta do you think?'

'Um…I suppose they *could*.'

'So what exactly stops a lion from climbing into our tree house?'

'Er…well…something must…or maybe…actually…nothing.'

'Hmm…that's what I thought. Leopards and cheetahs too you think?'

'They don't though Jacki,' I try to reassure her.

'*Why* don't they? It seems to me there is absolutely nothing stopping our friendly overgrown pussy cat from this afternoon popping in for a visit after lights out.'

'Well…maybe there is nothing *actually* stopping him, but they just…sort of don't…I think.'

'Thanks, Jac. That's very reassuring.'

'Don't worry. You'll be OK. Maria'll protect you.'

The stars are spectacular and the Southern Cross gleams at the end of the Milky Way. Sarah and I climb the stairs of our tree house where a single flame lights our room, the white mosquito net surrounding the bed shimmering in its light. I take Sarah's hand and we fall onto the bed lying side by side in cool night air. I lean over and gently kiss her neck. 'I love you,' I say.

'I love you too.'

Some time later—in the heat of the moment so to speak—we hear the unmistakable roar of a lion, and I have to say, I think that's a first.

It is Easter weekend and everything in Maun is closing down for four days. We cannot head north to Chobe and Victoria Falls until after the holiday, but have managed to hire the last four-wheel drive in town for close on two million dollars a day. I wait outside the Avis office while Sarah and Maria pay, and try not to think about what it's doing to our budget. Nothing that's geared towards tourists in Africa is cheap, especially not in southern Africa.

A couple of hundred kilometres from Maun are the Nxai and Makgadikgadi salt pans, formed around 10 000 years ago when the huge lake that covered them evaporated leaving a vast bed of cracked salt. They now form a remote and isolated national park that sits on the edge of the desert. There are no roads across the pans, as such, just the tracks of the vehicle that was there before you.

The guidebooks and tourist brochures are full of dire warnings in capital letters and bold font. You should only contemplate visiting the area in a four-wheel drive, and only if you are an experienced driver. You must take all your food and shelter and ensure you have more than sufficient water and fuel. As well as a basic wheel jack, you should carry chains and a winch.

The problem appears to be that the salt sometimes forms a hard crust and may look solid, but in actual fact is wafer thin and often conceals a gaping hole beneath. If you and your vehicle fall down the hole there is no way *at all* of getting out. 'Just like when the lakes freeze over at home,' says Sarah. 'Except if you fall in there, you die.'

'Oh and I'm sure we'd be completely fine if it happened here.'

Apart from the dangers of *literally* sinking without trace, there is also the problem of navigation. There are no signs, no maps, no clear or obvious paths to follow and no landmarks. The vast flat expanses of white have been known to have a strange affect on the psyche, especially in the heat if the day, and have left people lost and disorientated. 'A good sense of direction is a must,' reads Maria, exchanging a silent, knowing look with Jacki.

'Oh come on girls,' I say. 'I know it's not our best thing, but between us we should be OK. Two defective and two mediocre senses of direction must almost amount to one whole one surely?'

The problem is we have no desire to spend four days hanging out in Maun or taking day trips into the endless pale, yellow scrub that surrounds it. Driving isn't our best thing either, but Maria's brother owns a four wheel drive and once took her for a ride in it and showed her the switches and stuff, so I reckon we should be fine. Maria seems confident enough, and Jacki should be able to take care of the technical/mechanical details.

We load up the van with tents, jerry cans of water and petrol, and a giant cool box, and head to town for supplies. The supermarket is thoroughly Western and lined with all sorts of fresh and convenience foods we haven't seen for months. We decide on spaghetti and pesto and to be rash, splash out on the makings of a beef burgundy.

The road out of town is sealed and dead straight, but lined on either side with dozens of kamikaze donkeys. Apparently a bovine lung disease has spread throughout Ngamiland and thousands of cattle have been shot. The government has brought the donkeys in to help farmers with ploughing, but far from plodding neatly through the fields, they are running amok in the traffic. We sit on forty kilometres an hour, Maria braking suddenly every few minutes to let another untethered donkey amble across the road.

We breakfast on hot cross buns and practise pronouncing 'Nxai' and 'Makgadikgadi'. The 'k's represent 'a voiceless, click—a sound similar to that when approving of the taste of food'—and the 'g's are a kind of phlegmy throat clearing sound. Tricky enough in the first place, but according to our book, there are actually a number of *different* phlegmy throat clearing sounds and *five* different clicks. It all depends on where you place your tongue in relation to your palate and teeth and whether they all come together in an up or downward motion.

We attempt to match our own slurpy, dribbling, raspberry type sounds to the descriptions in the book, the most successful of which is a kind of 'gee-up-horse-y' click that emanates from the top left hand side of my mouth. I manage, finally, to get my tongue around the 'k's and 'g's, but the problem is putting them altogether without taking ten minutes to form the word, or sounding like I've contracted TB.

A few kilometres out of Maun we are stopped by armed personnel at a 'Veterinary Control Checkpoint' and I jump down from the cab and smile at the official who asks me to open up the back of our vehicle. He makes straight for the cool box and starts to rummage. 'Do you have any fresh meat?' he asks.

Bugger. We have a miniscule amount—just enough to prepare the first decent meal we've had in weeks—and it was bought in a very hygienic supermarket all nicely wrapped in cellophane and stored in a fridge and is really unlikely to contain any dodgy cow diseases.

'Er…well…sort of…I suppose…yes.'

'I'm sorry,' he says, dragging it out of the box. 'You can boil it here and take it with you cooked, or we must burn it. You cannot take it uncooked beyond this checkpoint.'

I reluctantly relinquish our precious dinner, and hop into the cab. 'Just remembered we forgot to buy wine girls, and as we have just lost our meat, I'm afraid there's no beef or burgundy in tonight's beef burgundy.'

The beautiful sealed road does not last long, and we turn onto a sandy track that leads into Nxai Pan. Jacki sits with the four-wheel drive manual on her lap and attempts to guide Maria through. 'OK Big Chica. You must adopt a relaxed, sitting posture and a loose grip on the steering wheel.'

'Yes. Thank you. I think I can manage that. Find the section on what to do when your nice firm road turns to soft, shifting sand.'

'OK. The first thing is to reduce the tyre pressure to increase the contact area of the tyres with the ground.'

Maria pulls over and we bail out fiddling with the valve on the wheels. 'Hang on girls,' I say. 'What do we do when we are back on the sealed road?'

'Put the air back in, *obviously*.'

'So there is a handy portable air pump in the boot then...?'

We pile back into the van and Maria starts up and drives onto the sand.

'OK. Next section,' says Jacki. 'Chica, you need to decide whether you want to travel in high or low ratio, and then adjust the wheels accordingly.'

Maria stops the van again.' Here's an idea, Jacki,' she says, 'try reading *ahead* a sentence or two.' We bail out, scrutinising the tyres and hub caps until we find something that looks like it can be adjusted and might take us into a different 'ratio'. As we pile back in, Maria whacks the red knob near the gear stick, which we suspect may also be of some importance to this process.

'OK,' says Jacki. 'Now you just avoid digging in or stalling by maintaining your momentum. That means lots of power and changing gear at high revs. You can do it, Chica!'

The three of us remain silent as Maria concentrates intently, manoeuvring the huge vehicle through the soft channels and sliding along the crumbling banks of the track. After a few minutes we settle into a rhythm—and as long as no one approaches from the opposite direction we should be just fine.

There is nothing between the vast blue sky and the flat yellow scrub except a few palm trees which, having lost their leaves, stretch like rows of telegraph poles towards the horizon. As we approach the pans, circles of white appear like so many ice rinks, silvery speckles sparkling in the sunlight. Slowly the circles come together, the salt overwhelming the scrub until the scorched, baked earth looks like it's been buried in a fresh fall of snow.

'Uh oh,' says Maria suddenly, noticing three large, shiny Range Rovers heading our way. It is the school holidays and Botswana is a favoured destination for South African four-wheel drivers.

'Just relax, Chica. You'll be fine,' says Jacki, gently resting a hand on Maria's back. Sarah and I glance nervously at the approaching convoy, at each other, at Jacki. The track is only wide enough for one vehicle, and beyond that the sand is deep and shifting. We slow to a crawl as they approach and Maria attempts to veer left in order to create some space. She fiddles with the gear stick, and keeps the revs high as instructed. Sarah and I offer sweet encouraging smiles to the oncoming driver whose face is florid and fearsome already. 'Di yi hif your wheels locked en?' he yells in a thick, clipped Afrikaner accent.

'Thank you. Yes,' Maria shouts back through gritted teeth.

He edges close, jerking along our right side as Maria attempts to haul us up the steep bank. The wheels spin and grind and with each lurch forward the angle of our van increases until we are inches from the Afrikaner's shiny blue paint work.

'Di yi kno' wet ya doin' girlie?' he yells.

'Don't even think about telling me,' mutters Maria.

'Yes, I know what I'm doing, *thank you*,' she yells back.

The rest of us hold our breath imagining a long deep scratch across the front panel, and the ugly scenario of a face off between Maria and the Voortrekker.

The wheels suddenly engage—some button we pressed must have kicked in—and we climb up the bank pulling away from the van. We skirt around the other two vehicles behind, and slide smoothly back down onto the track.

'*Well done*, Chica,' says Jacki. '*Excellent work!*' say Sarah and I.

The salt continues to encroach, until the track ceases to be a track, and becomes more a muddy white thoroughfare of dubious composition. The dried salt cracks beneath the tyres, and we rumble along never quite sure just what's holding us up.

We reach 'Baine's Baobabs,' a stand of ancient trees that appears to rise out of nowhere and float on a sea of white. Maria parks the van in the shade of their huge canopy, and we spill out onto baked dry earth. We hover by one of the sprawling trunks, joining hands to encircle it—even with our arms fully extended, the four of us cannot encompass its girth. The trees are thought to be over a thousand years old and have remained completely unchanged for at least the last one hundred and thirty. A young Englishman, Thomas Baines, painted them in 1862, and if you compare them with the painting now, apparently you can see that only one branch has fallen in all that time.

They are the only vegetation for miles and, if I stand with my back to them, there is nothing but a vast expanse of perfectly flat, dry white dirt—the long dried-up lake. Even the horizon is difficult to make out in the shimmering heat. It is eerily silent and absolutely still, no rustle of leaves, no flapping of wings and, once again, we have it to ourselves.

We run onto the salt pan, the surface dazzling like fresh snow in midday sun. It is incredibly hot and dry as the desert. I close my eyes, lifting my head to the sky and spin around in giant circles. My God! What an utterly beautiful, utterly pristine place. I flop down onto the salt and stare into the bright blue heavens. Sarah walks over and lies by my side and Maria squats down next to us. Jacki is setting up the self timer on the camera, and trying to balance it on her day-pack. She hits the button and dashes over to us, the Famous Four on their latest, greatest adventure.

CHAPTER 18

FROM COAST TO COAST

WE HAVE BEEN travelling for four-and-a-half months now and I am beginning to have chest-of-drawer fantasies: neat piles of fresh white knickers, and clean pressed shirts on long rows of wooden coathangers. I long to litter the bathroom with toiletries and not have to squeeze them dripping and oozing into a tiny wash bag. I want to dry my face on a cotton towel—not on the festering piece of polyester that lurks at the bottom of my pack pretending to be one. I want to lie in the bath and read a book. I want to take up space, to leave things lying around, to depart a place carrying only my wallet. I want order. I want familiarity. I want sameness.

I want, maybe, to go home, but then again, I don't. We have a huge push ahead of us: a long haul through the rough isolated terrain from Maun to Kasane in northern Botswana where we cross the Zimbabwe border into Victoria Falls. Then we have another long drive through the Caprivi Strip—the neck of land that joins Zimbabwe to Namibia—and down to the capital, Windhoek. Maria and Jacki have been coveting the luxury safari vehicles we've seen around town—padded armchair style seats, side tables with drink holders, and adjustable canvas flaps for shade—but we have ended up with an ex-British army four-wheel drive which could not, even in a generous moment, be described as luxurious.

We encounter only one mild hiccup *en route* in the form of an over zealous border official at Kasane who pokes his head through the window of our van and eyes us curiously. 'Only ladies?' he asks in a confused tone. 'You are only ladies?'

'Yes,' we reply in chorus. 'We are only ladies.'

'*Why* are you only ladies?'

Aah…well that's a pretty tricky question really, especially from a border official of a country whose president has declared lesbians and gays worse than dogs and pigs.

'Our husbands are busy at home…with business,' I say.

'Ah good. Husbands. Good,' he mutters. 'You may proceed.'

Over the past few weeks, Victoria Falls has taken on the status of a kind of Mecca, the place where our prayers will be answered—high-style toilets, beds and showers, chocolate, deodorant, batteries, international newspapers, even pizza maybe. When we arrive, the main shop-lined street is buzzing: dozens of backpackers and smartly turned out package deal-ers surrounded by eager locals waving brochures and wads of cash. 'Ooh! I see glossy magazines,' says Sarah. 'And a café with gourmet possibilities,' says Jacki. Maria has her nose pressed to window and is already undertaking a preliminary review of shopping opportunities.

We pile out of the van and are immediately inundated by hawkers trying to pass off bundles of Zambian kwacha as Zimbabwean dollars, but we are far too experienced travellers these days to be taken in by such a scam. We brush them aside and re-group on the pavement. The street is dominated by the Shearwater office, the big adventure company, which spreads across four shop fronts. There are a dozen other offices all advertising white water rafting, bungee jumping, canoeing, helicopter flights, and a variety of other adrenaline pumping activities. It is the sort of place your average independent traveller would declare 'really touristy' in a slightly disparaging tone, but—with its promise of good food and greater comfort—we quite love it.

From town, we can hear the falls and see the great clouds of spray that rise hundreds of feet above them and, as we draw nearer, a light mist blows across our faces. Outside the park entrance, groups of locals lounge by makeshift stalls offering umbrellas and raincoats for hire. We have been warned about the spray and have dressed accordingly in bathers and shorts, and I have wrapped the camera in a plastic bag sealed with elastic bands.

The falls are not the tallest in the world, but the longest and, many say, the most spectacular. The plume of spray above them extends half a kilometre into the sky and, on a clear day, can be seen from seventy kilometres away. The Zambesi continues to cut through the soft limestone and clay creating a long line of deep dramatic gorges. If conditions are good, you can spend half a day here watching the falls from the different vantage points.

We hover at the start of the track by a statue of David Livingstone— the first European to see them. In 1855 the young Scottish explorer set out to find the 'Mosi oa Tunya,'—'the smoke that thunders'. He was taken by dugout canoe to a small island on the northern side and, so the story goes, crawled out onto a precipice in order to see them. Overwhelmed by their beauty he declared: 'Scenes so lovely must have been gazed upon by angels in flight' and, as was tradition at the time, claimed them for his Queen, Victoria.

We head through the dense forest of mahogany and ebony that is nurtured by the continual spray above the falls. We can hear the water clearly enough, though all we can see through the trees is thick white cloud. 'Lovely forest,' says Maria, 'but can you see any *water?*'

The path cuts though the trees to a viewpoint atop a cliff edge where we pause at a wooden railing. We are completely engulfed by dense cloud and I can barely see Jacki only two metres away. The spray rains down on us from above, and splashes up from beneath our feet, and we hover, drenched and freezing. The problem, we have discovered, is that, like the Chobe River that feeds them, the falls are experiencing their highest volume of water for twenty years and, while we thought this might be a once in a lifetime viewing experience, the excessive spray caused by the deluge is so dense, we can't actually see *anything*.

We stand in a line *listening* to the mighty Zambesi cascading spectacularly one hundred metres into the vast basalt gorges below. 'Stunning view, eh girls?' I say.

We pause for a moment longer, defiantly looking at what *should be* one of the world's great natural spectacles. 'Maybe it's clearer further along,' Jacki suggests. We shuffle back to the track, out of the spray and into the rainforest. A wooden boardwalk leads to another viewpoint where we assemble, four bathing beauties in bright swimming costumes lined against a backdrop of dense white cloud. We step from foot to foot, arms flapping against the cold. On the track, ten metres away, it is warm and humid; here, the heat is forced out by the sheer volume of water and we stand, dripping and shivering. We wait for a break in the cloud and a chance to catch a glimpse of the legendary view.

As we linger, it clears, finally, and we can see the mighty Devil's Cataract—the western edge of the falls—cascading down a vast gaping fissure in the rock. This time, the view really is stunning: a huge white curtain sparkling in the sunlight, thundering against the rock, and a perfect rainbow arching high above, linking the ancient rainforests on either side.

In less than a minute the cloud rolls in, a cold spray whips across and we are enveloped in mist again. We stand, looking at each other, rain poring down our faces, huddling against the cold. 'That's it, my friends,' I say. '*That* was the famous Victoria Falls.'

We have been told that you can also view the falls from the other side—from Zambia—and we take the short taxi trip across the bridge that links the two countries. The change in the look and feel of our surroundings as we cross the border is remarkable. It's as if we are suddenly back in East Africa—unsealed, pot-hole ridden roads, shabby wooden shop fronts, and children begging on dusty street corners.

The small town of Livingstone which sits right on the border was once a thriving tourist centre where colonists came to amble though shady parks, and sip tea above the falls. The town fell into decline—along with the rest of the country—as a result of the political and economic turmoil of the 1970s. Decaying signs of its former glory are everywhere: a wide, almost elegant, street lined with what clearly used to be flower beds, now repositories for Coke cans and banana skins, a once stylish art deco cinema, its masonry crumbling, the paint-work chipped and flaking.

It's a shock to find ourselves suddenly back in Third World Africa, especially with the thriving Victoria Falls only a few kilometres away. There are none of the busy shops, none of the well-dressed pedestrians, none of the restaurants and fast food outlets. It's as if we are back at the start of our trip, in small town Kenya amongst the poverty and dirt, the modicum of order and familiarity that allowed us to feel a little more secure disappearing with one step across the border.

We search for somewhere that might provide lunch, but there are no cafés of any nature, nor even stalls selling kebabs or chapatis. I have done my dash with banana breakfasts and bread and margarine lunches, and will not entertain the possibility of mealie maize and sadza. We duck into a shabby corner store that, in a generous moment, might be called a bakery.

Our Baker's Delight is obviously the local hang-out of every homeless boy and ragamuffin in town, and we grab a couple of buns as quickly as possible and head for the door. A scruffy young lad, maybe twelve or thirteen, approaches me, edging to within inches of my face.

I shove him away, and we push through the crowd who have gathered in front of the exit to watch.

As we turn back towards the falls, Sarah notices the zip on the small pocket of my pack is open, and looks inside. 'Was there anything in here?'

'Just my glasses.'

'They're gone, Babe.'

'*Shit!*'

I realise to my despair that my much loved, beautiful black rim Italian specs with their expensive extra-specially-thin-lenses-ground-somewhere-in-Austria-at-enormous-expense, have been ripped off by some guttersnipe who will flog them for the price of a Coke. I have no spare pair, only the prescription sunglasses I am wearing.

'Oh Doll. What am I going to do?'

'I don't know. Let's go and report it. You never know. We have to get a statement for insurance anyway.'

The police station is dark and scruffy and filled with half uniformed young men sprawled across an old wooden desk. A scrappy piece of paper pinned to the wall behind them details 'Feeding times for prisoners,' and next to it, in primary school scrawl, another notice announces:

GUN SAFETY

You must know how it works.
Whether it is loaded.
Where it is pointing.
What your target is.
Where your bullet will go or stop.
You have a full time job. Don't guess. Don't forget.

Sarah and I read in unison and exchange glances. 'Oh dear,' I say, 'I think this could be tricky.' I take a deep breath and approach the desk. 'I'd like to report a theft,' I say.

The young officer looks at me blankly as I attempt to explain what's happened. He shuffles ash trays and Coke cans and after some time produces a crinkled, blank piece of a paper which he thrusts in front of me. It is a slow, tedious process involving my writing down the sequence of events, and the young officer copying out my statement word for word for me to sign. As the hours pass and the sun comes down, the office darkens and I realise what life's going to look like for the next few weeks. I can't not wear my sunnies. Even though they make everything darker, without them, I can't see a bloody thing.

By the time we leave the police station it is pitch-black and I'm squinting to make out my feet. I grab Sarah's arm and stumble along the rutted and uneven path. The young officer—AK47 slung casually over his arm—has been told to escort us back to the hostel and, having decided we must be extremely rich to own a pair of glasses worth a sum equal to the gross domestic product of his country, suggests we might like to give him some money for his trouble or, at least, buy him a beer. I suggest not, but tell him if he finds my specs I'll buy him a crate of beer.

We trek back through the unlit streets and I wonder how the hell I'm going to get a replacement pair of glasses, and how I'll manage until then. I really can't see much at all, and apart from anything else, I feel like a complete wanker wandering through town at night in a pair of Calvin Klein shades.

Back at the guesthouse we are greeted by Maria and Jacki who fail in their attempts to be supportive. 'It won't be too bad,' sniggers Maria. 'There are more daylight hours than dark.'

'And you're asleep for most of the dark ones,' says Jacki, with a not quite straight face.

'Apart from those when I eat, read, move about and am generally seen in company, you mean?'

While Sarah searches for the number of our insurance company, I head for the communal kitchen to prepare dinner. I lean over a chopping board carefully slicing onions with my head bowed. One guest after another wanders through doing a quick double-take as I raise my head and smile awkwardly. They shuffle around the fridge smirking at each other, thinking I can't see their eyebrow-raised looks.

I wander over to the stove and grab a saucepan. I could just make a general announcement explaining *why* I am preparing spaghetti bolognaise in a bright, fluorescently lit room in my sunglasses, but I can't do that every time I feel awkward. I resign myself to their smirks, stir my sauce and let them think I just fancy myself.

After dinner I manage to get through to my insurance company in Australia and speak to a terribly friendly older lady who I suspect has never ventured outside Glen Waverley, and whose idea of travelling overseas is taking the ferry to Tasmania for a weekend getaway. 'If you hold for a minute dear,' she says, 'I'll ask our medical people for the name of an optician in your area. Where are you again dear, Zimba?'

I try to explain that I'm in a Third World country—she may have seen something like it on the telly once—an ad for Community Aid Abroad perhaps, or a news bulletin about drought or famine—and that there are no such things as opticians in 'Zimba', and even if there were, I wouldn't be seen dead in pair of Coke bottle lenses that would undoubtedly be all they could provide. I thank her kindly for her inspired assistance and hang up.

'Not very helpful, Babe?' asks Sarah. I shake my head in despair. 'What am I going to do, Doll? *Why haven't I got a spare pair for Christ's sake?*'

'I'll call my parents. They'll sort it.'

I leave Sarah searching for the phone card and flop down on the couch to sulk. Why didn't I just buy a cheap pair before we left and chuck them in the bottom of my pack. I really can't function without them. It's embarrassing not recognising people, and having to hold things two inches from my nose and, apart from anything else, it's just not safe. I'd be over the edge of the bloody falls before the day's out.

A quarter of an hour later, Sarah emerges from the office and kneels by the side of the couch. 'It's sorted Babe. Mum called Sean in Melbourne and he has all the details of your prescription and frame on the computer. He'll organise a new, identical pair and courier them to Windhoek.'

'*Courier* them!?'

'There's no other way. *Don't* ask how much.'

I shuffle off to the bathroom and grab my toilet bag. At least I'm not going to be stumbling around forever, though Windhoek feels a long way off, and it's clearly costing a packet.

I stand in front of the mirror cleaning my teeth—boxers, T-shirt and sunglasses. Truly, it's *not* a good look.

There is no public transport from Victoria Falls to Namibia, and we toy only briefly with the idea of hitching through the Caprivi Strip. Instead, we organise a ride with a group, a night's accommodation and dinner provided *en route*. Maria and Jacki opt for a slightly more up-market version that promises a luxury coach and gourmet dinner, and we arrange to meet in Windhoek.

The road across the far north-west corner of Botswana is, as they all are, long and straight and seemingly never ending. As I watch it disappearing to a point on the horizon I realise I am beginning to tire of all this—the constant movement, the perpetual discomfort. I don't have many African bus rides left in me. And yet, do I really want to give it up? The absolute freedom that comes from carrying our lives in a backpack, from ridding ourselves of routine, from thinking only how to enjoy each day. For months now we haven't had to worry about work, bills, shopping, family. We haven't had to deal with any relationship but our own. Our biggest concerns have been our personal safety, keeping healthy, where we'll sleep at night, where our next meal will come from. In many ways, dealing with those things has been so much easier than negotiating the daily complexities of ordinary life. I've got used to things being a little simpler.

Well after dark we arrive in Otavi, a small farming community three hundred and seventy five kilometres north of Windhoek. There is a petrol station and two shops, but nothing that looks remotely like a backpacker's or a hostel, and we begin to wonder about the nature of our evening's accommodation. 'Are we staying here?' I ask the driver.

'Yes. Yes,' he says. 'Here.'

We head away from the small main road into what is clearly a residential street with no signs of the promised bed for the night. I speculate that perhaps the driver has pocketed the money for our quiet clean double room in a motel and vegetable curry dinner, and is taking us instead to the house of his uncle where his aunt and sisters will whip up a bowl of mealie maize and sadza, and we will all settle comfortably for the night on the back porch.

We pull into the driveway of a tidy suburban home with neat lawns and a white picket fence. A small, frail woman with a tight bun pops out the front door, and perches on the step. She looks vaguely alarmed, as if she's only just heard that twelve complete strangers are staying the night. She jerks her head sharply left and right and turns immediately back into the house like a cuckoo announcing one o'clock. 'This is…our accommodation?' I ask.

'Yes. Here. Accommodation.'

The twelve of us pile out of the bus and line up along the narrow garden path. Sarah and I enter first, wiping our boots carefully on the mat, and the others follow behind. The cuckoo lady has disappeared, and we hover awkwardly in the hallway like gatecrashers at a party. We can see into the adjacent living room, a settee and two chairs facing each other, an empty bookcase and two framed pictures leaning against a wall. There is a collection of dolls and a teddy bear on the floor, but no sign of the maps on the walls, the piles of safari brochures, the empty beer cans that might mark it out as a place frequented by budget travellers. It is in fact, as I suspected, not a hostel at all, but somebody's currently inhabited family home.

The cuckoo lady dashes down the hallway, turning abruptly at the end and marching back toward us. She pumps her arms vigorously, elbows at right angles, head twitching sharply from side to side. I try a gentle 'hi', and venture a smile, but she looks right through me, her eyes glazed, demonic.

She turns again and, without a word, dashes down the other corridor while we hover, eyebrows raised, politely suppressing the extraordinary urge to laugh.

Suddenly, a high pitched shriek emanates from one of the bedrooms down the hallway: 'ARE THERE ANY MARRIED COUPLES?'

There are no marrieds in our group, but Sarah suggests the Australians, Pip and John, might be able to wing it. They grab their packs hesitantly and hover in the hallway, reluctant to venture further into the house. 'It'll be fine,' says Sarah, ushering them towards what we presume is the double bedroom. 'You'll be OK.'

The cuckoo lady emerges a few moments later and, head still twitching, makes vague eye contact with the area around my left shoulder—maybe the sunglasses are a bit off-putting. I daren't look at Sarah who is hovering behind me. Suddenly, she snaps 'Come!' and Sarah and I are startled into action. We gather our bags quickly and trot down the hallway behind her.

We are shown into a small, pink bedroom which is completely empty except for a bed—*one* bed—a tiny, white-framed child's bed with matching Thomas the Tank Engine sheet and pillowcase. 'I will bring another,' she says, turning abruptly and leaving the room.

Sarah and I wait until her footsteps disappear down the hallway and splutter out the guffaws we have been suppressing since our arrival. We fall onto the still warm and, I suspect, until very recently inhabited bed. 'Maybe you'll get Bananas in Pyjamas, Doll,' I suggest, 'or perhaps Teletubbies.'

We emerge from our room and make a tentative inspection of the rest of the house. As there appears to be no other bedrooms, it seems the remaining members of our group are sleeping on the lounge floor. There's a kitchen that's obviously used, and a shower and toilet with a few plastic toys and a bottle of bubble bath. It *almost* seems like a normal family home, except it's completely devoid of anything personal. I would have said they'd just moved in and were in the process of unpacking, except that at the very end of the house there's a small sleep-out absolutely crammed full of everything one might reasonably expect to find in a home. It's like a whole house in one tiny room—a television, a couple of mattresses, a writing desk, a chest of drawers, a coffee table, a small wardrobe, two armchairs, some table lamps, sundry toys and games and, in the middle of the floor, a sleepy young girl in pyjamas—clearly, the rightful claimant to the Thomas the Tank Engine bed.

We shuffle hesitantly out the back where a middle aged man is leaning over a flaming *braai*. He nods 'hello' and offers a weak smile which almost, but not quite, involves eye contact. We hover in the tightly confined yard with our fellow passengers, struggling through stilted conversation about the region's rainfall and its potential to attract tourists. Our cook, it transpires, is the owner of the bus service, and the house in which we are staying is indeed his home where he lives with his daughter and girlfriend—the cuckoo lady. A few years ago, he noticed a gap in the market for this type of service and now, twice a week, he gives his house over to a dozen foreigners while, we presume, he and his family bed down on the remaining two inches of space in the sleep-out.

We sit, mostly in silence, picking at our charcoal coated *kudu* sausage, and passing around the 'salad' which appears to be made entirely of grapes. I catch Sarah's eye across the table, then Pip's and then John's. 'It's Africa,' I whisper.

'Yes,' they agree. 'It's Africa.'

By the time we reach Windhoek late the next day, I am exhausted. My body is giving me not so gentle hints that it could do with a few vitamin rich meals, occasional access to hot water, and a little more sleep. My skin is erupting in pimples where it's not dried and flaky. I have black bags under my eyes, and a crop of cold sores sprouting on my lips. I look shocking. So, for that matter, does Sarah.

Our clothes are stained and tatty, and my two T-shirts are covered in great green splotches where the patch Sarah used to mend my shorts ran in the wash. Our funds are much depleted which means, heaven forbid, we must start sleeping in dormitories and hanging out with the I-stayed-up-all-night-and-got-really-pissed-and-threw-up-and-it-only-cost-me-twopence-ha'penny crowd.

Between the two of us, we are lugging around half a dozen Shona stone carvings, a three kilogram mahogany hippo, a couple of wall hangings, an enormous wicker basket, some cushion covers, a bunch of *kangas* and sundry books and maps, in addition to the gear we set out with. Just lifting our packs is a challenge, and Sarah is clicking her joints daily in her own private chiropractic treatment.

I can't bear the thought of more camping, of those bloody awful squalid toilets, and of eating more crappy meals prepared in bacteria filled kitchens. I long to stay in one place for more than a night, and to eat something light and fresh and oil free. And, apart from all that, I am heartily sick of not being able to see my feet after sunset, and of people thinking that I think I must just be terribly cool.

It's not even as if conditions are really that bad, in fact, they're a lot better than they were at the beginning of the trip—to be honest, I'm not sure either of us could get through that now—its just that we've been on the road a long time. To make matters worse, when we finally catch up with Maria and Jacki, they describe, in some detail, their previous night in a cool, ceiling fanned lodge, eating pepper steak and salad, and sipping chilled Chardonnay. I think, maybe, we are nearing the end.

Windhoek, Namibia's capital, wins Africa's Tidy Town Award: neat, litter-free streets, graffiti free walls, and pavements unencumbered by beggars or street kids. It was formerly a German town, which may have something to do with it. The main street faces onto the new Supreme Court, a grand structure built in soft, pale sandstone which spreads out in a broad arc of arches and columns, reminiscent of North African desert architecture. Opposite, glitzy arcades and expensive Western-style shops line the pedestrian-only walkways, and smart-business suited men and women lick ice-cream cones and window shop.

Of all the places we have visited so far, it is certainly the most racially diverse: blacks and whites in more equal numbers, with a significant Asian—what used to be called 'coloured'—population. Almost everyone, regardless of their racial background, speaks English, German and Afrikaans, and many of the local Africans speak an additional two or three languages.

Our first stop is the DHL office where a nice lady hands me a large padded envelope. I carefully unwrap the outer padding to find an Australia Post Jiffy bag. Inside the bag is a cardboard box wrapped in bubble jet which I remove slowly. Inside the cardboard box is a beautiful, new, shiny chrome glasses case, and inside the case, a beautiful, new, shiny pair of glasses. I remove my sunnies, and slide the precious new spectacles over my ears, settling them carefully on my nose. I wiggle the arms gently adjusting them for comfort. 'How'd they look Doll?'

'Great Hon…bit like they used to.'

'Don't mock,' I say. 'You cannot begin to imagine just how wonderful it is to see daylight again.'

From Windhoek we take a bus through the *Speergebeit*, the 'Forbidden Zone' where the diamond mines spread out from the road. Vehicles are prohibited from stopping apart from two designated places, and we are warned that we risk being shot by security guards if we wander off. It leads us to Swakopmund, an isolated German coastal town that sits between the ocean and the desert.

The distinctive smell of an Atlantic coast seeps through the van as we approach. A light fog settles over the clapboard houses that litter the rocky shoreline and an ancient wooden pier disappears into the mist. We pass the Bakerei on Kaiser Wilhelmstrasse, the Beerhalle serving lager in Steins. Our hostel is the last building on a road that ends abruptly when it literally reaches the desert—'the edge of town' we call it. On one side of the street are suburban houses, and on the other, nothing; no trees, no scrub, just a flat expanse of sand leading to distant dunes.

We are picked up early the following morning by an American, Beth, who is taking us sand-boarding. We pile into the van with four large rectangular pieces of hardboard about a metre long and sixty centimetres wide with a coating of furniture polish on one side. 'They might not look like much,' says Beth, 'but they sure can move, don't you worry.'

We park in the middle of a vast area of nothing next to a group of one hundred metre dunes that rise sharply from the flat. I pick up a helmet and, just to be sure, fix the head-strap to my sunnies, sliding my lovely new specs into their chrome case and leaving them in the bus for safe-keeping. Maria and Jacki are eager to get started and grab their boards, holding them first in front, and then on their heads, trying to work out the best way to balance them. It's a bit of a traipse up the first dune, and the wind picks up, making the boards especially awkward to carry.

We pause for a breather at the top while Beth runs through the technique. 'Lie on your stomach,' she says. 'Grab the front of the board with both hands and keep your chin up. If you need to slow down, or adjust your direction, drop your toes into the sand. Be careful though, if you do that unevenly, or too quickly, you'll spin and come off. We'll start with "Little Nellie" here, a gentle training run.'

From the top, the descent looks rather steeper than I had imagined a 'gentle training run' might. I adjust my helmet, check my gloves and elbow pads, and position myself on the board. Beth sits crouched beside me and, at my nod, shoves me over the top. I tighten my grip, hold my breath, and begin to drop, picking up speed and skimming rapidly down the dune. The board shudders and I lose control, tumbling headlong into the sand and coming to an inelegant stop. It's enough to get the adrenaline pumping though, and in an instant I am up and ready for the next run. I grab my board and scamper out of the way as Maria and Jacki come hurtling down after me.

We try balancing the boards on our heads and schlep up to a higher part of the dune. 'This is "Lizzie" one of the Terrible Twins,' announces Beth. 'Bit steeper. Bit more fun.' I perch on the top looking down. The run starts with a steep drop of about twenty metres that smoothes out momentarily before dropping down a long sharp, forty-five degree angle into a wide bowl below. I lie on my board feeling faintly sick and wondering why I haven't grown out of thrill-seeking by now.

Beth gives me a shove, and I am away, dropping at thirty kilometres an hour, the wind whipping past my ears. I can see the big drop coming, and concentrate on keeping my body straight, the board as still as possible. I launch over the crest and plummet down the slope, the sand flying in my face, the board vibrating beneath me. I am speeding down at fifty kilometres an hour, my face inches from the ground. I drop into the bowl and swerve around, slowing gradually as the board starts to spin and I am tipped off into the dust. I stand up and brush myself down. 'Wow!' I say. 'More. I want more.'

As Maria and Jacki come hurtling towards me I grab the camera and attempt to catch them speeding down the slope. I focus on Jack as she hits the crest, flies through the air, swoops down and disappears from frame. All of a sudden I am seeing flying fish eagles again, and envisage a series of stunning shots of nothing. I drop the camera into its case, grab my board, and clamber back up the dune for another go at Lizzie.

After a couple of runs, we hang out in the 'Playground' where Jacki tries sand-boarding standing up, using her hands to steer, and Sarah and I have a go at tandem sand-boarding. Sarah, sitting behind me, is once again in control of steering, which she once again can't quite master. The board spins wildly halfway down the slope and we end up sprawled across the dune buried in sand. Maria and Jacki follow closely behind, taking a massive tumble where we have disturbed the sand, and falling on top of us, legs and arms and boards splayed everywhere. 'Well done, girls,' says Beth. 'I think you're ready for The Big One.'

Our final ride is called the 'Knuckle Eater', a one hundred metre drop down a virtually sheer slope which ends abruptly with a stretch of flat gravel. Beth estimates, if we keep our toes up, and don't try to slow down, we will reach eighty kilometres an hour.

I lie on my board at the top of the drop. I was right not to consider bungee jumping in Vic Falls; this is the outer limit of my fear. 'Whatever you do,' says Beth, 'do *not* lose control of the board as you hit the gravel—or you'll lose a layer of skin.'

'Thanks. I'll be sure to bear that in mind.'

I wrap my hands around the edge of the board and tuck my elbows in slightly, angling my face as far from the ground as is anatomically possible. I take a deep breath and launch myself over the edge, immediately picking up speed, the sand blurring past. Within seconds I am falling headlong into nothing at sixty kilometres an hour. I contemplate dropping my toes to slow down, but any shift in balance could send me spinning into high speed tumble turns across a gravel pit.

I cling tighter, my knuckles whitening, the sand flying up my nose, the ground speeding away like an Olympic luge run. Suddenly I am down, the soft sand hardens to baked earth and I shudder from head to toe. As I hit the gravel, the board starts to shake and I grip the edges, tensing my elbows to keep it straight. I shoot across the giant sand paper pit and as Beth's feet come into view I realise I have my mouth open and am screaming 'FUCK! FUCK! FUCK!' at the top of my voice.

Still shaking, and buzzing with adrenaline, we drag our scoured boards back to the bus and do hi-fives all around. 'Sensational!' says Maria. 'What do you reckon, Chica?

'Fantastic!' says Jacki. 'Like…totally thrilling.'

We pose for a photo at the bottom of the dune—the four of us decked in helmets and pads like an American football team. Doesn't get much more rugged than this.

Beth moves the bus around to provide a modicum of shade in which to eat lunch and we open up the back door and dive into the cool box. As we break open the Cokes and speculate on the speed of the last run, Jacki notices something shiny in the dirt just beyond the van. She walks towards it, leans over and hunkers down, brushing the sand away. I hear a sharp intake of breath and a muttered 'Oh no!' She gathers it in her cupped hands and walks towards me. 'Sorry Mate,' she says. 'Don't know how that happened.'

There, lying bent and buckled in her open palms, is my brand new glasses case. 'Oh please no,' I say.

I struggle to lift the top, a spring poking through the lining inside. The case is filled with sand, and buried beneath it my brand new, four hundred dollar, recently couriered all the way from Australia glasses, the arms contorted, a deep crack shattering the left lens. *'How the hell did they manage to get run over in five hundred square kilometres of empty desert?!'* I cry. *'There is only one van, for Christ's sake!'*

Beth leans over my shoulder staring into the twisted box. 'I am so sorry, Jacqui,' she says. 'They must have slipped out somehow when I turned the van around. I only moved it a few metres.'

I extricate the glasses from the mangled box and attempt to straighten them out. The arms no longer sit neatly across the lenses but poke at right angles as if doing the splits. The right lens is intact, though no longer attached to anything; the left is bisected by the San Andreas Fault.

On the way back to our hostel Beth drops us at an optician's where a well-meaning man explains he will have to send to Cape Town for a replacement. He's not sure they can find the same sort of frame, and the lenses will be a little thicker, and it will take at least two weeks. I thank him kindly for his trouble and fax Sean in Melbourne. *Love the new specs. Bit of an incident this end involving a small bus and a large desert. Please send replacement left lens.*

Another fucking two weeks in the dark.

Maria and Jacki have only a few days before they travel back to Melbourne, and they want to squeeze in as much as possible. We've decided to head to the famous Sossusvlei sand dunes, part of the Namib-Naukluft National Park; Sarah and I will join an organised group, and the girls will hire a car, leave us at the dunes and head back to Windhoek. I can't believe their time with us is almost over, and that we are only a few weeks from the end of our adventure.

There are twelve people on our tour and our guide explains that we will be moving around the bus regularly in order to get to know everyone. I roll my eyes at Sarah; the last thing I want at this stage is compulsory bonding with the Swedish ferals and earnest American Peace Corps volunteers who appear to comprise our group.

We head off across the Khomas Hochland, a rugged, thinly vege- tated area dissected by deep mountain passes that takes us from the high plateau around Windhoek down to the vast Sand Dune Sea that lies between us and the Atlantic. The steep gravel road descends through a series of bald outcrops, smoothed by the erosion of wind on the soft sandstone. Far below, we can see the vast plains of cream coloured nara grasses through a soft pink, sand-filled haze.

We drop sharply down Speetshoogte Pass, the steep winding track cutting its way through the sandstone to form deep dramatic 'S' bends. Our guide shifts into a lower gear, and we lean back, bracing ourselves against the seat in front. Behind us, Maria and Jacki bounce down in their tinny white Mazda. With each bend in the road we can see the russet and ochre hues of layered rock laid down millions of years ago, and far below, can just make out the edge of the Namib Desert, a vast plateau of dusty pink, edged north and south by the gentle shifting bumps of the Central Highlands.

When we finally reach the plateau, the desert spreads out before us like a scene from *Star Wars*. There is no vegetation, just a loose gathering of pink peaks rising from a perfectly flat floor. There are no clouds and the air is perfectly still. A soft haze hovers over the tiny mountains, and we linger, listening to the silence. As we drive across the desert, the peaks slowly flatten out, forming low rounded hills that eventually merge into a long line of smooth red dunes.

The air cools dramatically as evening approaches, and by the time we reach our campsite at Sesriem there is a definite chill. Maria and Jacki miraculously appear just a few minutes after us, their once white Mazda now the colour of the sand on which it's parked. We off-load our gear and quickly erect the tents. 'Come on girls,' I say. 'This is our last night.'

We race the declining light to a low sandy ridge and clamber up the side. We sit—four of us in a row—watching the sun drop slowly behind the giant, lonely Elim Dune. Talking doesn't seem necessary somehow, and we watch in silence as the bush turns shadowy and black around us.

We are up at four thirty for the drive to 'Dune 45'—so-called because it's forty-five kilometres from Sesriem. It is cold and dark—as it generally is anywhere at 4.30 a.m., especially in the desert—and I wonder if these early morning sun rises aren't just a little overrated. Like Meru and Mount Kenya, I have no doubt the dune will look just as lovely mid morning, and I wouldn't have to bounce around a crowded van for an hour, tired and cranky when I should still be tucked up in bed. Maria is slow to emerge and Jacki hovers by the tent making chirpy, 'Come on Chica' type noises. It's our last full day together, and it will be a while before we see them again.

The road is pitted with deep corrugations, and we are thrown about the bus. Sand bogs periodically sweep across the road and we fishtail wildly and, despite my best efforts, I end up sharing a number of intimate moments with the Swedish feral sitting on my left. I glance back at Maria and Jacki trying to negotiate the nightmare terrain in their tin-pot two-wheel drive. After the salt pans Maria has a reputation to maintain and, God knows how, she manages to keep up. They stall regularly, but somehow she manoeuvres them out of the ruts and on to firm ground.

Towards daybreak the shadowy Dune 45 appears in the distance, and we can just make out the line of smooth ridges that extends beyond it. The sand on the track is deep and shifting and, as we approach, the little Mazda finally gives up. We pile out of the van and watch the boys bounce it out of the dirt—just like Aberfoyle really, though they have rather more success.

We hover at the bottom of the dune, jackets turned up against the wind. We are standing on a grey gravel plain, the dune literally rising from the flat and extending some two hundred and fifty metres into the dark purple-blue sky. 'Ready for your last climb girls?'

We step hesitantly on the sand, the four of us ascending in an evenly spaced line, carefully treading in each other's footsteps. It's steep and slow and takes the best part of twenty minutes to reach the ridge at the top. We sit—four in a row for the last time—catching our breath and looking east towards the emerging light. As the sun rises the sky turns violet, then lilac, then pink, and white wispy cirrus emerge and float high above the horizon. Far below, a four-wheel drive weaves across the plain leaving a long thin spiralling dusty trail. The soft morning light slowly washes over the dunes and they emerge from the darkness, a vast sweeping mountain range of deep warm red.

We sit in silence, opening our jackets to the faint warmth of the early sun, and running the sand though our fingertips.

'Been fun,' says Maria. 'This trip. D'you reckon Chica?'

'Yeah. Been really fun,' says Jacki. 'Good to hang out with you girls.'

'Been fun having you,' Sarah and I say in unison. 'See you back in Oz, eh?'

We hover around the van at the bottom eating bread and jam, and using up film as the subtle shifts in light change the colours of the dunes. We take a short drive to Sossusvlei, the most accessible part of the three hundred kilometre long, one hundred and fifty kilometre wide sea of sand that covers western Namibia. The dunes—the highest in the world—originate from Kalahari sand washed down the Orange River millions of years ago.

We trek from the parking area along a deep sandy track that quickly turns into a gentle mound, and almost immediately are surrounded by a dozen gentle rolling dunes. The sun is scorching, despite the early morning breeze, and schlepping up and over each hill is hot hard work. There are no tracks up the dunes or obvious paths, and the sand swallows our feet at each step.

As we climb higher and head deeper into the pan, we are completely engulfed by vast mountains of sand towering behind and beyond us—broad sweeping parabola that swoop down from the sky, and sharp crescents that clash with the horizon. All around us alternating slopes in shadow and sunlight fall from the knife-edge ridges, and long smooth wind-sculpted arcs rise and fall and intersect.

It is quite beyond anything I have ever seen.

The slope of the dunes are vast, steep and empty like a fresh ski run and we cannot resist the temptation. We launch ourselves off the top, and slide and bounce like klipspringers all the way down. We tumble head first and gather ourselves up, and roll sideways, and slip and lose our feet and elbows in the sand.

At the bottom, we shake ourselves off and attempt to remove the sand from our ears and underwear. Ahead of us, looming and almost luminescent, is the tallest dune in Sossusvlei. We crane our necks to the top, and prepare ourselves for a final haul. 'This really is the last climb,' I say. 'Let's go girls.'

We step carefully up the side of the dune trying to match each other's footsteps; half the time they hold and we ascend smoothly, the other half they crumble and we struggle and stumble. The soft warm sand pours over the tops of our boots and filters through to our toes until our feet are leaden. Step-by-step we haul ourselves up the three hundred metre slip face, sweat dripping, the muscles in our calves tight and twitching.

At the top we balance astride the ridge and catch our breath. Far below, a dried-up riverbed meanders between the dunes, a few thin gorse bushes sprouting from the bleached, cracked earth. Pockets of white hide between the slopes, and an occasional camel thorn offers a glimpse of green. Towards the horizon, the dunes spread out as far as we can see, soft undulating hills sprinkled in dusty pink. It is absolutely silent; absolutely still. I cannot imagine a more barren landscape, yet of all the beauty I have seen in Africa, none compares with this.

I grab Sarah's hand and we look out towards the western horizon. Somewhere, just beyond those hills, is the Atlantic. In five months we have crossed an entire physical landscape. We have trekked from one coast of Africa to the other. We have been hungry and thirsty, and tired and dirty. We've been sick and scared, euphoric and miserable. We've seen the sun rise over the cradle of humanity one day, and watched a young woman die another. We have relied on ourselves, and on each other. We have struggled up mountains and reached the top.

'You know Doll,' I say, 'After this trip, I feel like I can do anything.'

'Me too, my love. Me too.'

CHAPTER 19

GUARDING MR MANDELA

WE CATCH AN overnight bus to Cape Town, an eighteen-hour trip on a posh double-decker with a toilet and the promise of 'steward service'. The seats are properly padded, covered in that ubiquitous pink and purple coach material, and actually recline. A young woman checks our tickets, and takes our order for tea and biscuits as we head out of the city. A movie flickers on a distant television screen and we wedge our knees against the seat in front and settle back. *Nell* is a bit of a struggle—love Jodie, truly, but she's made some shockers. When it's over, Sarah spends two hours waving her arms in the air and wailing 'Tay…tay in da win'. Yah OK Chikabee?' until I threaten to eject her through the pop-up window in the roof of the bus.

I sleep, fitfully, waking to fight Sarah for space and redirect blood to the particular part of my body that's running short. It's a million times more comfortable than the transport we're used to, but it's a long time since I could sleep sitting up. I check my watch regularly, hoping it just *feels* like I've only been asleep a few minutes.

In the dead of night we are awoken by a flickering light and an announcement that we have reached the South African border. It's 3.00 a.m., that time when human beings are said to be most vulnerable. I fumble for my boots, grab my jacket and passport and stumble off the bus into a mass of concrete, chain link and razor wire. We are directed towards a boom gate where we stand under a fluorescent light, a barbed metal fence separating us from the darkness beyond. It's bitterly cold—I had forgotten we are entering winter— and my breath circles in the air around me.

A dozen young white men with severe crew cuts and sharp eyes loiter on the other side of the gate. They are dressed in dark uniforms with high, military-style boots and waist belts that jangle with handcuffs and guns and batons like baseball bats. I edge towards Sarah, my eyes flitting between the line of metal toe-caps and the not so subtle display of weaponry. I have a sudden recollection of television images of Soweto school children clutching bullet wounds, and barefoot teenagers—bloodied and beaten—cowering beneath those very batons. Things are supposed to be different now, of course, and maybe they are, but somehow I can't see these guys helping an old lady across the road or organising a soccer game for the local kids. They exude contempt and violence, a palpable display of strength designed to frighten and overwhelm.

We are ushered through the checkpoint and, despite myself, I smile politely at the officer behind the mesh grate. He looks at me indifferently, stamps my passport and slides it back under the window. A string of guards, their arms folded tightly across their chests, lines our route along the razor wire fence. We walk in single file, silently, not daring to speak, or do anything that might draw attention to ourselves. A trickle of fear slides down the back of my neck; they are so indisputably, so overwhelmingly *white*.

As we step across the barrier into South Africa, we are ushered at rifle point through another boom gate and, finally, make a restrained dash to the coach. 'My God! Imagine being black and poor and up against these guys.' We watch the remaining passengers, black and white, edge sheepishly past them, their relief palpable as they step onto the bus. How did so many people find the courage to confront them? I wonder. 'Do you think you could lob a brick at those guys?' I ask Sarah. 'You know, stand up to them?'

'I don't know. I'd like to think we'd both be on the right side…'

'…but actually fighting back, putting yourself into the path of violence or danger, that's…something else.'

'Yeah, it is. Like that old saying: All it takes for evil to triumph is for good people to stand by and do nothing. I suppose, for me, it's about my family, you know, about being Jewish. Lots of people stood by then, but there were others, not just Jews, but all the righteous gentiles who did risk their lives to take a stand. That leaves you with a sense of obligation, but whether I'd have the courage to do the same? I don't know.

'Well, we all like to think we'd be brave, don't we? Fortunately, I doubt our courage, or lack of it, will ever be really tested.'

I awake with the sunrise to an early morning mist that rolls across a gentle valley and hovers above neatly cultivated fields. Bales of hay and tractors dot low-lying hills and a farmhouse nestles on the edge of a copse, smoke rising in a narrow plume from its chimney. My second glimpse of South Africa is an English pastoral scene straight out of Wordsworth—quiet, leisurely, undisturbed.

As the fog clears, a hamlet appears in the valley, and another a little further beyond, and as the hours pass, the hamlets turn to villages, and the villages to small towns. The fields give way to fenced houses and gardens, then to car yards, and furniture shops and, finally, to McDonald's. We drive through what might be the outskirts of any city in Australia or North America.

Cape Town itself, though, is unmistakable—the giant Table Mountain a staggering backdrop to a Western skyline of high-rise apartments and glitzy office blocks. The city is big and bustling, crammed with shops and cafés and cars and people, and as we head for the centre, the street corners fill with young men waving copies of the *Big Issue* and hauling sandwich boards advertising local jewellery outlets. Rows of plastic overnight bags and cheap perfume are spread on blue and green tarpaulins, and smartly dressed businesswomen tip-toe between them. We pass what appears to be a gay pub and wonder if our blotchy T-shirt and faded khaki pants combo would get us past the doorman.

A plethora of restaurants advertise dozens of different cuisines, and convenience stores display long lines of soft drinks in refrigerated cabinets. A jeans shop advertises *ten* different styles of Levis, and the Nu Metro cinema list *fourteen* movies currently showing at its multi-screen complex.

I am a little taken aback.

Whatever happened to beef and rice, or chicken and rice…or not, to Coke or Fanta…or not? How can anyone possibly choose between *fourteen* different films? Surely, you either see James Bond or you don't, you catch the latest adventure flick, or you stay at home. And aren't a pair of jeans just a pair of jeans? Do we really need *ten* different styles?

I realise with a sudden and overwhelming sense of loss that this is the end. We are back in the First World, and our time in Africa is done. From here our expectations and priorities change. In a day's time we'll be complaining that the salad dressing is off, that there's no soap in the toilets, or we've waited twenty minutes for our pizza. I think about everything we've been through, how quickly our lives changed when we first arrived. It was as if we pared life back to the core and some-how that gave us space to look around and view the world afresh. Now, all of a sudden, it feels crowded again with decisions and choices I really don't want to make.

I think about hauling myself up those mountains in the freezing darkness and breathing in the summit, about looking upon an exquisite landscape that's been here since time began, about those long weary hours with a young woman on a bus who never made it home. Those things felt important, *not* having fourteen movies to chose from.

It's not that I'm after some kind of simple, back-to-basics life—I want theatre and bookshops and smart cafés. I want to live in a decent house in a good neighbourhood. I want to travel and have enough money to make choices. But there *was* something about those days we had to struggle, albeit in a very small way, for food, shelter, safety—the fundamentals of human existence. When everything else is stripped away, when you stop worrying about work, bills, family or the myriad demands of ordinary life, you can finally start to understand what that ordinary life is actually about.

The bus driver drops us at a hostel where, fortunately, the cost of a double room is only slightly more than for two people in a dorm. We dump our gear, grab a map and head straight out. I find a telephone box in the centre of town that takes VISA and, while Sarah gorges on *People* magazines, I call Perth for Mother's Day.

'Ooh Jacqui! Where are you? How lovely to hear your voice.' She's had such a wonderful day: lunch with Sue and the girls, and dinner with Bob, Chris and the kids and oh...some flowers from John and Françoise, and now a call from Africa! Our postcards and letters have all arrived safely, and everyone has written. She's even spoken to Sarah's parents who promised to say hello with their Internet.

Before I have a chance to tell her Eva and Mike have indeed said hello with their Internet, we are interrupted by the pips and cut off after a blunted farewell. I hang up, annoyed by the shortness of the call; no news about the family, no details to fill in the sketchy correspondence. I kick the phone box and walk down the street feeling flat and frustrated.

Sarah is engrossed in some tedious Hollywood trivia, and I grab her magazine and sling it back on the shelf. 'Why do you read that crap?' I say. 'Let's get lunch.'

We walk down the main street and duck into an arcade where I plonk myself at the first available table. I snatch the only menu from Sarah's hand and flick the pages.

'You're always funny after you talk to your family,' she says.

'This has nothing to do with my family. I'm just hungry.'

We order a couple of sandwiches and I stare onto the street while Sarah fiddles with a napkin.

I know Sarah doesn't really want to live in Australia anymore; it feels like the edge of the world, she says, such a long way from home. She came for a year, and stayed for five. She likes Melbourne, genuinely, and knows we have a great life, but it's too far from her connections, from Canada. She'd like a change, somewhere different, somewhere closer to home. Perhaps a year or two in London.

London for me is drizzle and damp, crowds and chaos, but it's also my home, where Ian and Kate and Ali—the friends I've had for almost thirty years—still insist on having dinner parties without me. My roots are there, but my family—and there are a lot of them—is now in Australia. Sarah's parents, her sister and old friends are in Toronto, other friends sprinkled around the world: Russia, the UK, the US.

I grab a bottle of water and pour us both a glass.

It's been a while since I've had the where-are-we-going-to-live conversation in my head. Travelling really did put it on hold. I've realised while on this trip it's easier to like England, especially London, when you're not living there—you forget the hard slog, the day-to-day struggle, and just remember the good things: the theatre, the history, the long summer nights strolling along the canal, oak trees and bluebells and green hills. But the opposite is true of Australia. When you're away it's easy to criticise: miles from anywhere, an unsophisticated, anti-intellectual culture built on a male tradition of 'mateship'. But when you're there, day-to-day living is easy—more than easy. The sun shines from that vast blue sky and somehow life just works better. There's an optimism about Australia I think England has lost. Truly, it's a seductive place to live.

I push my sandwich around the plate and mumble into my glass. 'I'm not funny about my family.'

'You are, but that's OK.'

' Well…it's just so frustrating. Where we going to live, Doll? We can't be with all the people we want to be with. It's just not physically possible.'

'I know Babe.'

'I just keep going around in circles.'

'I know. So do I.'

'We have to make some decisions.'

'Later, Jac. We'll make some decisions later.'

We have booked a 'Freedom and culture tour' which includes a visit to a community museum, a drive through the townships, and an afternoon on Robben Island, home of the infamous prison that held Mandela and a number of the country's current Cabinet Ministers. I'm not terribly comfortable about cruising around the townships in a shiny minibus looking at other people's—*black* people's—poverty and despair. But *not* seeing it means Cape Town becomes just another rich, Western capital full of well-to-do middle-class whites ambling leisurely through the expensive shops and wine bars of the Victoria and Alfred Waterfront. 'Cape Town is a rich and beautiful place,' says our guide, Mohammed. 'We have more BMWs than America, but if you only see the city, you'll only know half the story. I'm going to show you the other half.'

Mohammed drives us, a couple of Australian backpackers and Mr and Mrs Educational Holiday and their two children, to District Six, a once thriving working class suburb, home to Jews, Christians and Muslims, blacks, whites and 'coloureds', merchants, teachers and artisans who lived side by side peacefully for decades. In 1966 the area was declared 'Whites Only' under the *Group Areas Act*—one of the corner-stones of apartheid legislation—and, during the next fourteen years, 60 000 of those merchants, teachers and artisans and their families were forcibly removed to the townships, and their homes bulldozed. District Six was flattened—literally. Only the churches and mosques were allowed to remain.

We shuffle up the wooden stairs of an old Methodist 'freedom church' which now houses the District Six Museum, squashed between two crumbling and grafittied tenement blocks. The wooden walls are lined with black and white photographs of life before the *Act*: jazz musicians playing in the street, workers pouring out of factories, kids playing in the yard, the dairy and fish market, the public washhouse. Next to them are photographs of bulldozers, of huge piles of rubble, of the remains of demolished houses and shops, the thousands of families who were evicted to make way for whites who wanted to enjoy the easy access to the harbour and city that the district afforded.

Above us, suspended from the ceiling, is a line of rusting black and white street signs: Ashley, Rutger, Pontac, Reform, Cowley. 'When the legislation was passed,' explains Mohammed, 'the foreman in charge of demolition was told to dump District Six into Table Bay. He did just that, but as each street was destroyed he rescued its sign, and kept them secretly hidden under his house for almost thirty years. He told no one until 1994 when it was safe to unearth them.' There must be sixty or seventy signs hanging there, each one representing hundreds of families who were evicted from the homes they'd occupied for generations. It's a remarkably powerful display, such a tangible symbol of destruction and resurrection. Beneath them, on the rough floorboards where we stand, a large map of the district has been painted. Now, former residents write their names where those homes used to be. 'It's a way of starting to reclaim what was taken,' says Mohammed.

We leave the museum and head south out of the city. As we drive, Mohammed explains how people were categorised depending on the exact shade of their skin, the shape of their nose, the texture of their hair. He points to people in the street and asks us to guess whether they would be 'black', 'coloured', or 'mixed'. No one feels much like playing this game, and we listen with undisguised embarrassment as he dissects the physical characteristics of an old man crossing the road, of a group of teenagers on the sidewalk. 'You begin to get some idea of what it was like,' he says.

We reach the edge of the bleak sprawling plain that is Cape Flats, home to hundreds of thousands of non-whites, including many of the former residents of District Six. Mohammed drives slowly through Langa, the oldest formal black township, home to around 200 000 people. Small, grey, featureless two-roomed houses—like municipal toilet blocks—line the main unsealed road, and sagging wire fences surround the rough dirt patches that pass for gardens. It's not like anything I've seen before—certainly not in Australia—and it's more desperate, more *insignificant* somehow than even the most run down estates in the East End of London. But what is most shocking is that these tiny boxes used to be, and to a large extent still are, the homes of *middle-class* blacks: doctors, journalists, lawyers. This is where the rich people live.

With the end of apartheid some have moved to better neighbourhoods, but others have remained. They've tried to personalise their homes by painting them in bright colours or planting window boxes. If anything though, the occasional blue or pink house, the odd drooping flower, only serve to enhance the sense of drab cold poverty.

On the edge of the Langa townships is a legal squatter camp—the next level of housing down—a sea of one-room corrugated iron shacks with bare electric light bulbs strung between houses like washing lines. Children splash by the stand-pipes outside the communal toilets, and old men sit on up-turned crates, smoking and chatting. A few women fire up charcoal stoves behind makeshift food stalls, while their kids kick around a deflated soccer ball. These are the familiar images I recall from television—the vast shanty towns home to the majority of black South Africans.

It strikes me that the task of rehousing all these people is phenomenal, and I ask Mohammed if the government can ever expect to achieve it. 'It is huge,' he says, 'and will take many years, but new houses and clinics are built every month.' He pulls over at a site of some construction, a housing project started by a group of women who pooled their limited resources to build one house. Other women joined the project and built more houses, until they attracted the attention of the government and, more recently, Bill and Hilary Clinton on their African tour. 'They now have state funding, and a donation from the American people,' Mohammed explains. 'Families are moved from the legal camps to these and other new houses, then people can be moved from the illegal camps to the legal ones—where they at least have water, electricity and toilets—and the old shacks are bulldozed. This way, slowly, our people will be housed.'

Beyond the corrugated iron huts are the illegal squatter camps that spread out around the edges of the flats. The houses here are no more than temporary shacks erected out of cardboard boxes and plastic bags. There is no sanitation, and heat and light are provided by kerosene lanterns that frequently cause devastating fires. There is no road or track and we weave awkwardly amongst the people squatting in the dirt around their fragile homes.

I have always resisted the notion of 'white guilt'—I thought it never really helped anybody—but here, staring into the eyes of these old men, of these young women with pot-bellied babies hung on their hips, I can't help but feel, somehow, I am on the wrong side of all this. It's not that I feel responsible. I don't. It's just that in this particular place, at this particular time, being white doesn't feel so good.

On our way back to town we stop at a community school named after Chris Hani, a charismatic black activist gunned down in front of his home in 1993. Hani's killer, a Polish immigrant, was found to have strong connections with the organised Right and the national Conservative Party. His assassination, at a time when the apartheid regime was being dismantled, sent shock waves through the country, and over a hundred thousand people attended his funeral.

The school that bears his name is run entirely by a volunteer staff who provide an education for two hundred of the poorest neighbourhood children. It was established by a middle-aged woman, Maureen Jacobs, who raised money for furniture and equipment by taking the children to town every Saturday to sing to tourists in the city square. Now, the tourists come to her through an arrangement with our tour company. Part of our fee for today's trip goes to the school, and visitors can also make donations. 'When I bring you here,' says Mohammed, 'you learn a little about the real South Africa, and we help the school.'

Many of the Chris Hani kids can't be enrolled in government schools because they have no birth certificate, because they come from a different township, or because their parents are illiterate and unfamiliar with the official procedures. Here, the kids learn some basic skills, while Maureen helps their parents with the necessary paperwork required to enrol them in the state system.

We hover in the doorway of the one large room, a kind of dusty church hall with a dog-eared alphabet chart and a few drawings pinned to the wall. Four classes are in progress, each facing into a corner. There must be a hundred and fifty kids, most aged between five and ten, plus a handful of teenagers. Dozens of heads turn as we enter, and a line of faces looks towards us as each kid nudges the one next to him. They are bright and lively, shuffling in their seats and sneaking 'thumbs up' signs when their teachers aren't looking. Maureen interrupts their lessons and they gather at the front of the room for 'music practice'. Only when they line up do I realise they are wearing a uniform of sorts: old and tatty shirts and jumpers in various shades of maroon and off-white.

We stand with our backs against the wall, facing the kids who are clearly delighted to have an audience. Maureen raises her hand and they fall silent. On her command they begin to sing and sway, arms swinging in perfect time—the familiar *toyi toyi* so often danced at funerals and demonstrations. The strange white visitors begin to sway too, and the kid's struggle to conceal their laughter. We step, hopelessly out of time, knocking each other's elbows and banging into the wall.

As Maureen brings the song to a close we cease our awkward shuffling and hover, the kids smirking and sending Chinese whispers down the line. With a barely perceptible flick of her wrist Maureen regains their complete attention. The faces of a hundred and fifty children shift suddenly from bright smiles to a deadly seriousness. They puff out their chests and stand a little taller, place their hands on their hearts and begin to sing 'Nkosi Sikelele iAfrica', 'God Bless Africa', for so long the banned song of black resistance, now the national anthem.

Their voices echo around the wooden hall with a beauty and earnestness that is almost overwhelming. They are, at the same time, hauntingly melancholic and utterly hopeful and, as I listen, my eyes fill with tears. I'm not sure if it's sadness I feel, or joy, or something in between. More than anything, I feel *humble*. It's as if these kids—impoverished and barely educated as they are—understand exactly the struggles of their country's past, and know that because of them, their futures will be brighter. I remember the words in English: '…Sounds the call to come together,/ And united we shall stand/ Let us live and strive for freedom/ In South Africa our land.' In this dusty room, amongst a handful of ragged kids I feel the hope of the new South Africa. And if South Africa can be hopeful, so can we all.

They finish their song and file back to their desks as we linger by the door. I wipe my eyes discreetly, taking one last look around the room and, in what feels like an act of supreme inconsequence, empty my wallet into the donation box.

Half an hour later we are sitting on a low wall on the edge of the beautiful city waterfront eating chicken and avocado sandwiches, and looking out across the bay. I feel breathless somehow, like the weight of the morning is bearing down on me. I breathe the chill air blowing in from Robben Island, and try to sift through the myriad images of poverty and squalor, and the contrasting sense of hope and renewal that I've witnessed this morning. It strikes me that's been our experience, not just here, but everywhere we have travelled in Africa.

The island is a vast, barren rock sitting in the icy Atlantic eleven kilometres from the city. It has long housed South Africa's undesirables: slaves, lepers, the mentally ill, tribal chiefs who opposed colonialism and more recently, of course, Nelson Mandela and other political prisoners. What strikes me most about being here is that the history of this place is so recent, that Mandela was imprisoned here in my adult lifetime, that it was only in 1994 that black people actually got to vote for the first time.

Anti-apartheid campaigns were raging when I was teaching in London in the eighties and some of my students—fifteen, sixteen, seventeen year olds, black and white—were actively involved. After class one day, a couple of fifth years, Louise and Adi, started telling me about the twenty-four hour picket outside the South African Embassy in Trafalgar Square. They gave me a history lesson on the South African liberation struggle, and how people in the UK were supporting South African exiles. 'What you doin' Sunday afternoon, Miss?' asked Louise. 'Maybe you could come down?' And so, at a time when the Thatcher government was worried about left-wing teachers influencing kids, I was invited to a demonstration by a fifteen-year-old who knew more about racial politics than I was ever likely to.

There were at least a hundred people outside the embassy when I arrived, handing out leaflets and chanting, and a guy on a megaphone calling for the release of Nelson Mandela from his prison on Robben Island. There were pictures of Mandela on placards everywhere— about twenty years younger than he was at the time. There were none available of him as an older man. Louise and Adi were clearly chuffed to see me, and we lined up in front of the embassy in a peaceful demonstration, the crowd growing to a few hundred as the afternoon wore on.

The police had been there from the start, but slowly their numbers increased until they were lined three deep in front of the picket. Almost before I knew what was happening, two people on either side of me linked my arms, and I was in the middle of a line of protesters looking eye-to-eye with a row of batoned, uniformed policemen.

One of the senior cops warned us, through a megaphone, that we were 'obstructing the highway' and told us if we didn't disperse we would be forcibly removed. The arms on either side of me gripped tighter, and everyone shuffled closer. By now, there were a lot more people behind me, and two more rows in front, and I could just make out the line of police helmets above their heads, and the vast sea of huge black boots below.

Suddenly, everyone in front surged back, and I had to struggle to stay upright, the two fellow protesters on either side still hanging onto my arms. An immense weight bore down on my shoulders and I fell to my knees, instinctively wrapping my arms around my head as feet flew everywhere. In an instant, I was yanked up, a policeman's hand grabbing my collar and hauling me, half-standing, through the crowd and onto the street. I was marched around the corner and shoved in to an awaiting van.

The van was already half full, a policeman sitting between each protester. I must have looked completely terrified, as one of the other demonstrators asked me if this was the first time I'd been arrested, and started telling me my rights. The policeman next to her told her to shut up, that we weren't allowed to speak to each other.

It was certainly not the afternoon I had planned. After being questioned and charged I was transferred to a cell while they 'confirmed my identity.' I had given them the number of an old friend of mine, Alison, who I said would confirm who I was and where I lived. I found out later Ali had thought it was someone playing a practical joke, and had asked the WPC who'd called if it was 'a wind up'.

I recall the cell was really quite unpleasant—unsurprisingly—a filthy toilet in one corner, and a bed with a rotting vinyl mattress in the other. My only consolation was that I had a copy of *Of Mice and Men* with me that I'd shoved in my pocket to read on the train. I was studying it with my fifth years, and spent my two-hour imprisonment preparing a few lesson plans in my head.

Nineteen charges were brought against protesters in total that day, all of which were eventually withdrawn—after some eighteen months—for lack of evidence, except one. Somebody had grabbed a police helmet and was charged with 'possession of police property.' But the police had ensured that the organisation that backed the picket, the City of London Anti-Apartheid Group, had wasted a huge amount of time and money on legal fees required to answer the charges. Breaking up the picket was a deliberate political act, one of the many ways the police suppressed this sort of dissent under Thatcher.

When I finally read my charge sheet I was stunned. In the whole course of my arrest there had been absolutely no communication whatsoever between me and the arresting officer, but reading his statement you might be forgiven for thinking otherwise. I can't remember the exact words, but it went something like this: 'Statement of Police Constable Plod, Cannon Row Police Station. I was standing on the pavement outside the South African Embassy in Trafalgar Square on such and such a date when I noticed that Tomlins was obstructing the highway. I told her she was causing an obstruction and asked her to move. She replied: 'Fuck off you fascist bully-boy pig dog.' I then repeated my warning to Tomlins, telling her if she refused to move I would be forced to arrest her. She replied: 'Piss off Pig, you racist bastard. You're the enemy of the people, you fascist scum.' I then told Tomlins I was arresting her for obstructing the highway and escorted her to an awaiting van.'

There was a lot of talk at the time about the fact that the police were dodgy, especially when it came to political demonstrations. My brother had been telling me for years the Birmingham Six *were* framed though I don't think I really believed him. But then, when your everyday plod could make up such whoppers, it did make you wonder. And here I am, ten years later, a long way from Trafalgar Square, staring out towards Robben Island; Mandela is the President of a free South Africa, and his former prison cell is now a tourist attraction. Oh, and it turns out the Birmingham Six were framed after all.

I join the large crowd of people from a dozen different countries gathering on the dock and shuffle onto the ferry for the twenty-minute trip. We are met at the other end by a middle-aged man in a bright floral shirt and Fremantle Dockers beanie who introduces himself as Peter and welcomes us to the island. He tells us, with an air of casual ease, that he is an ex-political prisoner who was incarcerated here for twenty years. Now he works as a guide, as do many of the former inmates.

He ushers us through the old prison gates into a long, grey corridor. Rectangles of light shine through barred windows and fall like latticework on the concrete walls and floor. We gather in front of a small bare office of what used to be the 'censor room', where officers read inmates' letters—the one or two a year they were allowed. 'Only family news and local gossip was permitted,' says Peter, 'and if there was any hint of information about the outside world the letters would be cut. Sometimes I received letters that just said 'Dear Peter' and everything else was removed except the signature. Information was important to us, and this is how they controlled it. Occasionally, notes could be smuggled in and out by inmates who had contact visits—messages would be written on toilet paper, wrapped in plastic and transferred via kisses. Sometimes, a priest might help by smuggling a letter in a Bible.'

He leads us out of the administration building into a concrete court-yard where the prisoners worked and exercised. A photograph shows two rows of men seated on either side, one line sewing clothes, the other breaking rocks. 'This is where we spent most of the time when were weren't in our cells,' he says. 'The work was tedious or back-breaking, or both. During the occasional breaks we played football or tennis here. We would slip a message into a ball and hit it across the wall to prisoners in the other sections—the political prisoners were strictly segregated from everyone else and this was one way we could communicate.'

Peter directs us to the wall enclosing the yard and hunkers down. 'Here is where Mandela buried his autobiography, before it was discovered by the wardens. Fortunately, a copy had already been smug-gled out by the man who is now the Minister for Transport. Nelson lost privileges for four years for writing that book, because he used paper that was provided for study.'

The courtyard—the whole prison complex—is bleak and depress-ing, but what is almost more disconcerting is Peter's matter-of-factness about it all, his gentle, easy manner. He spent almost half his life incar-cerated here, for things most of us wouldn't even have the courage to contemplate. And yet, here he is showing us around with no hint of bitterness or anger. 'Why does he do this?' I whisper to Sarah. 'Surely you'd never want to see the place again.'

'I don't know. Ask him.'

'It was a policy amongst the inmates,' he continues, 'to educate each other. Those who could read and write taught those who couldn't. The men who had studied at university taught history or political science.

Some prisoners arrived at Robben Island with a grade one education and left with a degree. Sometimes, even the wardens—many of whom were ill-educated themselves—sat in on classes, taking care their supervising officer didn't see them.'

Beyond the courtyard, we are led into the cell block where prisoners spent most of their time—often twenty-three hours a day. Tiny, six by five feet concrete rooms with floor to ceiling bars line either side of a long thin corridor. Mandela's cell remains as it was when he was first imprisoned: a thin, black blanket folded on the floor, a mug and cup on a square wooden box, and a metal bucket in the corner. Beds were only provided years later after a lengthy petition to the government.

Our group files slowly past as Peter calmly looks on, each person craning their neck to see around the bars. I linger at the back of the crowd trying to fathom how anyone could endure this kind of privation and emerge a sane human being, let alone lead some forty million people to a new democracy. Twenty-seven years he was imprisoned, thirteen of them in this suffocating little box. And yet he emerged on that historic day in February 1990 talking of peace and unity, of reconciliation. I am overwhelmed, and humbled once again, not only by the thought of Mandela, but by the colossal grace and dignity of Peter who, I am confident, would baulk at the suggestion that he was anything other than an ordinary man who happened to get caught up in some extraordinary events.

Back at the entrance, I ask what motivates him to return daily to a place of such misery. 'People often ask that,' he says. 'Do I not feel bitter? Am I not resentful? This is what I say: There is no point dwelling on the past. We must remember it to ensure it never happens again, but we must move forward. Now I talk to the ex-warders, we work together and pray together. You cannot correct a wrong thing by doing another wrong thing. Fighting does not build, it destroys. We must create a foundation for the next generation to build upon. Let's make it strong. Let's make it united. Let's make it peaceful. For the future of South Africa we must come together now and join hands so the terrible things that happened here never happen again.'

On the ferry back to the mainland Peter's words echo around my head. I'm not sure where that kind of magnanimity comes from, that capacity to acknowledge a brutal past, but still look optimistically to the future. It's not a forgiveness as such, but more an acceptance—that was then and this is now and we must move on for the benefit of humanity. I reflect on Australia's diabolical relationship with its indigenous people—the current frustrated attempts at reconciliation, the debates raging around saying 'sorry'—and can't help thinking we might just be able to learn something here.

Back on the mainland, our group disperses and Sarah and I wander around the waterfront and duck into the Robben Island Museum shop. While part of me wants to take something home as a reminder of this extraordinary day, buying a replica prison mug or plate seems vaguely obscene, though I am quite taken with the Nelson Mandela fridge magnet with three different outfits: a green floral print shirt, another with the national flag, and a South African soccer team strip.

There is no one else in the shop, and the middle-aged man behind the desk is clearly at a loose end and keen to chat. It turns out he is Christo Brandt, an ex-warder who worked on Robben Island for four years, and who once guarded 'Mr' Mandela on a visit outside the prison grounds. He grabs a copy of Mandela's autobiography, *Long Walk to Freedom*, and shows us the page where he is mentioned. 'You know, Mr Mandela sends a Christmas card to my family every year,' he says proudly.

As he flicks through the pages of the book, a young black man drops into the shop and introduces himself as Vusumzi Mcongo. He is another ex-prisoner who was sentenced to fifteen years in 1978 for sabotage. Now he runs the ticket office. The two of them knew each other before—once when Christo was escorting Vusumzi to the Groote Schuur hospital for a check-up, Christo bought a newspaper and left it lying where Vusumzi could pick it up. They laugh at the recollection of the story. 'Things are very different these days,' says Christo. 'Vusumzi here is my colleague, and my boss is an ex-inmate too.'

The four of us lean against the counter and chat about life in the prison, about Mandela, about reconciliation. They see Robben Island now as a place where positive relationships between black and white can be fostered. Over the past couple of years the two of them have developed a genuine friendship, and they want people to follow their example—if a former inmate and warder can become friends, anyone can.

Listening to them chatting away like old buddies from way back, I am struck by how remarkable they are. In fact, I am struck by how remarkable everyone is who we have met today: the children of the Chris Hani School, Maureen Jacobs and her teachers, Mohammed and Peter. All of them have a fundamental faith in the capacity of the individual to influence things bigger than themselves which leaves me feeling both powerful and inadequate. Despite their astonishing histories, there is no desire for vengeance, no hint of bitterness. Scratch the surface and maybe it's there—I don't know—but today we've seen only an acceptance of the past, and an optimism about what's to come. God knows the country is a mess—homelessness, hunger, crime, unemployment and disease—and the capacity of any government to fix it is doubtful at best, but for the time being at least, there is a real faith in the future, a belief that whatever happens, nothing will ever be as bad as it was.

For our last night we book a table at Morton's on the Wharf, an expensive restaurant on the waterfront. It's packed with an exclusively white clientele leaning up against the mirrored bar and hovering around a display of fresh-cream desserts. Despite our best efforts, we are woefully underdressed and clunk across the floor in our heavy, muddied boots. Our waiter, Craig, is charming however, and we settle into the plush padded chairs and order from the extensive menu.

We sip ice cold beers, silently, unaccustomed to the order and affluence of our surroundings, and contemplate the last six months of our lives. Kenya seems so long ago, but at the same time, it feels like half a year has passed in the click of a finger.

We have ventured into eight countries, climbed mountains, kayaked across lakes, canoed down rivers, trekked through jungle and cessnaed into a delta.

We've traversed the land by train, coach, minibus, four-wheel drive, taxi, bicycle and sand-board, and covered many, many miles on foot.

We've travelled through desert, savannah, woodland, steppe and rainforest, skirted flood plains, walked along the coast and above the timber line.

We've met Masai, Kikuyu, Luo, Shona, Xhosa, Tswana, Indians and Afrikaners, and Westerners from all over the world.

And now we are done—and sitting in a fancy restaurant that's a world away from any of that—eating marinated chicken wings and seafood terrine.

'Ready for home, my love?' I ask.

'I suppose so…in some ways…but part of me can't bear to leave. I'll miss the freedom. The thrill of waking each day and not knowing what will be in it. I feel like…I've been alive for the past six months in a way I never have before. It's as if Africa has opened me to the possibilities of life, and my life will forever be different because of it. Truly, it's the best thing I've ever done. I will always be in Africa's debt.'

'I think it was the smartest decision we ever made. It's like, whatever happens from here on in, we'll always have done this trip. When we look back on our lives, Africa will always be there. I feel like I touched the very edges of life, and somehow, because of that, I understand the world—and my place in it—a little better.'

Craig clears our plates, refills our glasses and returns with two fresh Table Bay sole served with creamed potato, asparagus and a green salad. 'Food's fantastic,' I say. 'I won't miss the fried eggs, and the dog bones, and the endless bottles of warm Coke. I'm hanging out for cheese and a rare steak…'

'…and a bath, and new clothes, and some books, and a firm mattress and a visit to the chiropractor.'

'So back to Melbourne, Doll and what then?'

'Don't ask difficult questions.'

'I must say, I'm quite looking forward to being in the same place for a while, unpacking, spreading out a bit.'

'Me too.'

'We'll rent somewhere nice eh? Bit more space. Backyard maybe.'

'Yeah. And once I'm working again we should be able to save some money.'

'We can open a separate bank account and, you know, put a big chunk in there every month. Shouldn't take long to build up. Maybe, if you become a Senior Associate and I do some freelance work we could save enough…'

I stop myself mid sentence, and we both laugh out loud. 'Uh oh. Isn't this where we came in?' I grab my beer and raise my glass. 'A toast,' I say.

'To what?'

'To Africa, of course.'

'To Africa.'

We've come a long way since that first terrifying night in Nairobi when Africa was scary and squalid and dangerous, and even further from those days in Melbourne when it was no more than a handful of guidebooks and glossy safari brochures. Now, knowing how unique each country is, it's difficult to talk about 'Africa' at all. Someone at home asked us if, after a while, all the countries become a bit of blur, but the opposite is true. The mountains that edge the Great Rift Valley couldn't be more different from the desert and dunes of Namibia, the infrastructure and economy of Botswana share little with its bordering Zambia, and while there is poverty all over, nowhere is it more desperate than in Tanzania and Malawi. Perhaps we are so used to hearing 'Africa' talked about as a monolithic entity, we take too little account of the individual countries that it comprises.

And yet, there are commonalities: everyone we met, wherever they were from, had a deep understanding of their country's history, and was acutely aware of the problems their country faced. And, despite those problems, they shared a strong sense of pride and an enormous love of the place they were born. No one ever looked to outsiders for affirmation of the worth or integrity of their country. No one ever doubted why we might choose to visit. We never felt unwelcome anywhere, and the generosity of spirit towards us—towards rich, white Westerners, was unfailing. If these diverse countries share anything, perhaps it is a resilience, a tenacity, a capacity to keep faith with life when, so often, life refuses to keep faith with them.

In truth, in our six months we have done little more than totter across the continent, a superficial stroll that offered a glimpse into some people's lives. We haven't stayed in one place for more than a week, we haven't lived or worked anywhere, and our relationships with local people were friendly, but rarely intimate. I cannot say that in this time I have even begun to understand Africa—I suspect it is beyond knowing to anyone who is not born here—but I have glimpsed its shadow, and know where that understanding might be found.

Perhaps there is an answer somewhere in its ancient landscapes that harboured man before man even knew who he was; in its ferocious sun and wind and rain that perpetually heap drought and flood and famine on peoples most unable to bear it; in its history of European colonialism with its legacy of white land ownership and alien religions; and in its people who, despite all this, continue to endure. We barely touched Africa, but Africa touched us deeply.

And yes, Africa is in my blood.